Color and Money

SUNY series, The New Inequalities

A. Gary Dworkin, editor

Color and Money

Politics and Prospects for Community Reinvestment in Urban America

Gregory D. Squires
Sally O'Connor

State University of New York Press

Photo of Liberty Bank building, Milwaukee. Photo by Alan Magayne–
Roshak/UWM Photo Service. Used with permission of the Board of
Regents, University of Wisconsin.

Published by
State University of New York Press, Albany

© 2001 State University of New York

For information, address State University of New York Press
90 State Street, Suite 700, Albany, NY 12207

Production by Judith Block
Marketing by Anne M. Valentine

Library of Congress Cataloging-in-Publication Data

Squires, Gregory D.
  Color and money : politics and prospects for community reinvestment in urban America
  / Gregory D. Squires, Sally O'Connor
    p. cm. — (SUNY series, the new inequalities)
  Includes bibliographical references and index.
  ISBN 0-7914-4951-3 (alk. paper)—ISBN 0-7914-4952-1 (pbk. : alk. paper)
    1. Discrimination in mortgage loans—Wisconsin—Milwaukee.   2. Race
  discrimination—Wisconsin—Milwaukee.   3. Community
  development—Wisconsin—Milwaukee.   4. Milwaukee (Wis.)—Economic
  conditions—Regional disparities.   I. O'Connor, Sally, 1947–   II. Title.   III. Series.

  HG2040.2.S65   2001
  332.7'22'0977595—dc21   2001016519

10 9 8 7 6 5 4 3 2 1

Contents

Tables and Illustrations

Tables

viii   **Tables and Illustrations**

Figures

Maps

Preface

This book is a result of long-term-research interests in, and strategic organizing around, community reinvestment issues. For many years we have conducted research projects and worked with various actors in the community reinvestment debate (e.g., community organizations, lenders, regulators, policymakers, and others in housing related industries, government agencies, and nonprofit groups). Much of our work could be characterized as "advocacy research." Our objectives throughout have been to conduct the best research we could while having an impact on the subjects we were studying. These are not always the most compatible goals. Readers will have to decide for themselves how successful we have been.

As trained social scientists, we have struggled to be objective, or at least as objective as possible. We have made every attempt to accurately report available facts, to interpret them as fairly as possible (which sometimes means offering several possible alternative explanations), and to suggest reasonable and feasible policy recommendations. At the same time, we have tried to change the environment we are researching. Our basic objective is to increase access to credit in markets that have long been underserved in urban America generally but particularly in our hometown of Milwaukee, Wisconsin.

Many of the findings reported in this book were the result of research projects that were launched in conjunction with the needs of various community organizations. Our most frequent partner has been Milwaukee's Fair Lending Coalition which is described in chapter 9. We were involved in starting that organization and have worked with it since its inception. Consequently, most of the chapters that follow were initially prepared at a particular point in time in the mid- to late 1990s to respond to specific organizations' strategic needs. Collectively, however, they tell a good part of the community reinvestment story in one fairly typical urban community in the United States at this point in time. We have learned a great deal about banking, government regulation, community organizing, and the actors who inhabit these arenas. More importantly, we have learned something about the barriers to credit in certain markets and what types of actions might ameliorate those barriers. We have written this book in an effort to share the lessons we have learned. Again, the readers will have to judge for themselves the validity and utility of these thoughts.

Some of the following chapters are revisions of papers that have previously appeared elsewhere. We want to thank the publishers for granting their permission for allowing us to use these materials. Portions of the first chapter were taken from Gregory D. Squires' essay, "Friend or Foe? The Federal Government and Community Reinvestment," which appeared in *Revitalizing Urban Neighborhoods*, edited by W. Dennis Keating, Norman Krumholz, and Philip Star and published by the University Press of Kansas in 1996. Chapter 6 is a revision of a paper by Gregory D. Squires and Sally O'Connor titled "Access to Capital: Milwaukee's Small Business Lending Gaps," presented at the Federal Reserve Board's conference on "Business Access to Capital and Credit" in Arlington, Virginia on 8 March, 1999. Chapter 7 expands upon two papers by Squires and Sunwoong Kim, an associate professor of economics at the University of Wisconsin-Milwaukee; "Does Anybody Who Works Here Look Like Me?" published by the University of Texas Press in *Social Science Quarterly* (Vol. 76, No. 4, pp. 823–838) in December 1995 and "The Color of Money and the People Who Lend It," published by the Fannie Mae Foundation in the *Journal of Housing Research* (Vol. 9, No. 2, pp. 271–284) in 1998. Chapter 8 is drawn from our article, "Fringe Banking in Milwaukee" which was published in *Urban Affairs Review* (Vol. 34, No. 1) in September 1998. Chapter 9 is a revision of a paper written by Squires and Dan Willett, the first Executive Director of the Fair Lending Coalition, entitled "The Fair Lending Coalition: Organizing Access to Capital in Milwaukee," which was published in *Building Community: Social Science in Action*, edited by Philip Nyden, Anne Figert, Mark Shibley, and Darryl Burrows and published by Pine Forge Press in 1997.

Several people have assisted us throughout. Graduate students at the University of Wisconsin-Milwaukee (UWM) who have contributed to our work include Brenda Hicks-Sorensen, David Somerscales, and Leah Sweetman. Donna Schenstrom, head cartographer of UWM's cartographic services laboratory prepared our maps. Charles Finn, a researcher with the Hubert Humphrey Institute at the University of Minnesota has supplied us with the mortgage lending data on which much of our research has been based. Glenn Canner, an economist with the Federal Reserve Board, provided data on small businesses. Lois Quinn and John Pawasarat of the UWM Employment and Training Institute supplied us with survey data on banking practices of Milwaukee residents. Thomas Longoria, a political scientist at the University of Texas-El Paso, assisted us in parts of the statistical analysis. Financial assistance was provided by the HUD-funded Milwaukee Community Outreach Partnership Center at UWM, the Center for Urban Initiatives and Research at UWM, the Milwaukee Campaign for Human Development, the Community Development Block Grant Program of the City of Milwaukee, and the Fair Lending Coalition.

This book is, fundamentally, about a nationwide social movement. Redlining and disinvestment are now being met with a community reinvestment movement that is creating access to capital in communities where economic opportunity has long been limited. As with any successful social movement, it has been a long and difficult struggle for thousands of people and organizations to realize the achievements that have been made. As is also often the case, such heroes rarely get the recognition and gratitude they deserve. We would like to take a small step toward rectifying this. Gale Cincotta and her many colleagues over the years with the National Training and Information Center were pioneers who launched this movement and continue to provide leadership and strength. Cal Bradford, who probably knows more about banking and community reinvestment than anyone else in the country, has provided research, advocacy, and other counsel from virtually the beginning of this movement. ACORN has empowered some of the nation's most marginalized communities, making some of the most powerful respond more effectively to their needs as a result. The Center for Community Change and the Woodstock Institute have long provided research and advocacy tools that community organizations, lenders, and regulators alike have used to ameliorate disinvestment and nurture reinvestment. John Taylor and the National Community Reinvestment Coalition have provided data analysis and related technical assistance to hundreds of community organizations and made community reinvestment a prominent nationwide issue;

one which lenders, regulators, and elected officials understand better and respond to more effectively than had ever previously been the case. To these people, their organizations, and the thousands who have worked for justice and to make their communities better places in which to live, work, and play, we dedicate this book.

1

Opening Doors
The Community
Reinvestment Movement

Guaranty believes that not only does adherence to nondiscriminatory practices comply with the law of the country, but that also equal access to credit enhances our profitability potential.

—U. S. Department of Housing and
Urban Development and Guaranty Bank 1999: 1

WHEN THE *ATLANTA JOURNAL-CONSTITUTION* reported in January 1989 that Milwaukee had the nation's highest racial disparity in mortgage loan denial rates, it reignited a smoldering community reinvestment movement in that community (Dedman 1989). The city's Democratic Mayor John O. Norquist and Republican Governor Tommy Thompson quickly brought together a collection of lenders, regulators, community groups, and civil rights organizations to develop a plan for closing this racial gap. The group, referred to as the Fair Lending Action Committee (FLAC), held several contentious meetings and in October of that year issued its then controversial report, "Equal Access to Mortgage Lending: The Milwaukee Plan." That plan called for several lending, marketing, training, and counseling goals and programs, many of which have subsequently been implemented.

The *Atlanta Journal-Constitution* story was the first systematic investigation of mortgage loan denial rates. It triggered strong reaction across the country. Fair housing and community advocacy groups claimed it confirmed the discrimination and redlining they had long accused lenders of practicing. Lenders responded that the investigation revealed little more than the fact that racial minorities and residents of lower income neighborhoods generally have poorer credit records.

But in Milwaukee and across the country much has subsequently happened to alter the terms of the redlining debate. Lenders and community groups have formed partnerships for reinvestment. Regulators and other law enforcement officials have settled fair lending discrimination complaints. Mortgage lending institutions in particular and financial services industries in general have experienced substantial restructuring and more appears to be on the way.

But what has changed? What has happened to the racial gap in denial rates and the distribution of mortgage loans? How has the restructuring of financial institutions affected the availability of loans and other financial services and products? What does the future portend?

This book examines what has been a national community reinvestment social movement (Squires 1992) through the lens of a typical urban community. Milwaukee, Wisconsin is an older, industrial area that has experienced the loss of thousands of manufacturing jobs but a rise in service industry positions in recent decades. Like many other metropolitan areas, Milwaukee's suburbs are growing while numerous city neighborhoods are stagnating (Levine 1998). Milwaukee has long been torn by racial strife (Trotter 1985; Coleman 1997). And it is home to active community organizations struggling with issues of redlining and disinvestment and, more recently, working with financial institutions to nurture community reinvestment (Glabere 1992). The following chapters focus on what has changed in the delivery of mortgage loans in the Milwaukee metropolitan area. There is no single benchmark, index, or "bottom line" that can reveal how successful these efforts have been. Community reinvestment, the changing structure of financial institutions and the impact on reinvestment, and the role of various actors (lenders, regulators, fair lending and fair housing advocates) are explored in diverse ways in an effort to understand how these struggles have played out in one community. Hopefully, this multifaceted approach to illuminating this recent history will facilitate future efforts to turn a tradition of disinvestment into ongoing, effective partnerships for reinvestment.

Community Reinvestment: A National Social Movement

More than one trillion dollars have been committed for community reinvestment objectives in 360 agreements negotiated by neighborhood organizations with lenders nationwide since the federal Community Reinvestment Act was enacted in 1977, according to the National Community Reinvestment Coalition (NCRC), a Washington, D.C. based membership group of more than 680 community organizations (Silver 1999). The community reinvestment movement has come a long way in the thirty years since Gale Cincotta and her troops blocked bank doors with picket lines, slowed business by opening and closing accounts for one dollar on Saturday afternoons, or stopped all business by scattering pennies across lobby floors, because those institutions would not make credit available to their depositors on Chicago's Northwest side (Pogge 1992). To understand this evolution from redlining to reinvestment, it is important to begin with an examination of the issue of race. Indeed the history and politics of mortgage lending and race are inseparable.

The Role of Race

Race has long been an explicit and central factor in mortgage lending markets in urban America. Almost seventy years ago, University of Chicago sociologist and federal housing policy advisor, Homer Hoyt ranked fifteen racial and ethnic groups in terms of their impact on property values in a report he prepared for the Federal Housing Administration (FHA). Those having the most detrimental impact were Negroes and Mexicans (Hoyt 1933). Following the advice of its expert, in its 1938 underwriting manual the FHA concluded, "If a neighborhood is to retain stability, it is necessary that properties shall continue to be occupied by the same social and racial classes. A change in social or racial occupancy generally contributes to instability and a decline in values" (U.S. Federal Housing Administration 1938, par. 937).

The FHA was also a leading advocate of racially restrictive covenants which virtually guaranteed that properties would be occupied by the same classes over time. These covenants were enforceable in court until the U.S. Supreme Court ruled them unenforceable in the 1948 case of *Shelley v. Kraemer*.

The FHA was a major source of home financing from its inception in 1930 through the 1950s when it financed 60 percent of all home purchases, virtually all of which were in suburban communities (Lief and Goering 1987: 229). During the 1960s, the FHA turned around and flooded central cities with federally insured mortgages. Liberal loan terms and lower costs made these loans attractive to low-income buyers. Since the costs were paid up front and were insured by the federal government, they were attractive to many lenders. Often working with local realtors, lenders would solicit home purchases from families who could not, in fact, afford the acquisition. Exploiting racial fears in many cases, blockbusting resulted in the swift racial transition of urban communities. Thousands of families shortly defaulted on the loans contributing directly to the deterioration of once vibrant neighborhoods. The linchpin of such destruction was the availability of federally insured loans which guaranteed the profits of lenders and realtors but cost many families their homes and life savings. The operation of the dual housing finance system—conventional loans for white suburbanites and FHA loans for nonwhite inner city residents—cemented the division of American society into the predominantly white and affluent suburbs and largely poor nonwhite central cities forewarned by the Kerner Commission in 1968 (Bradford 1979; Bradford and Cincotta 1992).

The racist policies and practices of the federal government were matched by those of the private housing industry. In 1932 a leading real estate theoretician, Frederick Babcock, observed "there is one difference in people, namely race, which can result in very rapid decline. Usually such declines can be partially avoided by segregation and this device has always been in common usage in the South where white and negro populations have been separated" (Bradford 1979). The American Institute of Real Estate Appraisers used the following example to illustrate neighborhood analysis into the 1970s, "The neighborhood is entirely Caucasian. It appears that there is no adverse effect by minority groups" (Greene 1980: 9). Until 1950 the National Association of Realtors stated in its code of ethics that

> A Realtor should never be instrumental in introducing into a neighborhood a character of property or occupancy, members of any race or nationality, or any individual whose presence will clearly be detrimental to property values in the neighborhood. (Judd 1984: 284)

And in 1988 a sales manager for the American Family Insurance Company offered, in a tape-recorded statement,

> . . . I think you write too many blacks . . . You gotta sell good, solid premium paying white people . . . they own their homes, the white

works . . . Very honestly, black people will buy anything that looks good right now . . . but when it comes to pay for it next time . . . you're not going to get your money out of them. (NAACP v. American Family Insurance Company 1992)

The explicit attention paid to race has been a key factor accounting for the dual housing market and rigid patterns of racial segregation in urban areas throughout the United States (Jackson 1985; Massey and Denton 1993).

Fighting Back

At the urging of fair housing and related community-based advocacy groups around the country, in the late 1960s the federal government began an about face in its approach to the dual housing finance market and the dual housing market generally (Bradford and Cincotta 1992). The Federal Fair Housing Act in 1968 and the Equal Credit Opportunity Act in 1974 prohibited discrimination in housing and housing finance markets.

The Home Mortgage Disclosure Act (HMDA, 1975) requires most mortgage lenders to publicly report the number of loans, the type and purpose of those loans, and dollar volume of its mortgage lending activity in urban areas by census tract. As amended in 1990 HMDA requires lenders to disclose the race, gender, and income of all applicants and the disposition of all applications (Federal Financial Institutions Examination Council 1996a). A substantial amount of research, including this book, utilizes HMDA data, but there has been some controversy surrounding this data set. Because there is no information on the credit record of the borrower or condition of the home, it is difficult to determine from HMDA reports the extent to which racial disparities in lending reflect discrimination, legitimate risk-based underwriting and pricing, or other factors (Galster 1991; Benston 1997). But HMDA data are quite useful in documenting credit flows and identifying disparities associated with the race and income of borrowers and racial composition, income levels, and other socioeconomic characteristics of communities.

Under the Community Reinvestment Act (CRA) passed in 1977, most federally regulated depository institutions "have a continuing and affirmative obligation to help meet the credit needs of the local communities in which they are chartered." Federal financial regulatory agencies (the four principal regulators are the Federal Reserve Board, the Office of the Comptroller of the Currency, the Federal Deposit Insurance Corporation, and the Office of Thrift Supervision) periodically evaluate lenders under their jurisdiction. Those evaluations and a final rating (outstanding, satisfactory, needs to improve, or substantial noncompliance) are to be kept on file and also made available to the public upon request. Regulators are required to take lenders' CRA performances into account when evaluating applications from those institutions they supervise whenever the lenders seek permission to open a new branch, merge or purchase another institution, increase their depository insurance, or make almost any other significant change in their business practices. The key provision of the CRA is that third parties can challenge such applications. These challenges often delay consideration of the application and, therefore, can be quite costly for the financial institution. Regulators rarely deny applications on CRA grounds, but often they take time to review the challenges and frequently ask the lender and the organization filing the challenge to attempt to seek a voluntary solution. This challenge process provides leverage that several groups have used to negotiate reinvestment or CRA agreements. Community organizations, often in conjunction with supportive public officials, sympathetic reporters and academics, and friendly lenders have exploited the opportunities created by the information made available through HMDA and the affirmative requirements established by the CRA (Marsico 1996). This is the basic procedure by which community organizations in Milwaukee (see chapter 9) and throughout the United States negotiated the one trillion dollars in lending agreements reported by NCRC.

Although each CRA agreement is unique, most include a combination of the following provisions. Generally they include commitments for home purchase and home improvement loans for single family and multifamily units. Some are at below market rates, others waive various closing costs, while others reduce points, and still others eliminate or reduce mortgage insurance requirements. Underwriting standards have been altered and made more flexible. Counseling, second reviews of rejected applications, and self-testing for discrimination are other elements of some agreements. Business loans are frequently incorporated often targeting small businesses, minority and women-owned businesses, and other commercial development projects. Participation in public and privately formed loan pools is featured in some agreements. Consumer and farm loans are required by others.

Improved banking services are a feature of many programs. They include new branch banks, free checking accounts, cashing of government checks, hiring bilingual staff, and other affirmative action to diversify lender workforces. A variety of new marketing and educational programs are also frequently incorporated. Specific elements include advertising in minority media, call programs to meet with local realtors in minority areas, seminars on homeownership, individual and family counseling, and various reporting programs to increase accountability (National Community Reinvestment Coalition undated).

Perhaps the most concrete evidence of the shifting role of the federal government is a series of settlements that the Department of Justice has entered into with diverse lenders in all regions of the country. Since 1992 the Department has brought thirteen lending cases resulting in more than $33 million in monetary relief and adoption of new policies and procedures to provide for equal treatment of bank customers (Lee 1999: 39).

In 1992 the Department settled the first pattern and practice lawsuit brought by the federal government against a mortgage lender. Following up Bill Dedman's Atlanta research, the Department launched an investigation of one of Atlanta's largest mortgage lenders, Decatur Federal Savings and Loan. Among the evidence obtained by Justice was the fact that between 1985 and 1990 over 97 percent of the lender's mortgage loans were made in predominantly white census tracts and not one of the institution's forty-three branch offices were in black census tracts. Little marketing was done in minority areas and few minorities were employed in professional positions. Black applicants were rejected more than four times as often as whites and a multivariate analysis of more than two thousand loan files found race to be a significant factor in determining whether or not to approve the loan after controlling on relevant socioeconomic characteristics. The settlement included $1 million for forty-eight plaintiffs and changes in the lender's underwriting practices, commitments to increase advertising in minority media and marketing efforts in minority communities, affirmative action commitments to increase minority employment, and changes in the compensation structure of loan officers to encourage more inner-city lending (United States v. Decatur Federal Savings & Loan Association C.A., No 1:92-CV-2198 [N.D. Ga. 1992]).

In its lawsuit against Shawmut Mortgage Company in Boston, the Justice Department charged that the company required black and Hispanic applicants to provide more information than whites, applied more stringent underwriting requirements to blacks and Hispanics by failing to consider compensating factors that were taken into consideration with white applicants, and failed to approve the applications of blacks and Hispanics that did not meet all the lender's underwriting standards but which were equal to or better than applications from whites that were approved. Justice also charged that the lender utilized several underwriting guidelines that exerted a disparate impact on black and Hispanic applicants including failure to consider the stability of an applicants' income as opposed to employment stability, prior record of rent and utility payments, and nontraditional sources of cash for downpayments. Terms of the settlement included, the creation of a $960,000 compensation fund for those injured by the lender's previous practices, opening a new branch in the predominantly minority community of Roxbury, more advertising in minority communities, training of loan officers in the principles of fair lending, and expansion of its mortgage review board that reevaluates qualifications of rejected minority applicants (United States v. Shawmut Mortgage Company C.A., No. 3:93 CV 2453 [D. Conn. 1993]).

The Department of Justice charged First National Bank of Vicksburg in Mississippi with charging higher interest rates and offering different terms and conditions to minority borrowers than were offered to whites. The bank agreed to develop new loan policies that would provide for nondiscriminatory loan terms, implement a loan review process to assure compliance with fair lending requirements, develop an educational program on fair lending for loan officers, contract with a qualified organization to conduct paired testing of the bank in the future, and deposit $750,000 into a trust account to be administered jointly with Justice for loans to those aggrieved by the bank's past practice (United States v. First National Bank of Vicksburg C.A. No. 5:94 CV 6[B][N][W.D. Miss. 1994]).

Blackpipe State Bank in South Dakota was charged with discriminating against American Indians by refusing to make loans on properties located on Indian reservations and providing different terms and conditions on loans it did make for American Indians. The lender agreed to expand its service area to include reservations, train its loan officers in fair lending practices, recruit Indian employees, market its loan products to American Indian communities, and provide $125,000 in compensation to victims of past practices (United States v. Blackpipe State Bank C.A. No. 93-5115 [D. S.D. 1994]).

In its case against Chevy Chase Federal Savings Bank in Maryland, Justice did not find evidence of discriminatory treatment in the underwriting of applications from minority borrowers, but rather charged the bank with discriminating in its marketing practices due to its failure to market its products in minority communities within the Washington D.C. metropolitan area. Over 97 percent of the bank's loans were in white areas, in part because only four of its seventy-seven branches and eighteen mortgage offices were in predominantly black census tracts. Justice also charged the bank with failing to solicit loans in black neighborhoods, advertising primarily to white customers, and using a commission structure discouraging small loans, which adversely impacts on minority areas. The bank agreed to pay $11 million to redlined areas through a special loan program and to open three branch banks and one mortgage office. Chevy Chase also agreed to extensively advertise and target sales calls in black areas, recruit black loan officers, and take steps to obtain a market share in black communities comparable to its share in white areas (United States v. Chevy Chase Federal Savings Bank et al., C.A. No. 9-1-1824JG [D. D.C. 1994]).

In the spring of 1995 the Department settled a case against the Northern Trust Company in Chicago. Relying primarily on a review of loan files the Department found that the bank provided white applicants, but not black or Hispanic applicants, with an opportunity to explain adverse items on their credit reports. The bank also often helped white applicants find offsetting qualifications to compensate for those negative factors but did not provide the same assistance for blacks and Hispanics. As a result, sixty victims received $566,500 in damages, an additional $133,500 was placed in a fund to compensate additional victims who may be identified, and the bank agreed to take actions to assure that all applicants have the opportunity to fully present their qualifications (United States v. Northern Trust Company C.A. No. 95C3239 [E.D. Ill. 1995]).

Subsequent cases in Ohio, California, New Mexico, Nebraska, and New York have resulted in similar relief and institutional change (Lee 1999:49).

Justice is not alone in its efforts to combat discrimination and redlining. In 1993 the Office of the Comptroller of the Currency (OCC) announced that it would soon be using paired testing as part of its investigatory tools. In 1998 OCC also created a new economics unit to bolster its fair lending enforcement efforts (Office of the Comptroller of the Currency 1998). That same year HUD pledged to double its enforcement efforts and in April announced the largest settlement of a lending discrimination case in U.S. history. Dallas-based AccuBanc Mortgage Corporation agreed to target $2.1 billion in mortgages to minorities and low- and moderate-income families in three years. This nationwide lender will also provide closing cost assistance and training for its staff on diversity issues (U.S. Department of Housing and Urban Development 1998).

The Federal Housing Enterprises Financial Safety and Soundness Act passed in 1992 established specific numerical goals for the purchase of loans by the Federal National Mortgage Association (Fannie Mae) and the Federal Home Loan Mortgage Corporation (Freddie Mac) to finance mortgages for low- and moderate-income families and in central cities. These two private government sponsored enterprises are major actors in the secondary mortgage market which purchases loans from loan originators and in doing so increase the pool of funds available for mortgage loans. In 1998 Fannie Mae announced a $2 billion initiative to increase minority homeownership with downpayments as low as 3 percent. And in 1999 it announced new products that will lower mortgage insurance costs for qualified low-income buyers (Fannie Mae 1999). Freddie Mac announced a five-city (including Milwaukee) initiative that will provide for downpayments as low as $1,000, mortgages for single family and two-family houses, and rehabilitation loans. In Milwaukee alone $50 million have been set aside for this program (New Opportunities for Homeownership in Milwaukee 1998a).

In January 1994, President Clinton issued Executive Order 12892 calling for all relevant federal agencies to develop rules assuring that their programs will be administered in a manner that affirmatively furthers fair housing. Among the specific mandates of this order is a directive to HUD to promulgate detailed regulations describing the nature and scope of lending conduct that violates the Federal Fair Housing Act. Although discriminatory lending practices have been explicitly prohibited since the Act was passed in 1968, HUD (the agency charged with primary responsibility for enforcement and the only agency with authority to issue clarifying regulations) had never previously promulgated such rules.

An Interagency Task Force on Lending Discrimination was also created in 1994. (The Task Force consists of eleven agencies including the Departments of Justice, HUD, and the Treasury, as well as the Federal Reserve Board, Comptroller of the Currency, Office of Thrift Supervision, Federal Deposit Insurance Corporation, Federal Housing Finance Board, Federal Trade Commission, National Credit Union Administration, Office of Federal Housing Oversight.) The Task Force issued a Policy Statement on Discrimination (1994) to provide guidance for lenders, consumers, and others on the types of practices that would constitute illegal lending discrimination. Although this statement does not supplant the detailed regulations of each regulatory agency, it represents an initial step to provide a more coordinated response to the problem of discrimination.

Perhaps the most significant component of the statement is the conclusion that unlawful discrimination can occur as a result of disparate impact as well as by intentional discrimination or disparate treatment. Under the disparate impact standard, particular policies or practices that are applied uniformly across all applicants and are neutral on their face may exclude a disproportionate share of protected class members and, therefore, may constitute unlawful discrimination. Where such a practice can be justified as a business necessity and where no less discriminatory alternative is available that would serve that business purpose, there would be no violation. But, as the Chevy Chase case cited above indicates, intentional discrimination against black or Hispanic applicants, or individual members of any protected class, may not be necessary to establish the presence of unlawful discrimination and to trigger remedial and affirmative actions by lending institutions.

Several voluntary initiatives have followed from the pressure generated by community groups and law enforcement authorities. The word "voluntary," of course, must be used advisedly in this context. But for whatever reason, several lenders have initiated efforts, sometimes in collaboration with community organizations and regulators, and often on their own to increase their presence in low-income areas and minority communities.

A recent survey of 130 lenders by the Consumer Bankers Associations indicates how widely at least certain changes have been institutionalized (Harney 1994). Of those surveyed, 96 percent had lowered their downpayment requirements for moderate-income buyers with the average downpayment on "affordable housing" being just 4.2 percent. Over 93 percent reported they had developed more flexible standards for their front end ratio (monthly housing payment compared to monthly income) and back end ratio (total monthly debts compared to income). Industry standard ratios are approximately 28 percent and 36 percent. For moderate-income buyers these ratios average 33 percent and 39 percent among those reporting more flexible standards.

Lenders are also utilizing new approaches for evaluating credit and work histories. More than 94 percent of the respondents to this survey report that they now take into consideration rent and utility payments in addition to conventional credit reports. Almost 80 percent reported they now look beyond length of employment with current employer and consider such factors as length of time employed generally and income stream over time.

The Mortgage Bankers of America (MBA) and HUD (1994) announced a collaborative effort to stimulate more lending activity in minority areas. In a Fair Lending—Best Practices Master Agreement, HUD and the MBA set out a series of "Best Practices" that they will encourage mortgage lenders to pledge to follow. The MBA will encourage its members to sign an agreement to pursue these policies and objectives. This is strictly a voluntary initiative that has no force of law.

Under this agreement the MBA will assist its members in conducting self-testing, The association will also foster closer working relationships between its members and real estate agents, developers and others active in minority communities. The association will develop educational and other outreach programs to increase minority employment in the industry. It will also foster education and training programs for consumers and current loan officers. And the association will assist in the development of more flexible underwriting standards and market analysis tools for lenders.

Individual lenders will be asked to sign a pledge to pursue "best practices" to improve their performance in minority and low-income neighborhoods. These include setting goals to increase lending activity in such areas, promotion of more flexible underwriting guidelines, establishment of second review programs to reconsider rejected loan applications to assure compliance with fair lending principles, self-monitoring efforts to assess market share in previously underserved areas, establishing outreach programs to work with local business and community groups, and minority recruitment and training efforts to increase minority employment. Performance targets will be established to permit evaluation of these efforts in the future.

James McLaughlin, a lobbyist for the American Bankers Association stated, "It's pretty clear the mortgage bankers were hoping to fend off CRA-type regulation" (Knight 1994). (Independent mortgage bankers not tied to federally regulated depository institutions are not covered by the CRA.) Unquestionably, there are a variety of motives that stimulate such "voluntary" actions. But these are steps that would not have been contemplated just a few years ago.

Persistent Barriers

Not surprisingly, enactment of these statutes and implementation of these programs have not eliminated discrimination in mortgage lending. Racial disparities have been documented by several academic researchers (Bradbury et al. 1989; Shlay et al. 1992), government agencies (Munnell et al. 1996; Canner and Smith 1992), journalists (Dedman 1989: Everett et al. 1988), community and policy advocacy groups (Immergluck and Wiles 1999; National Community Reinvestment Coalition undated) and others (Carr and Megbolugbe 1993; *Housing Policy Debate* 1992).

Nationwide black mortgage loan applicants are rejected approximately twice as often as whites with the Hispanic rejection rate falling between that of blacks and whites. This gap can be partially explained by differences in the socioeconomic status and, therefore, credit worthiness of these groups. But other factors, including discrimination, also contribute to this gap. The most comprehensive study of mortgage lending discrimination was conducted by the Boston Federal Reserve Bank (Munnell et al. 1996). In examining over three thousand loan application files with 131 Boston area lenders, the researchers found that among black and white applicants with identical credit records, debt histories, income, and other financial characteristics, the black applicants were rejected 60 percent more often than the white applicants.

Among the discriminatory practices that contribute to the racial gap in mortgage lending is the differential "coaching" that black and white applicants receive. Marginal white applicants (e.g., those whose current debt to income ratios slightly exceed traditional guidelines) are more likely to be counseled during their application so that the final application can be approved whereas black applicants will simply be rejected. White applicants, for example, may be advised to pay off or consolidate certain debts. Loan officers may also look more closely for compensating factors in the application of white borrowers or simply be more familiar with existing compensating factors of white applicants (Munnell et al. 1996; Hunter and Walker 1995). Concentration of bank offices in suburban communities, underwriting guidelines that have a disparate impact on minority applicants though no racial animus is intended (e.g., minimum loan amounts that exclude a disproportionately higher number of racial minorities than whites), and the relatively small number of black employees in lending institutions (see chapter 8) are some of the contributing factors (Cloud and Galster 1993; Williams and Nesiba 1997; Squires 1992).

In Chicago Calvin Bradford of Community Reinvestment Associates recently found that among comparable middle- and upper-income neighborhoods and borrowers, black borrowers and those seeking homes in black communities were being steered to Federal Housing Authority (FHA) loans, contributing to the financial distress of those communities (Dedman 1998). The Fair Housing Council of Greater Washington found that among equally qualified white and nonwhite testers, nonwhites were treated less favorably in more than 40 percent of all tests (Haggerty 1998). And the National Bureau of Economic Research found in a 1993 survey that black business owners were three times as likely as whites to be turned down for small business loans. Among businesses that were comparable in terms of credit rating, age, size, geographic location, and experience of owner, black-owned firms were still twice as likely to be rejected. Black businesses that were approved paid an average of one percent more in interest (Blanchflower, Levine, and Zimmerman 1998).

Recent evidence does suggest that, despite continuing barriers, lending to low- and moderate-income and minority markets has increased and that community reinvestment advocacy and fair lending law enforcement are, at least in part, responsible. Partisan declarations and, more recently, econometric evidence point in this direction. John Taylor, Executive Director of the National Community Reinvestment Coalition, reported that the share of loans to low- and moderate-income borrowers increased from 18 percent to 28 percent in 1997. For blacks and Hispanics the increase was from 10 percent to 14 percent (Taylor 1999a). Evanoff and Segal (1996) found that since the Community Reinvestment Act was passed lending activity to low-income individuals and neighborhoods has increased faster than it has in other areas. Schwartz (1998) found that lenders with CRA agreements have larger market shares in low-income and minority markets than those who have not entered into such agreements. Shlay (1999) examined lenders with and without CRA agreements and communities where there had been high and low levels of organizing. Although she did not find significant differences between these two sets of lenders, she concluded that local organizing created an impetus for more effective CRA enforcement nationwide. In its assessment of the impact of the CRA the U.S. Department of the Treasury found substantial increases in lending activities in traditionally underserved communities, particularly by institutions covered by the law. CRA covered institutions and their affiliates increased their lending to low- and moderate-income borrowers and communities by 39 percent between 1993 and 1998 while their loans to other borrowers increase by 17 percent (Litan et al. 2000: 68).

Members of the Federal Reserve Board have testified to this effect as well. Governor Edward M. Gramlich has frequently stated his belief in the need for further empirical evidence on the effect of CRA yet he concluded,

> CRA does seem to have generated a large amount of new loans . . . There seems to be little doubt that most of these outcomes would not have occurred in the absence of CRA and other fair lending laws. All of these conclusions, however, are based on fragmentary data, and it would certainly be productive to conduct some new surveys to verify the results. (Gramlich 1998)

More recently he observed that CRA lending appears to be profitable for lenders. He pointed to a survey of large lenders in which 98 percent concluded that their CRA loans were profitable and 24 percent found them as profitable or more profitable than other loans (Gramlich

1999). Governor Laurence H. Meyer concurred stating, "At no time in our history has credit been more available and more affordable to virtually all income groups, than it is today. The Community Reinvestment Act has contributed to this increase in the availability and affordability of credit" (Meyer 1998a).

Not everyone agrees. Some contend that enforcement pressure by regulators may have forced some lenders to make loans to low-income borrowers who were not able to handle the payments and, therefore, who subsequently lost their investments when they went into default (Benston 1997). Three researchers with the Dallas Federal Reserve Bank have argued that market pressures and improved technology providing for more information on potential borrowers account for increasing lending in previously underserved areas rather than CRA and related enforcement efforts (Gunther, Klemme, and Robinson 1999). And one of these Dallas Federal Reserve Bank staff members suggested that there may be a conflict between the safety and soundness standards lenders are required to meet and the objectives spelled out in the CRA (Gunther 1999).

But most of the empirical evidence indicates that attitudes and behaviors of many lenders have changed and that community reinvestment advocacy and enforcement efforts have contributed significantly to these developments. And it appears these changes have not come at the expense of unprofitable lending. In a recent Federal Reserve Board survey 82 percent of financial institutions reported that their CRA related home purchase and refinance lending was profitable or marginally profitable. While overall home purchase and refinance lending was reported to be more profitable, 56 percent said their CRA related loans were just as profitable as their other home purchase and refinancing loans (Federal Reserve Board 2000: v). The extent and permanency of these changes, however, remain in doubt.

New programs have been created, law enforcement actions have been initiated, partnerships among lenders and community groups have been formed, and financial institutions have launched their own unilateral efforts. The question that remains is whether or not lending patterns and practices have significantly changed. Despite major national policy developments and consolidation among financial service providers, lending is predominantly a local issue. If mergers, buyouts, and concentration generally are the hallmarks of financial industry restructuring today, lending decisions are still made principally by local actors in response to local conditions. If lending has changed, it is at the local level that these changes must be evident.

The Milwaukee Case

Like cities throughout the United States, Milwaukee has experienced diverse trajectories of uneven development and the social costs associated with that development. Throughout the latter half of the twentieth century cities have been losing people, business, jobs, and other resources to their suburban rings and beyond. Deindustrialization, the loss of manufacturing jobs, and the rise of both high-wage professional service positions and low-wage personal-service jobs have contributed to inequality throughout urban America. Poverty has become increasingly concentrated. Segregation persists. Urban sprawl has exacerbated a longstanding spatial mismatch which has resulted in jobs being increasingly distant from and out of reach of those urban residents most in need. A combination of private investment practices and public policies have fueled the uneven development of metropolitan America. These patterns have been clearly manifested in Milwaukee.

Nationwide the share of central city residents within metropolitan areas declined from 43.0 percent in 1970 to 33.8 percent in1994. Jobs have shifted in a similar pattern (Wyly, Glickman, and Lahr 1998: 20). In 1970 the income of city and suburban residents was comparable. In 1989 suburban residents earned 22 percent more than urban residents and by 1996 the gap reached 31 percent (U.S. Department of Housing and Urban Development 1998: 9). Between 1970 and 1990 the number of census tracts with concentrated poverty (more than 20 percent of the residents living on incomes below the poverty line) doubled as did the number of people living in them. One consequence has been the increasing unaffordability of housing. In 1976 44.8 percent of households could afford the median priced home nationwide. By 1996 this dropped to 36.5 percent (Wyly, Glickman, and Lahr 1998: 23–25). Metropolitan areas continue to be highly segregated with the vast majority of whites and nonwhites living in racially homogeneous neighborhoods in part because blacks continue to be denied twice as often as whites in their mortgage loan applications (Massey and Denton 1993; Denton 1999). A relatively strong national economy has improved the economic condition of most cities during the 1990s, but many communities are still left behind. Suburbs are still growing faster than cities and poverty rates remain higher than 20 percent in 170 cities, nearly one-third of all cities nationwide (U.S. Department of Housing and Urban Development 1999: 2). And many inner ring suburbs are starting to experience the kinds of problems that previously had been associated with central cities. (U.S. Department of Housing and Urban Development and Guaranty Bank 1999: 2–5; Orfield 1997; Rusk 1999).

Milwaukee fits this pattern. The city's population peaked at approximately 740,000 in the 1950s and dropped to 640,000 in the 1990s. Meanwhile, the metropolitan area has continued to grow to more than 1.3 million (Squires 1998). In the past two decades the City of Milwaukee lost more than 14,000 jobs while the suburban ring gained more than 100,000 (White et al. 1995: 24). Per capita income in the city was 83.6 percent of suburban per capita income in 1970 and this dropped to 63.4 percent in 1990 (Levine 1998: 36). Among the nation's one hundred largest metropolitan areas the concentration of poverty is highest in Milwaukee (Coulton et al. 1996). The number of high poverty census tracts grew from eleven in 1970 to fifty-nine in 1990, one of the largest increases nationwide (Jargowsky 1996: 225). The percentage of households that could afford the median priced home in the Milwaukee metropolitan area dropped from 83.5 percent in 1991 to 68.9 percent in 1998 (Sharma-Jensen 1998). Massey and Denton (1993) included Milwaukee among their list of sixteen hypersegregated cities. In 1990 black median family income was just 39.5 percent of the white median, down from 65.1 percent in 1970. Black poverty and unemployment rates are four times higher than white rates (Levine 1998: 110–111). And according to HMDA reports, mortgage loan applications from blacks are consistently denied four or five times as often as whites, which is twice the national average.

A variety of forces have nurtured these patterns of development in Milwaukee and urban communities around the nation. The increasing mobility of capital, the globalization of the economy generally, and the deindustrialization of city neighborhoods have reinforced preexisting forms of inequality (Harrison and Bluestone 1988; Wilson 1996). Schlitz, Pabst, Allis-Chalmers, Allen-Bradley, American Motors, and Briggs and Stratton are just some of the former household names that have either shut down or greatly reduced their operations in Milwaukee. Racial discrimination and segregation have hindered opportunities for educational attainment, job advancement, homeownership, accumulation of wealth, and participation in virtually every sphere of society (Massey and Denton 1993; Darity Jr. and Mason 1998; Oliver and Shapiro 1995). The structure of racial inequality has given rise to an oppositional culture characterized by drug use, criminal activity, nonwork, out of wedlock births and other forms of so-called "underclass" behavior (Wilson 1987; Anderson 1999).

Public policy has also contributed to the uneven development of metropolitan areas. Urban sprawl has been driven by federally funded highways, federal subsidies of homeownership via income tax deductions for property taxes and interest on mortgage payments, and locally funded infrastructure (e.g., schools, sewer systems) all of which have gone disproportionately to white suburbanites (Jackson 1985; Orfield 1997; Norquist 1998). Local officials have used a variety of economic development subsidies (e.g., tax increment finance districts, below market-rate loans, urban renewal funds, urban development action grants, enterprise zone funds) primarily to support downtown development (Norman 1989). New office towers, convention centers, and sports arenas are the types of projects that have generally been the targets of such development. Consequently, downtown development, and the suburban residents who staff the professional services industries concentrated downtown have benefited, often at the expense of surrounding urban neighborhoods (Keating, Krumholz, and Star 1996; Cummings 1988; Squires 1989).

One area where private practice and public policy overlap is housing and particularly housing finance. As indicated above, the practices of mortgage lenders, often operating under the requirements of federal policies, have favored predominantly white suburban communities over urban and particularly minority neighborhoods. In Milwaukee, as in cities around the country, people have begun to fight back.

Redlining is an issue that community organizations in Milwaukee have organized around for many years, and in recent years several financial institutions have responded, often at the prodding of public officials, the media, and regulatory agencies. The 1989 report of the Fair Lending Action Committee (FLAC) noted above reflected long years of confrontation and triggered several positive developments.

After Park State Bank announced in 1964 that it was closing its office in a lower-income neighborhood on the west side, three community organizations emerged to combat similar actions in the future. While it took many years for these organizing efforts to bear fruit, in 1980 Cooperation West Side Associates (COWSA) was able to block a closing announced by Midtown Bank. Agreements with M & I Bank, Bank One, and First Financial Savings followed between 1985 and 1991 totaling more than $100 million in loan commitments, a branch bank, and "lifeline" rates to make basic banking services more affordable to low-income residents (Glabere 1992). Organizing efforts increased after the release of the FLAC report and the formation of the Fair Lending Coalition (FLC) (see chapter 9). FLC is an interracial coalition of labor, civil rights, and other community groups which has negotiated agreements with eleven lenders totaling over $160 million, three new branch banks, affirmative action commitments, and other efforts to increase access to credit in the central city and for racial minorities throughout the metropolitan area.

The Wisconsin Housing and Economic Development Authority (WHEDA), a state affiliated organization that provides resources to stimulate community development, has become much more active in Milwaukee's central city in recent years. Over the past seven years WHEDA has provided $50 million in home loans to encourage homeownership in that community (Wisconsin Housing and Economic Development Authority 1998: 4). This has translated into 177 loans for the Target Area in 1997, up from 122 in 1990 (Wisconsin Housing and Economic Development Authority 1999).

Under the Greenline Homeowners Assistance Program, financed by the American Family Insurance Company as part of its 1995 settlement of a fair housing lawsuit, $9.5 million in below market-rate loans for homeownership and property maintenance became available for residents of the central city. More than nine hundred families have received subsidized loans or grants through this program (NAACP Insurance Settlement Class Committee 1999).

The City of Milwaukee has assisted these efforts. It provides financial support for the FLC and each year the Comptroller issues a report on mortgage lending which serves as an annual reminder of persisting credit gaps in Milwaukee. Milwaukee's mayor also assisted in the development of a consortium of lenders whose primary objective is to nurture homeownership among low- and moderate-income residents through housing counseling and other partnership activity among lenders, government agencies, and community groups. New Opportunities for Homeownership in Milwaukee (NOHIM) has fifty-five members including many lenders and community organizations. Among its achievements was the $50 million Freddie Mac program noted above (New Opportunities for Homeownership in Milwaukee 1998a). A focus of much NOHIM activity is the homebuyer counseling provided by seven affiliated community organizations. One of those organizations is the Walkers Point Community Development Corporation which serves primarily Milwaukee's Hispanic community on the south side. According to Denise Wise, the Executive Director, clients have no difficulty securing a mortgage loan after they have been through the counseling program: "one of the things that we don't have any problems with banks is mortgages . . . We take our applicants in . . . We experience no denials" (Wise 1998).

In 1999 Guaranty Bank renewed the "Best Practices Agreement" it initially signed with HUD in 1996. (Guaranty is also one of the lenders that negotiated a community reinvestment agreement with the Fair Lending Coalition.) Among the commitments Guaranty Bank made in the agreement are the following: maintaining a minority and low-income denial ratio that currently ranks among the lowest quartile for home mortgage lenders; utilizing flexible underwriting standards that contain valid indicators of creditworthiness; ensuring fair consideration of nontraditional sources of income like child support payments and disability income; providing a "second look" review to assure that all loan standards are applied consistently; conducting and participating in educational programs and other partnership activities with real estate agents, churches, and other neighborhood organizations; and maintaining a diverse work force. Guaranty sees no conflict between its community reinvestment objectives and its normal business goals. As noted above, the bank concluded that "equal access to credit enhances our profitability potential" (U. S. Department of Housing and Urban Development and Guaranty Bank 1999).

In one of the boldest developments, three veteran bankers opened up a new bank in the heart of Milwaukee's central city in August 1999. Three African American women raised the capital to launch Legacy Bank, a full service commercial bank that will provide a full range of business and home lending products along with financial education services for its customers. Legacy's target market is 97 percent African American and the median family income is just over $19,000 (Causey 1999).

It is evident that the CRA has encouraged these and related voluntary initiatives on the part of lenders. As Denise Wise observed "if it wasn't for CRA the investment wouldn't be here" (Wise 1998). She also sees continuing barriers. For example, she claims some lenders still question where a minority could get money for a downpayment particularly when it is in cash. She has had to explain to more than one lender that in her culture (she is Latina) some Mexicans do not trust banks. So they keep money at home "in coffee cans." But Wise says she is having success in convincing lenders that "mattress money" is acceptable.

Pam Smith, vice president and affordable lending manager at Firstar Bank and former NOHIM chairperson also sees considerable progress in Milwaukee, but believes part of the community remains to be convinced. "So I think while credit is certainly available I think part of the population needs to be still convinced and made aware that it is available" (Smith 1998). Tim Elverman, former Wisconsin director of government relations for Bank One, echoed these sentiments when he responded to a question about remaining barriers: "I would still put up more than anything else in my humble view, perception; people not thinking they can get credit" (Elverman 1998). He also maintained that there have been dramatic positive changes in large part because of the improved perception of lenders. He conceded that discrimination was widespread in the 1970s:

> lending institutions were part of this whole game of steering people in certain geographies and we just wouldn't approve credit. Banks understood they wouldn't approve credit for people who were violating somehow these unwritten rules we had about where people were going to live. So the realtors wouldn't bring the people to the banks, the banks of course wouldn't reach out to the people and when by chance an application actually crossed the desk it was coded by the realtor so the banker knew that they were not to approve the credit and that was a practice in the institutions as late as the 1970s. (Elverman 1998)

But, he maintains, attitudes have changed in terms of both racial and geographic discrimination.

Margaret Henningsen, a veteran participant in and observer of Milwaukee's real estate and housing finance industries, is not so sure. Henningsen is a former realtor and banker who is one of the principals at Legacy Bank. When asked about remaining barriers, she also pointed to the industry's attitude, but observed, "I think it's regressing" (Henningsen 1998). To the extent that progress has been made, she claims it is due more to some of the people that have been brought into financial institutions than policies of the banks themselves. She is particularly ambivalent about the mortgage counseling programs that have been started. For those who need the counseling, that is good, but others who do not need counseling are simply being asked to meet requirements others do not have to meet. She stated:

> The programs that have been structured where banks have said "Okay, if you have to do this, then we're going to make you do things that your other customers don't have to do if you want these loans" . . . So, if you're in one of these programs that are designed for lending in the central city or for minorities, then they had different criteria . . . To me it was good, but it was still discrimination. My push all along was to treat every customer the same. If you had bad credit, you didn't get a loan. If you had no credit everybody had to follow the same rules. If you had good credit, of course, you got approved. (Henningsen 1998)

Perhaps the clearest indicator of her perspective on credit barriers in Milwaukee is her involvement with Legacy Bank. One of the motivations for starting the bank, she said, is "the fact that it still is very hard for minorities to get capital to start small businesses, to maintain the existing ones that they own and to become a homeowner (Henningsen 1998).

Henningsen also expressed some concern with CRA. She credits the law for getting several lenders involved in central city lending, but believes "the law needs to have much bigger teeth." In particular, she fears that community groups do not have the power to block the major mergers that are occurring and lenders are becoming less concerned with the law (Henningsen 1998). At the same time, she acknowledges that CRA has been a significant boost to her efforts to launching Legacy Bank. As a minority- and female-owned institution, other financial institutions have provided loans and investments in order to enhance their own CRA records (Federal Reserve Bank of Chicago 1999).

Perhaps Leo Ries, former deputy commissioner of the Department of Neighborhood Services of the City of Milwaukee, captured recent developments in Milwaukee best when he pointed to the value of collaborative and confrontational approaches. In commenting on NOHIM and the FLC he observed, "you have to work both the positive and the collaborative efforts as well as the more confrontational approaches in order to move things along" (Ries 1999). Ries, who is active with and a strong supporter of NOHIM, also expressed a desire for a stronger CRA. He noted ". . . it does make an impact on the lenders . . . that the lenders keep trying to challenge Congress and water it down suggests that they must be threatened by it" (Ries 1999).

A range of initiatives has been launched in Milwaukee to increase lending in previously underserved areas. Attitudes appear generally more supportive of community reinvestment. Local organizing coupled with more aggressive law enforcement at the national level have brought more partners to the negotiating table. A combination of local, state, and national initiatives have created new loan products and services, built new branch banks, and created an overall environment that is more attentive to community reinvestment concerns. A question that arises, however, is whether and to what extent changes have occurred in the delivery of financial services. Are low- and moderate-income neighborhoods receiving better service? Are racial gaps closing? What developments, economic and political, are in the offing that may affect recent efforts? The following chapters examine what has happened in Milwaukee from several different perspectives.

The following chapter examines the distribution of loans and loan dollars by race and ethnicity as well as by neighborhood income level during the 1990s. It finds that large gaps remain between the share of households in these groups and the share of mortgage loans and loan dollars they receive. And while lending to blacks and Hispanics as a proportion of all lending in the metropolitan area has increased noticeably, lending to low-income areas has improved, but almost imperceptibly.

How Milwaukee compares with other metropolitan areas around the country and with similar large communities in the nation's Frostbelt is the subject of chapter 3. It finds that Milwaukee is roughly at or above average on most indicators of community reinvestment but is at or near the top and bottom on a number of key measures.

Race and ethnic disparities in Milwaukee's suburbs are examined in chapter 4. It finds that while lending has increased slightly to blacks and Hispanics, at current rates of progress it would take 141 years to eliminate the black/white lending gap and seventeen years to close the Hispanic gap.

How individual lenders compare with each other is the topic of chapter 5. Dramatic variations among lenders are found in the distribution of mortgage lending activity by race, ethnicity, and income.

Similar disparities are found in the allocation of small business credit. Chapter 6 finds that small business lending activity in Milwaukee is concentrated in middle- and upper-income areas and is concentrated in such communities more heavily than is the case nationwide. Large racial disparities are also found along with substantial differences among lending institutions on each measure of small business lending.

One change in the financial landscape nationwide is the emergence of so-called "fringe banking" institutions. In Milwaukee check-cashing services have recently become significant actors in the financial services marketplace. Chapter 7 finds that in Milwaukee, as is generally the case nationwide, these services are heavily concentrated in minority and low-income communities though they are beginning to spread throughout the metropolitan area. While check-cashing services are not sources for mortgage or business loans, their presence reflects critical structural changes in the financial services industry that do reflect access to these services. When check-cashers become the banker of choice (or forced choice) it becomes more difficult to establish relationships with conventional banking institutions and secure access to conventional mortgage and small business loans.

Many factors account for uneven lending patterns. Chapter 8 examines one potential cause; employment of minorities among lending institutions. The basic finding is that lenders who employ relatively more minorities, particularly in professional occupations, are more responsive to applications from minority borrowers.

If the CRA has been a linchpin for community reinvestment activity, it is organizing at the local level that has made it work. Chapter 9 analyzes the role of the Fair Lending Coalition which was created to utilize leverage provided by the CRA to encourage banks to meet their obligations under that act.

The numbers show some progress. But that progress is fragile. Legislation to limit CRA is introduced annually and the bank modernization bill recently enacted by Congress does, in fact, roll back some provisions of this statute. The national wave of consolidation and merger activity, which will increase considerably under the new law, threatens local community reinvestment commitments. Milwaukee has not been unaffected by these developments. No doubt further proposals to "reform" the CRA will be forthcoming and do not bode well for community reinvestment. Predatory lending and "reverse redlining" may have already exacerbated disinvestment problems in some communities. These issues are addressed in the final chapter.

Community development will persist as an economic development challenge, a contentious subject of political debate, and a national social movement. But the terms of that debate, the relative power of various actors, and the outcomes for American communities remain very much in doubt. Information alone will not resolve any of the impending matters. But hopefully, a more informed discussion will enhance the likelihood of more favorable outcomes for all parties involved.

2

Race, Ethnicity, and Income
The Persistent Lending Gaps

S INCE THE 1989 *ATLANTA JOURNAL-CONSTITUTION* story was published reporting that Milwaukee had the highest racial disparity in mortgage loan rejection rates of any large city in that decade, lending regulators, city and state officials, civil rights groups, and other community-based organizations have all responded, as indicated in chapter 1 (Dedman 1989). Some lenders have opened new branch offices and initiated ongoing relationships with real estate agents and community groups in neighborhoods where they previously conducted little business. Lender consortia have been formed to develop new products and seek out new markets. Regulators have stepped up their monitoring of lending activity. The mayor of Milwaukee and governor of Wisconsin have called for more aggressive actions to respond to allegations of discrimination and redlining. Community groups have taken legal actions against particular lenders. New partnerships, organizations, and lending programs have been created. And disparities associated with race, ethnicity, and income persist. Although some gaps have closed, substantial disparities remain.

This chapter documents the gaps in Milwaukee's mortgage lending market that have continued into the 1990s. The purpose is not to provide a detailed explanation for the racial disparities or to offer a blueprint for changing current practices. Rather, the objective is to examine the extent to which lending practices and patterns have changed since the *Atlanta Journal-Constitution* story was published.

The intensive and extensive reaction to the Atlanta story and subsequent activity reflect the essential nature of credit, particularly for homeownership, in urban communities. Without mortgage loans most families simply cannot buy or maintain a home. Credit is also essential to start, maintain, or expand a business. Community development, by any definition, depends on an adequate supply of affordable credit. In part for these reasons racial discrimination is prohibited by law under the Federal Fair Housing Act, the Equal Credit Opportunity Act, and many other federal banking regulations and state laws and regulations. For similar reasons redlining is prohibited by the Community Reinvestment Act (CRA) of 1977 which requires federally chartered depository institutions to ascertain and respond to the credit needs of their entire service areas, including low- and moderate-income communities. Refusing to provide credit or varying the terms and conditions under which credit is available due to the geographic location or neighborhood racial composition of a risk is just as problematic as denying service due to the race or any other characteristic of an individual applicant unrelated to credit-worthiness.

It is important to distinguish between racial disparities and racial discrimination. The fact that racial disparities exist in a market does not automatically mean that racial discrimination accounts for those differences. But understanding the basic facts of the experiences of different racial groups is a critical starting point for determining if there is a problem and, if so, the extent to which discrimination might be a factor. To that end, this chapter provides information on applications, loans, loan amounts, and denial rates for whites, blacks, Hispanics, and residents of distressed neighborhoods in the four-county (Milwaukee, Waukesha, Ozaukee, Washington) Milwaukee metropolitan area.

The Data

Information on lending practices and patterns are derived from Home Mortgage Disclosure Act (HMDA) reports that most mortgage lenders (e.g., commercial banks, savings institutions, credit unions, mortgage bankers) must submit annually (Federal Financial Institutions

Examination Council 1996a). These reports provide a variety of types of information for each mortgage loan application including: loan purpose (e.g., home purchase, home improvement, refinancing, and multifamily); dollar amount of loan; census tract of property; race, gender, and income of applicant; and disposition of loan (e.g., denied, approved).

Information on individual loan applicants has been made available to the general public since 1990. From 1976 through 1989 HMDA required disclosure of lending activity by census tract. This chapter is based on HMDA reports from 1990, 1994, and 1997. The number of HMDA reporting institutions has grown from 156 Milwaukee metropolitan area lenders in 1990 to 438 in 1997. The following pages document the number of applications received from, and loans and loan dollars that went to, whites, blacks, Hispanics, and residents of what the comptroller of the City of Milwaukee has defined as the Target Area during these years. It also examines denial rates for these groups. More significant are the percentages of all Milwaukee metropolitan area applications, loans, and loan dollars accounted for by these residents which are also reported.

The Target Area is a set of eighty-one census tracts in Milwaukee's central city that meet the following criteria:

1. Median assessed property value of one- and two-family dwellings is less than or equal to 80 percent of the median assessed property value of similar dwellings in the City of Milwaukee.

2. Median family income is less than or equal to 80 percent of the median family income for the City of Milwaukee.

3. The proportion of owner-occupied dwellings in the area is less than or equal to 80 percent of the proportion of owner-occupied dwellings in the City of Milwaukee

4. The vacancy rate of dwellings in the area is greater than or equal to 120 percent of the vacancy rate in the City of Milwaukee. (See map 2.1 and figure 2.1.)

The Findings

Several benchmarks provide the basis for measuring racial, ethnic, and income disparities in Milwaukee's mortgage market. The percentage of households in the metropolitan area that are black, Hispanic, or located within the Target Area constitute one frame of reference.

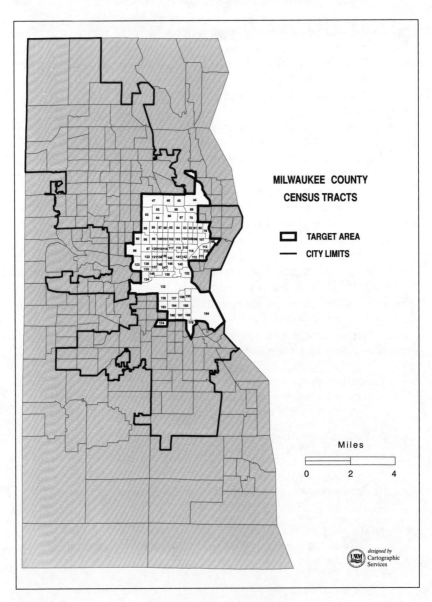

Map 2.1 Target Area and the City of Milwaukee

44	45	46	47	63	64	65	66	67
68	69	70	79	80	81	82	83	84
85	86	87	88	89	90	96	97	98
99	100	101	102	103	104	105	106	107
108	110	111	112	113	114	115	116	117
118	119	120	121	122	123	132	134	135
136	137	138	139	140	141	142	145	146
147	148	149	150	152	154	155	156	157
158	163	164	165	166	167	168	174	178

Figure 2.1 Census Tracts in City Target Area

According to the 1990 census, blacks constitute 11.5 percent, Hispanics account for 2.6 percent, and Target Area residents are 11.7 percent of all Milwaukee metropolitan area households. The Target Area also has a disproportionate share of the area's minority population. Blacks constitute 59.7 percent and Hispanics account for 11.4 percent of Target Area households. In examining progress or change of any kind over time, the place to begin, however, is with the share of resources received by the respective groups at different points in time. The question that arises is the following: How have these groups fared in Milwaukee's mortgage lending market during the 1990s?

Table 2.1 Mortgage Applications by Race and Target Area: Milwaukee Metropolitan Area, 1990, 1994, and 1997

	1990	1994	1997
Total Applications	28,120	56,064	72,018
White	22,591	43,514	48,995
Percent White	80.3	77.6	68.0
Black	1,753	5,015	7,208
Percent Black	6.2	9.0	10.0
Hispanic	501	1,455	1,874
Percent Hispanic	1.8	2.6	2.6
Target Area	1,481	3,226	4,586
Percent Target Area	5.3	5.8	6.4

SOURCE: 1990, 1994, and 1997 HMDA Data

Applications

The total number of applications received by HMDA reporting institutions increased substantially between 1990 and 1997. As shown in table 2.1, the applications grew from 28,120 to 72,018.

Loan applications from blacks grew faster than did the number of total applications. Consequently, the percentage of all applications from blacks grew from 6.2 percent to 10.0 percent. Hispanics accounted for a larger share of applications in 1997 (2.6 percent) than in 1990 (1.8 percent) as well. Applications from the Target Area rose from 5.3 percent in 1990 to 6.4 percent in 1997.

In every case, the percentage of applications (and the proportion of loans and loan dollars) is far below the representation of these respective groups among all households in the Milwaukee metropolitan area.

Loans

The surge in loan applications, not surprisingly, resulted in significant increases in the number of loans that were originated with loan volume increasing from 22,553 in 1990 to 47,193 in 1997. Blacks received a much higher percentage of all loans in 1997 (7.4 percent or 3,493 loans) than they did in 1990 (5.1 percent or 1,140 loans) as did Hispanics (2.4 percent or 1,130 loans compared to 1.6 percent or 369 loans) (see table 2.2).

Table 2.2 Mortgage Loans by Race and Target Area: Milwaukee Metropolitan Area, 1990, 1994, and 1997

	1990	*1994*	*1997*
Total Loans	22,553	43,445	47,193
White	19,563	36,968	38,058
Percent White	86.7	85.1	80.6
Black	1,140	3,003	3,493
Percent Black	5.1	6.9	7.4
Hispanic	369	1,028	1,130
Percent Hispanic	1.6	2.4	2.4
Target Area	867	1,732	1,977
Percent Target Area	3.8	4.0	4.2

SOURCE: 1990, 1994, and 1997 HMDA Data

Lending activity in the Target Area as a proportion of all loans in the metropolitan area showed a moderate increase from 3.8 percent or 867 loans in 1990 to 4.2 percent or 1,977 in 1997. The increased number of loans in this community reflects the significant increase in lending throughout the metropolitan area.

Overall, a closing of critical lending gaps has occurred. But this progress must be viewed in light of the substantial gaps that remain.

Loan Dollars

The total dollar volume of HMDA reported loans in the metropolitan area increased from $1.4 billion to $4.5 billion between 1990 and 1997. Just as the percentage of loans to blacks and Hispanics increased, so did the percentage of all loan dollars. For blacks the increase was from 2.8 percent or $40 million in 1990 to 3.5 percent or $156 million in 1997 and 1.0 percent or $15 million to 1.4 percent or $63 million for Hispanics (see table 2.3).

The percentage of loan dollars to the Target Area declined from 1.9 percent in 1990 to 1.7 percent in 1994, but increased to 2.0 percent in 1997. The dollar volume of lending in the Target Area increased from $27 million to $88 million; again this reflects the total increase throughout the metropolitan area. The share of lending in the Target Area remained virtually unchanged.

Table 2.3 Mortgage Loan Dollars by Race and Target Area: Milwaukee Metropolitan Area, 1990, 1994, and 1997

	1990	1994	1997
Total Loan Dollars	$1,407,692	$3,275,271	$4,469,946
White	$1,267,343	$2,939,256	$3,774,250
Percent White	90.0	89.7	84.4
Black	$39,688	$112,459	$156,432
Percent Black	2.8	3.4	3.5
Hispanic	$14,631	$47,079	$63,323
Percent Hispanic	1.0	1.4	1.4
Target Area	$27,353	$56,181	$87,744
Percent Target Area	1.9	1.7	2.0

SOURCE: 1990, 1994, and 1997 HMDA Data

Overall, racial minorities are submitting many more loan applications and the proportion of applications from minorities has increased. The denial rates for racial minorities are also increasing and at a faster rate than for white applicants. Racial minorities received a higher percentage of all loans and loan dollars in 1997 than they did in 1990, but the share of loans and loan dollars to predominantly minority and low-income areas—Milwaukee's Target Area—changed only slightly during these years.

Clearly, there has been an effort to direct more credit to distressed and underserved markets. Sporadic progress appears to have been made in reaching racial minorities in some communities. But those areas that are most racially identifiable have gained little ground relative to the rest of the metropolitan area. If pockets of progress can be identified, serious gaps persist in Milwaukee's mortgage market.

Denial Rates

Denial rates increased steadily for all groups from 1990 to 1997 (see table 2.4). Although ratios of nonwhite to white, and Target Area to Nontarget Area denials increased between 1990 and 1994, they were lower in 1997 than in either of the two earlier years. The black/white denial ratio increased from 3.9/1 in 1990 to 4.5/1 in 1994 but dropped

Table 2.4 Mortgage Loan Application Denial Rates and Ratios by Race and Target Area: Milwaukee Metropolitan Area, 1990, 1994, and 1997

	1990	1994	1997
White Denial (Percent)	6.9	7.1	11.6
Black Denial (Percent)	26.8	31.8	35.0
Hispanic Denial (Percent)	17.5	20.2	23.7
Target Area Denial (Percent)	23.6	32.3	31.8
Nontarget Area Denial (Percent)	8.7	8.9	13.9
Black/White Denial Ratio	3.9/1	4.5/1	3.0/1
Hispanic/White Denial Ratio	2.5/1	2.8/1	2.0/1
Target Area/Nontarget Area Denial Ratio	2.7/1	3.6/1	2.3/1

SOURCE: 1990, 1994, and 1997 HMDA Data

to 3.0/1 in 1997. Comparable figures for the Hispanic/white denial ratio were 2.5/1, 2.8/1, and 2.0/1. The Target Area/Nontarget Area denial ratio during these years was 2.7/1, 3.6/1, and 2.3/1.

A Word on Causes, Counteractions, and Policy Implications

Several factors are likely contributors to these racial gaps in mortgage lending. A significant consideration is the credit-worthiness of loan applicants. In general, racial minorities and residents of distressed areas have lower incomes, own fewer assets, and pose greater financial challenges in their applications for mortgage loans. But other factors are likely to be operating as well.

Disparate Treatment and Disparate Impact in Mortgage Lending Markets

As indicated in chapter 1, a substantial body of research has uncovered several reasons for racial disparities in mortgage lending markets. The Boston Federal Reserve Bank found that blacks were rejected 60 percent more often than similarly qualified white applicants in that city. The researchers indicated that loan officers were more likely to counsel marginal white applicants to help them prepare approvable applications but similarly qualified minorities were not provided the same service (Munnell et al. 1992). The Chicago Federal Reserve Bank suggested that the "cultural affinity" between white loan officers and clients might contribute to a higher approval rate for white applicants (Hunter 1995). In Milwaukee, there is statistical evidence that lenders who employ more minority workers are more likely to approve loan applications from minority homebuyers (see chapter 8).

Prescreening by loan officers frequently discourages racial minorities from submitting loan applications when comparable white applicants are encouraged to apply. In evaluating applications that are submitted, many appraisal and underwriting guidelines are utilized that have a disparate impact on minority applicants, even though no intentional discrimination may be occurring. Minimum loan amounts, requiring a specific length of time in a particular job (as opposed to spells of continuous employment or income), and restricting use of gifts or other lawful sources of income for a downpayment are just some examples. Underwriting barriers may be presented by the secondary mortgage market (e.g., Fannie Mae and Freddie Mac) as well as by loan originators (Cloud and Galster 1993).

In the cases settled by the U.S. Department of Justice discussed in chapter 1, lenders were found to be charging different interest rates to blacks and whites for comparable loans, providing different types of counseling to white and nonwhite applicants, and failing to place branch offices or to market in predominantly nonwhite neighborhoods. In other words, unlawful discrimination, resulting either from disparate treatment or adverse impact, occurs nationwide and may be contributing to the racial disparities in Milwaukee's mortgage market.

Local Responses

The patterns and practices documented in this report have not gone unnoticed in Milwaukee. Immediately following the *Atlanta Journal/ Constitution* report in 1989, Mayor John Norquist and Governor Tommy Thompson created a Fair Lending Action Committee (FLAC) to develop responses to Milwaukee's racial gap. FLAC included lenders, regulators, and representatives of various civil rights and community-based organizations. The group proposed a series of actions including expansion of housing counseling for first-time homebuyers, creation of a loan application review board, more branch banks and marketing in the central city, more financial support to assist low-income homebuyers, greater utilization of minority employees in financial institutions and other steps to increase services to distressed areas. The committee also set numerical goals calling for 13 percent of all residential, commercial real estate, and business loans, and the dollar volume of these loans to go to racial minorities by 1992. (This figure was chosen because racial minorities constituted 13 percent of the four-county metropolitan area population when the report was released in 1989.)

Many of these proposals have been pursued in varying degrees. Several lenders came together to form New Opportunity for Homeownership in Milwaukee (NOHIM), which provides support for additional housing and mortgage counseling. The Milwaukee Area Housing Initiative was created to provide multiple reviews by various institutions to assure that qualified applications are not denied.

In 1991 the Fair Lending Coalition was formed (see chapter 9). This interracial coalition of central city churches, unions, and other community groups has used the leverage of the Community Reinvestment Act to negotiate reinvestment agreements with twelve lenders. These agreements call for over $110 million in new loans to racial minorities and residents of the Target Area, creation of three new central city branch banks, affirmative action commitments to increase minority employment, increases in contracts for goods and services with minority vendors, and other initiatives to better serve previously underserved markets.

The Wisconsin Housing and Economic Development Authority and Milwaukee's Department of City Development have expanded housing and loan programs aimed at low-income homebuyers. The city also implemented a Socially Responsible Investment Ordinance requiring depositories of city funds to develop effective reinvestment programs.

Despite these efforts, significant gaps persist. With blacks and Hispanics together receiving less than 10 percent of HMDA reported loans and less than 5 percent of loan dollars in 1997, the 13 percent goal for 1992 set by the Fair Lending Action Committee remains an elusive target. And there are no simple solutions. More lenders could voluntarily participate in some of the partnerships that have been created or launch more effective reinvestment programs on their own. Some may be encouraged to do so by federal financial regulatory institutions (i.e., Federal Reserve Board, Comptroller of the Currency, Federal Deposit Insurance Corporation, Office of Thrift Supervision). Counseling more potential homeowners on the responsibilities of homeownership and their rights under the law would help. Research evaluating the various initiatives that have been started is critical to find out what works and what does not, and why.

The objective of this chapter, however, is not to specify the causes or provide detailed prescriptions for the persistent racial gap in Milwaukee's mortgage market. The primary purpose is to delineate how critical gaps have changed since the *Atlanta Journal/Constitution* story broke in 1989. The answer provided by the statistical data is mixed. Compared to their representation among all Milwaukee metropolitan area households, blacks, Hispanics, and residents of predominantly minority communities (the Target Area) submit a small share of applications and receive a smaller share of all loans and loan dollars. Lending to blacks and Hispanics, as a proportion of all metropolitan area lending, was greater in 1997 than in 1990 but was considerably lower during intervening years. Lending activity in the Target Area, however, has changed little. If some progress has been made during the 1990s, much more remains to be accomplished.

What has clearly changed in a positive direction is the local milieu in which mortgage lending issues are debated and lending activity is conducted. Far more attention is being paid by all sectors to these issues. More commitment has been expressed by lenders, public officials, and community groups to address the racial gap and related credit availability problems. If the spirit of the conclusion drawn by the Fair Lending Action Committee in 1989 prevails, there can be cause for optimism. As that committee maintained ten years ago:

> Building on the relationships that have been established among lenders, public officials and community groups, neighborhood revitalization throughout the city and prosperity throughout the entire metropolitan area can and will be achieved. (Fair Lending Action Committee 1989)

3

Community Reinvestment in Milwaukee

An Ambiguous Comparative Legacy

T HE RESPONSE OF MILWAUKEE AREA mortgage lenders to redlining debates has resulted in a schizophrenic community reinvestment record in recent years compared to lenders in other communities throughout the United States and in the frostbelt. When comparing Milwaukee area lenders with those in the fifty largest metropolitan areas nationwide and in fourteen similar frostbelt communities, Milwaukee ranks at, or just above, the average on most indicators. But Milwaukee is also at or close to the top and at or near the bottom on several key indicators.

This chapter examines the record of Milwaukee area mortgage lenders on several measures of community reinvestment compared to their counterparts in other metropolitan areas. Focusing on conventional home purchase mortgage loans, as provided by Home Mortgage Disclosure Act (HMDA) reports (Federal Financial Institutions Examination Council 1996a), this chapter examines the distribution of mortgage applications, loans, and loan dollars, along with denial rates, by race of applicant and census tract income level. A five-year time frame—1992 to 1997—is examined to document trends on selected variables.

Two sets of comparisons are drawn. First, Milwaukee is examined in relation to the fifty largest metropolitan areas in the United States. Second, in order to compare Milwaukee with other similar cities in terms of size and economic development, the fourteen largest frostbelt communities, excluding New York, are examined (Levine 1998: 4).

The following pages present a series of benchmarks with which to compare community reinvestment efforts in Milwaukee and other comparable communities. No attempt is made to formally test various potential causes of these patterns, though some possible explanations may be suggested by these descriptive statistics. These findings show areas where Milwaukee has been relatively more successful and where it is falling behind, and it provides a benchmark for measuring future progress.

Overall, Milwaukee area lenders approximate the average (that is Milwaukee ranks between tenth and thirty-seventh) for the fifty largest communities on the following measures: applications from and loans as well as loan dollars to blacks, Hispanics and low- and moderate-income communities; the ratio of denial rates in low- and moderate-income areas compared to upper-income areas; and the rate of increase in lending to low- and moderate-income areas between 1992 and 1997 (see table 3.1). Milwaukee has the lowest white denial rate but the forty-ninth highest black/white denial ratio and the forty-seventh highest Hispanic/white denial ratio. At the same time, Milwaukee ranks fifth in terms of the increase in lending to blacks during these years.

Among similar frostbelt cities, Milwaukee's ranking is more polarized. It ranks in the top three of these fourteen communities in terms of applications from, and loans to, blacks and Hispanics and denial rates for whites, blacks, and Hispanics. It is second in the increase in lending to Hispanics and to blacks. However, the black/white denial rate is last or the highest among these fourteen areas. And Milwaukee ranks ninth or worse in terms of loan dollars to blacks and Hispanics; applications from and loans to low- and moderate-income areas; and the increase in loans to low-income areas. More detailed findings are provided in table 3.1.

Applications

In the Milwaukee metropolitan area, the percentage of total applications filed by potential black and Hispanic borrowers is considerably below their share of the total population. For blacks this was true in every metropolitan area and for Hispanics this pattern held in most,

Table 3.1 Milwaukee MSA Ranking on Selected Indicators

	Black		Hispanic	
	All 50 MSAs	Frostbelt Cities	All 50 MSAs	Frostbelt Cities
Ratio of Percentage of Applications to Percentage of Population	11	2	11	3
Ratio of Percentage of Loans to Percentage of Population	14	3	10	3
Ratio of Percentage of Loan Dollars to Percentage of Population	37	9	26	11
Denial Ratios	49[a]	14[a]	47[b]	12[b]
Percent Change in Loans between 1992 and 1997	5	2	16	2

	Low Income		Moderate Income		Low and Moderate	
	All 50 MSAs	Frostbelt	All 50 MSAs	Frostbelt	All 50 MSAs	Frostbelt
Percentage of Applications for Property in Low and Moderate Income Tracts	30	11	31	11	32	12
Percentage of Loans for Property in Low and Moderate Income Tracts	25	10	20	8	24	9
Percentage of Loan Dollars for Property in Low and Moderate Income Tracts	24	9	17	8	16	7
Denial Ratios	NA	NA	NA	NA	21[c]	3[c]
Percent Change in Loans for Property in Low and Moderate Income Tracts between 1992 and 1997	18	10	10	2	13	4

[a]Ratio of the black denial rate to the white denial rate.
[b]Ratio of the Hispanic denial rate to the white denial rate.
[c]Ratio of the lower- and moderate-income denial rate to the upper-income denial rate.

SOURCE: 1997 HMDA, and 1990 U.S. Census Bureau

but not all, areas. In comparison to other communities nationwide and in the frostbelt, Milwaukee fared relatively well. The share of applications from low- and moderate-income areas, however, was considerably smaller in Milwaukee than elsewhere, particularly among frostbelt communities.

Because the proportion of blacks and Hispanics in the local population differs substantially among these fifty communities, the distribution and ranking of applications by race and ethnicity was calculated by dividing the percentage of all conventional home purchase mortgage applications by the percentage of the total population accounted for by the respective group. (Similar procedures are utilized below in examining loans and loan dollars.) A ratio of 1.0 would mean that a given group submitted the same share of applications as it accounted for in the population. A ratio below 1.0 would mean it submitted a share of applications that was below its share of the population while a ratio above 1.0 would indicate it submitted a higher share of applications than it accounted for in the population. (Obviously, population alone would not be expected to predict mortgage application or lending patterns. Financial status, demand, and many other factors contribute to a family's decision to consider purchasing a home and a lending institution's ability to approve a loan application. This benchmark is utilized as a convenience for drawing comparisons across metropolitan areas while taking into consideration some key demographic differences among those communities.)

In the Milwaukee metropolitan area, blacks accounted for 8.0 percent of all applications and 13.8 percent of the total population for a ratio of 0.6. Hispanics submitted 2.9 percent of all applications and accounted for 3.4 percent of the total population for a ratio of 0.9 (see table 3.2). In other words, blacks submitted slightly more than half the applications they would submit if applications were distributed according to population. Hispanics accounted for almost 90 percent of what they would be expected to supply on the basis of total population. As indicated in table 3.2, this means that Milwaukee ranked eleventh nationwide in terms of the share of conventional home purchase applications that came from blacks and Hispanics. Among the fourteen frostbelt communities, Milwaukee ranked second for blacks and third for Hispanics.

Because the share of low- and moderate-income census tracts does not vary anywhere near to the extent that race and ethnicity does, applications (and in the following pages, loans and loan dollars) from these communities are measured simply in terms of the percentage of all applications submitted by residents of these communities. In the

Table 3.2 Ratio of Percentage of Black and Hispanic Applications to Percentage of Black and Hispanic Population*

	Black	Rank	Hispanic	Rank
Atlanta, GA	0.6	12[&]	1.1	8
Baltimore, MD	0.5	19[5#]	0.7	18[6]
Bergen/Passaic Counties, NJ	0.3	44	0.4	45
Boston, MA	0.5	18[4]	0.5	34[11]
Buffalo, NY	0.3	46[13]	0.3	49[14]
Charlotte, NC	0.6	13	2.0	3
Chicago, IL	0.4	33[10]	0.6	27[9]
Cincinnati, OH	0.3	48[14]	0.7	20[7]
Cleveland, OH	0.5	17[3]	1.3	7[1]
Columbus, OH	0.4	31[9]	0.6	29[10]
Denver, CO	0.4	36	0.6	25
Detroit, MI	0.3	45[12]	0.4	42[12]
Fort Worth/Arlington, TX	0.3	43	0.6	23
Ft. Lauderdale, FL	0.8	1	2.1	2
Greensboro, NC	0.7	5	3.7	1
Hartford, CT	0.6	10	0.5	36
Houston, TX	0.5	24	0.7	17
Indianapolis, IN	0.4	42[11]	0.8	14[5]
Kansas City, MO	0.4	35	0.6	28
Las Vegas, NV	0.4	32	0.7	19
Los Angeles, CA	0.5	16	0.5	35
Miami, FL	0.4	39	1.3	6
Milwaukee, WI	0.6	11[2]	0.9	11[3]
Minneapolis, MN	0.7	4[1]	0.8	12[4]
Nashville, TN	0.4	41	1.9	4
Nassau/Suffolk Counties, NY	0.8	2	0.3	50
New Orleans, LA	0.5	15	0.4	43
New York, NY	0.6	8	0.4	40
Newark, NJ	0.4	40	0.6	26
Norfolk/VA Beach/Newport News, VA	0.5	14	0.5	33
Oakland, CA	0.4	34	0.6	30
Orange County, CA	0.6	9	0.4	48
Orlando, FL	0.4	28	1.7	5
Philadelphia, PA	0.4	27[7]	0.9	9[2]
Phoenix, AZ	0.5	22	0.5	37
Pittsburgh, PA	0.4	30[8]	0.4	47[13]
Portland, OR	0.4	38	0.5	32

(continued)

Table 3.2 *(continued)*   Ratio of Percentage of Black and Hispanic
Applications to Percentage of Black and Hispanic Population*

	Black	Rank	Hispanic	Rank
Providence, RI	0.4	37	0.7	16
Riverside/San Bernadino, CA	0.7	3	0.6	22
Rochester, NY	0.4	29	0.5	38
Sacramento, CA	0.5	21	0.4	46
Salt Lake City, UT	0.7	6	0.7	15
San Antonio, TX	0.6	7	0.8	13
San Diego, CA	0.3	47	0.5	39
San Francisco, CA	0.2	49	0.4	44
San Jose, CA	0.5	26	0.4	41
Seattle, WA	0.5	23	0.5	31
St. Louis, MO	0.5	25[6]	0.6	24[8]
Tampa/St. Petersburg, FL	0.5	20	0.9	10
Washington, DC	0.2	50	0.6	21

Note:
*For example, in Milwaukee, 8.0% of applications came from blacks and 13.8% of the
metropolitan population is black. Therefore, the ratio is 8.0 to 13.8 (8/13.8) = .6
[#]Rank among the fourteen frostbelt cities.
[&]MSAs are ranked from 1 to 50 where the lowest number indicates the highest ratio
of percent applications to percent population for the respective group. What may
appear to be ties are numbers that have been rounded to the nearest tenth.
SOURCE: 1997 HMDA, and 1990 U.S. Census Bureau

Milwaukee metropolitan area 26.5 percent of all applications were
submitted by residents of low- and moderate-income census tracts
(see table 3.3). Milwaukee was just below average, ranking thirty-
second, among the nation's fifty largest communities. But Milwaukee
ranked twelfth among fourteen frostbelt areas. Only Boston and Buffalo
ranked behind Milwaukee on this measure.

Loans

Not surprisingly, the distribution of loans generally reflected the distribution of applications. Nationwide, Milwaukee ranked slightly better than average in the rate of lending to blacks and Hispanics and to
low- and moderate-income neighborhoods. Among frostbelt communities, Milwaukee was well above average in lending to blacks and
Hispanics, but below average in lending to low- and moderate-income
communities.

Table 3.3 Percentage of Applications from Low- and Moderate-Income Tracts%*

	Low Income	Rank	Moderate Income	Rank	Low and Moderate Income	Rank
Atlanta, GA	11.7	13[&]	21.8	15	33.4	13
Baltimore, MD	9.5	24[19#]	17.7	37[14]	27.2	30[10]
Bergen/Passaic Counties, NJ	4.2	43	17.3	40	21.5	40
Boston, MA	6.2	35[14]	19.4	29[9]	25.6	35[13]
Buffalo, NY	6.7	32[12]	18.5	33[12]	25.3	36[14]
Charlotte, NC	16.7	4	25.5	4	42.3	4
Chicago, IL	6.6	34[13]	20.1	24[8]	26.7	31[11]
Cincinnati, OH	13.3	9[4]	22.5	13[5]	35.8	9[4]
Cleveland, OH	10.7	17[6]	22.9	11[4]	33.6	12[5]
Columbus, OH	10.5	20[7]	19.2	30[10]	29.7	22[8]
Denver, CO	11.2	16	21.1	17	32.3	19
Detroit, MI	14.1	8[3]	23.5	10[3]	37.6	8[3]
Fort Worth/Arlington, TX	19.8	1	26.2	3	46.0	2
Ft. Lauderdale, FL	7.3	31	20.6	21	27.9	29
Greensboro, NC	19.8	2	27.9	2	47.7	1
Hartford, CT	8.8	27	23.6	9	32.4	18
Houston, TX	15.2	5	24.4	6	39.6	6
Indianapolis, IN	12.1	12[6]	21.0	20[8]	33.1	15[6]
Kansas City, MO	12.7	10	21.1	16	33.8	11
Las Vegas, NV	8.7	28	20.0	25	28.7	26
Los Angeles, CA	2.2	49	10.0	49	12.2	49
Miami, FL	3.6	46	13.9	43	17.5	44
Milwaukee, WI	7.4	30[11]	19.1	31[11]	26.5	32[12]
Minneapolis, MN	14.4	7[2]	24.0	8[2]	38.4	7[2]
Nashville, TN	12.5	11	22.7	12	35.2	10
Nassau/Suffolk Counties, NY	4.3	41	17.7	38	22.0	39
New Orleans, LA	10.6	19	17.8	36	28.4	28
New York, NY	1.8	50	8.0	50	9.8	50
Newark, NJ	5.0	39	17.3	39	22.3	38
Norfolk/VA Beach/ Newport News, VA	11.6	14	21.0	18	32.6	17
Oakland, CA	4.3	42	13.1	45	17.5	45
Orange County, CA	4.2	45	13.2	44	17.4	46

(continued)

Table 3.3 *(continued)*   Percentage of Applications from Low- and Moderate-Income Tracts%*

	Low Income	*Rank*	*Moderate Income*	*Rank*	*Low and Moderate Income*	*Rank*
Orlando, FL	9.3	25	19.8	26	29.1	24
Philadelphia, PA	10.3	21[8]	18.3	34[13]	28.6	27[8]
Phoenix, AZ	9.2	26	19.6	27	28.8	25
Pittsburgh, PA	9.7	23[8]	20.1	22[7]	29.8	21[7]
Portland, OR	4.9	40	18.1	35	23.0	37
Providence, RI	6.1	36	20.1	23	26.2	33
Riverside/						
San Bernadino, CA	5.6	38	12.9	46	18.5	43
Rochester, NY	11.3	15	22.1	14	33.3	14
Sacramento, CA	5.9	37	14.4	42	20.3	41
Salt Lake City, UT	8.6	29	24.3	7	32.9	16
San Antonio, TX	14.8	6	28.0	1	42.8	3
San Diego, CA	4.2	44	10.7	47	14.9	47
San Francisco, CA	2.4	48	10.3	48	12.6	48
San Jose, CA	3.5	47	15.3	41	18.8	42
Seattle, WA	6.6	33	19.5	28	26.1	34
St. Louis, MO	16.9	3[1]	24.9	5[1]	41.8	5[1]
Tampa/St. Petersburg, FL	10.2	22	21.0	19	31.2	20
Washington, DC	10.7	18	18.8	32	29.5	23

Note:
%The FFIEC has defined income categories as follows: Low Income = Less than 50% of MSA Median Income, Moderate Income = 50–79% of MSA Median Income, Middle Income = 80–119% of MSA Median Income, and Upper Income = 120% or more of MSA Median Income.
*For example, of the 20,279 applications for the Milwaukee MSA, 1,497 or 7.4% were for property located in low income tracts.
#Rank among the fourteen frostbelt cities.
&MSAs are ranked from 1 to 50 where the lowest number indicates the highest percent of applications from low- and moderate-income tracts. What may appear to be ties are numbers that have been rounded to the nearest tenth.
SOURCE: 1997 HMDA

Among the fifty largest metropolitan areas nationwide, Milwaukee ranked fourteenth in terms of the loans-to-population ratio for blacks and tenth for Hispanics. Among the fourteen frostbelt communities Milwaukee was third in lending to both blacks and Hispanics (see table 3.4).

Table 3.4 Ratio of Percentage of Black and Hispanic Loans to Percentage of Black and Hispanic Population*

	Black	Rank	Hispanic	Rank
Atlanta, GA	19.5	11[&]	1.0	8
Baltimore, MD	0.4	19[4#]	0.4	34[11]
Bergen/Passaic Counties, NJ	0.5	10	0.6	14
Boston, MA	0.4	13[2]	0.4	33[10]
Buffalo, NY	0.2	45[13]	0.2	49[14]
Charlotte, NC	0.4	27	1.3	6
Chicago, IL	0.3	39[11]	0.5	21[6]
Cincinnati, OH	0.2	46[14]	0.5	25[8]
Cleveland, OH	0.4	20[5]	1.2	7[1]
Columbus, OH	0.4	31[9]	0.4	30[9]
Denver, CO	0.3	34	0.4	37
Detroit, MI	0.3	43[12]	0.3	47[13]
Fort Worth/Arlington, TX	0.3	44	0.5	22
Ft. Lauderdale, FL	0.7	1	2.0	2
Greensboro, NC	0.5	8	2.6	1
Hartford, CT	0.5	6	0.4	35
Houston, TX	0.2	47	0.4	39
Indianapolis, IN	0.3	37[10]	0.7	12[4]
Kansas City, MO	0.3	41	0.5	28
Las Vegas, NV	0.4	25	0.5	20
Los Angeles, CA	0.4	12	0.4	32
Miami, FL	0.3	32	1.3	5
Milwaukee, WI	0.4	14[3]	0.7	10[3]
Minneapolis, MN	0.6	3[1]	0.6	13[5]
Nashville, TN	0.3	42	1.4	3
Nassau/Suffolk Counties, NY	0.7	2	0.2	50
New Orleans, LA	0.3	33	0.5	29
New York, NY	0.5	7	0.4	40
Newark, NJ	0.3	40	0.5	24
Norfolk/VA Beach/Newport News, VA	0.4	24	0.4	36
Oakland, CA	0.3	36	0.5	26
Orange County, CA	0.5	9	0.3	48
Orlando, FL	0.4	30	1.4	4
Philadelphia, PA	0.4	29[8]	0.8	9[2]
Phoenix, AZ	0.4	18	0.3	46
Pittsburgh, PA	0.4	28[7]	0.4	38[12]
Portland, OR	0.3	38	0.4	31

(continued)

Table 3.4 *(continued)*   Ratio of Percentage of Black and Hispanic
Loans to Percentage of Black and Hispanic Population*

	Black	Rank	Hispanic	Rank
Providence, RI	0.3	35	0.6	16
Riverside/San Bernadino, CA	0.6	4	0.5	18
Rochester, NY	0.4	23	0.4	42
Sacramento, CA	0.4	17	0.4	44
Salt Lake City, UT	0.6	5	0.6	15
San Antonio, TX	0.4	16	0.5	19
San Diego, CA	0.2	48	0.4	41
San Francisco, CA	0.2	49	0.4	45
San Jose, CA	0.4	22	0.4	43
Seattle, WA	0.4	21	0.5	27
St. Louis, MO	0.4	26[6]	0.5	23[7]
Tampa/St. Petersburg, FL	0.4	15	0.7	11
Washington, DC	0.2	50	0.6	17

Note:
*For example, in Milwaukee, 6.0% of all loans went to blacks and 13.8% of the
metropolitan population is black. Therefore, the ratio is 6.0 to 13.8 (6.0/13.8) = .4
[#]Rank among the fourteen frostbelt cities.
[&]MSAs are ranked from 1 to 50 where the lowest number indicates the highest ratio
of percent loans originated to percent population for the respective groups. What
may appear to be ties are numbers that have been rounded to the nearest tenth.
SOURCE: 1997 HMDA, and 1990 U.S. Census Bureau

Milwaukee was just about in the middle, ranking twenty-fourty, in
lending activity to low- and moderate-income areas nationwide but
ninth in lending to low- and moderate-income neighborhoods in the
region (see table 3.5).

Loan Dollars

Milwaukee's rankings differed in the allocation of loan dollars. Its
rankings in terms of loan dollars to blacks and Hispanics were considerably lower but its rankings in terms of loan dollars to low- and
moderate-income areas were somewhat higher. These patterns held
nationwide and within the region.

Among the fifty largest metropolitan areas nationwide, Milwaukee
ranked thirty-seventh in loan dollars to blacks and twenty-sixty in
loan dollars to Hispanics (see table 3.6). Among the fourteen frostbelt

Table 3.5 Percentage of Loans to Low- and Moderate-Income Tracts%*

	Low Income	Rank	Moderate Income	Rank	Low and Moderate Income	Rank
Atlanta, GA	6.4	23[&]	18.9	12	25.3	17
Baltimore, MD	7.0	18[8#]	16.1	36[14]	23.1	29[12]
Bergen/Passaic Counties, NJ	3.5	41	16.5	32	20.0	38
Boston, MA	5.2	32[13]	18.7	15[7]	23.9	25[10]
Buffalo, NY	4.3	38[14]	16.9	29[11]	21.2	34[14]
Charlotte, NC	8.0	9	18.8	13	26.8	11
Chicago, IL	5.3	31[12]	19.3	10[6]	24.6	22[8]
Cincinnati, OH	8.3	7[4]	19.4	9[5]	27.7	7[5]
Cleveland, OH	7.9	10[5]	21.0	4[2]	28.9	5[3]
Columbus, OH	6.8	20[9]	16.7	30[12]	23.5	26[11]
Denver, CO	7.1	17	18.1	18	25.2	18
Detroit, MI	7.6	11[6]	20.2	7[4]	27.8	6[4]
Fort Worth/Arlington, TX	9.7	4	17.5	24	27.2	8
Ft. Lauderdale, FL	6.2	24	19.7	8	25.9	13
Greensboro, NC	10.1	3	20.9	6	31.0	3
Hartford, CT	7.4	12	23.0	1	30.4	4
Houston, TX	8.1	8	17.9	21	26.0	12
Indianapolis, IN	7.3	13[7]	17.4	25[9]	24.7	21[7]
Kansas City, MO	8.6	5	18.4	16	27.0	10
Las Vegas, NV	86.0	27	15.8	37	21.8	32
Los Angeles, CA	1.5	49	9.3	49	10.8	49
Miami, FL	2.7	46	12.8	42	15.5	46
Milwaukee, WI	6.1	25[10]	17.9	20[8]	24.0	24[9]
Minneapolis, MN	10.7	2[2]	22.4	2[1]	33.1	1[1]
Nashville, TN	7.2	14	17.9	22	25.1	20
Nassau/Suffolk Counties, NY	3.3	43	17.2	26	20.5	36
New Orleans, LA	5.2	34	12.2	45	17.4	41
New York, NY	1.1	50	6.8	50	8.0	50
Newark, NJ	3.8	39	16.3	34	20.1	37
Norfolk/VA Beach/Newport News, VA	5.4	29	15.4	38	20.8	35
Oakland, CA	3.6	40	12.3	44	15.9	44
Orange County, CA	3.2	44	12.6	43	15.8	45

(continued)

Table 3.5 *(continued)*   Percentage of Loans to Low- and Moderate-Income Tracts%*

	Low Income	Rank	Moderate Income	Rank	Low and Moderate Income	Rank
Orlando, FL	6.0	26	16.3	35	22.3	31
Philadelphia, PA	8.5	6[3]	17.2	27[10]	25.7	14[6]
Phoenix, AZ	6.4	22	16.9	28	23.3	27
Pittsburgh, PA	5.4	30[11]	16.4	33[13]	21.8	33[13]
Portland, OR	3.4	42	15.0	39	18.4	39
Providence, RI	5.2	33	19.1	11	24.3	23
Riverside/San Bernadino, CA	4.5	37	11.8	46	16.3	43
Rochester, NY	6.9	19	18.7	14	25.6	15
Sacramento, CA	4.7	36	13.2	41	17.9	40
Salt Lake City, UT	5.8	28	21.3	3	27.1	9
San Antonio, TX	6.8	21	16.5	31	23.3	28
San Diego, CA	3.1	45	9.9	47	12.9	47
San Francisco, CA	1.8	48	9.6	48	11.4	48
San Jose, CA	2.5	47	14.3	40	16.8	42
Seattle, WA	4.8	35	17.7	23	22.5	30
St. Louis, MO	10.9	1[1]	20.9	5[3]	31.8	2[2]
Tampa/St. Petersburg, FL	7.1	16	18.2	17	25.4	16
Washington, DC	7.2	15	17.9	19	25.2	19

Note:
%The FFIEC has defined income categories as follows: Low Income = Less than 50% of MSA Median Income, Moderate Income = 50–79% of MSA Median Income, Middle Income = 80–119% of MSA Median Income, and Upper Income = 120% or more of MSA Median Income.
*For example, of the 16,886 loans in the Milwaukee MSA, 1,031 or 6.1% went to low income tracts.
#Rank among the fourteen frostbelt cities.
&MSAs are ranked from 1 to 50 where the lowest number indicates the highest percent of loans to low- and moderate-income tracts. What may appear to be ties are numbers that have been rounded to the nearest tenth.
SOURCE: 1997 HMDA

communities, Milwaukee ranked ninth in loan dollars to blacks and eleventh in loan dollars to Hispanics.

Milwaukee ranked sixteenth nationwide in the share of loan dollars that went to borrowers in low- and moderate-income tracts; well above its thirty-second and twenty-fourth ranking for applications and loans. And Milwaukee was seventh among frostbelt communities; also higher

Table 3.6 Ratio of Percentage of Black and Hispanic Loan Dollars to Percentage of Black and Hispanic Population*

	Black	Rank	Hispanic	Rank
Atlanta, GA	0.4	9[&]	0.7	7
Baltimore, MD	0.3	30[5#]	0.4	20[7]
Bergen/Passaic Counties, NJ	0.4	8	0.5	13
Boston, MA	0.3	18[2]	0.3	36[12]
Buffalo, NY	0.2	47[14]	0.2	50[14]
Charlotte, NC	0.3	26	0.9	5
Chicago, IL	0.2	41[11]	0.4	23[9]
Cincinnati, OH	0.2	45[13]	0.7	9[2]
Cleveland, OH	0.3	29[4]	0.7	8[1]
Columbus, OH	0.3	25[3]	0.4	19[6]
Denver, CO	0.3	23	0.3	37
Detroit, MI	0.2	40[10]	0.2	47[13]
Fort Worth/Arlington, TX	0.2	39	0.3	34
Ft. Lauderdale, FL	0.6	2	1.9	1
Greensboro, NC	0.4	13	1.3	2
Hartford, CT	0.3	17	0.2	46
Houston, TX	0.3	28	0.4	29
Indianapolis, IN	0.3	31[6]	0.6	11[3]
Kansas City, MO	0.2	43	0.3	35
Las Vegas, NV	0.4	12	0.5	14
Los Angeles, CA	0.3	16	0.3	41
Miami, FL	0.2	38	1.2	3
Milwaukee, WI	0.2	37[9]	0.4	26[11]
Minneapolis, MN	0.4	10[1]	0.4	18[5]
Nashville, TN	0.2	35	0.9	6
Nassau/Suffolk Counties, NY	0.5	3	0.2	49
New Orleans, LA	0.2	44	0.4	27
New York, NY	0.4	7	0.3	32
Newark, NJ	0.2	46	0.4	28
Norfolk/VA Beach/Newport News, VA	0.3	24	0.3	43
Oakland, CA	0.2	34	0.4	31
Orange County, CA	0.4	6	0.3	38
Orlando, FL	0.3	21	1.0	4
Philadelphia, PA	0.2	42[12]	0.4	24[10]
Phoenix, AZ	0.4	5	0.2	48
Pittsburgh, PA	0.2	33[7]	0.4	21[8]
Portland, OR	0.3	22	0.3	33

(continued)

Table 3.6 *(continued)*   Ratio of Percentage of Black and Hispanic
Loan Dollars to Percentage of Black and Hispanic Population*

	Black	*Rank*	*Hispanic*	*Rank*
Providence, RI	0.2	32	0.4	22
Riverside/San Bernadino, CA	0.6	1	0.4	16
Rochester, NY	0.3	27	0.3	40
Sacramento, CA	0.4	14	0.3	39
Salt Lake City, UT	0.4	4	0.4	17
San Antonio, TX	0.4	11	0.4	25
San Diego, CA	0.2	48	0.3	44
San Francisco, CA	0.1	50	0.3	45
San Jose, CA	0.3	20	0.3	42
Seattle, WA	0.3	15	0.4	30
St. Louis, MO	0.2	36[8]	0.5	12[4]
Tampa/St. Petersburg, FL	0.3	19	0.6	10
Washington, DC	0.1	49	0.5	15

Note:
*For example, in Milwaukee, 3.1% of all loans went to blacks and 13.8% of the
metropolitan population is black. Therefore, the ratio is 3.1 to 13.8 (3.1/13.8) = .2
[#]Rank among the fourteen frostbelt cities.
[&]MSAs are ranked from 1 to 50 where the lowest number indicates the highest ratio
of percent loan dollars to percent population for the respective groups. What may
appear to be ties are numbers that have been rounded to the nearest tenth.
SOURCE: 1997 HMDA, and 1990 U.S. Census Bureau

than its twelfth and ninth ranking for applications and loans (see
table 3.7).

Denial Rates

Milwaukee exhibited a peculiar pattern in denial rates. Overall, denial
rates are quite low in Milwaukee for all groups compared to other
communities. But the racial disparities continue to be among the highest in the nation and among frostbelt communities.

Milwaukee leads the nation in its approval of white mortgage applications. Only 6.0 percent of white applicants were denied, the lowest denial rate among the fifty largest communities (see table 3.8).
Blacks and Hispanics also have relatively low denial rates in Milwaukee,
but the black/white racial disparity of 3.2 ranks forty-ninth; higher than
in any other community except Newark, New Jersey. The Hispanic/

Table 3.7 Percentage of Loan Dollars to Low- and Moderate-Income Tracts[%*]

	Low Income	Rank	Moderate Income	Rank	Low and Moderate Income	Rank
Atlanta, GA	2.5	23[&]	11.4	13	13.9	13
Baltimore, MD	2.5	26[10#]	8.7	36[13]	11.1	34[13]
Bergen/Passaic Counties, NJ	1.5	40	9.9	26	11.4	32
Boston, MA	2.3	29[11]	11.3	14[7]	13.5	17[8]
Buffalo, NY	1.8	36[13]	10.1	22[8]	11.9	31[12]
Charlotte, NC	2.8	13	10.3	21	13.2	18
Chicago, IL	2.3	30[12]	11.4	12[6]	13.7	14[6]
Cincinnati, OH	3.4	7[4]	11.6	11[5]	15.0	9[4]
Cleveland, OH	3.5	6[3]	12.8	4[2]	16.3	3[2]
Columbus, OH	2.6	20[8]	9.6	30[12]	12.2	28[11]
Denver, CO	3.1	8	11.6	10	14.8	11
Detroit, MI	2.8	15[6]	11.9	8[4]	14.6	12[5]
Fort Worth/Arlington, TX	3.7	4	9.2	34	12.9	20
Ft. Lauderdale, FL	2.3	28	10.5	20	12.8	21
Greensboro, NC	3.8	3	11.8	9	15.5	6
Hartford, CT	3.0	11	14.4	2	17.4	2
Houston, TX	3.1	9	9.3	31	12.4	25
Indianapolis, IN	2.7	18[7]	9.9	25[10]	12.6	23[8]
Kansas City, MO	3.6	5	11.2	15	14.8	10
Las Vegas, NV	2.8	16	10.0	24	12.7	22
Los Angeles, CA	0.5	50	4.0	49	4.5	49
Miami, FL	0.9	48	5.9	45	6.7	45
Milwaukee, WI	2.5	24[9]	11.0	17[8]	13.6	16[7]
Minneapolis, MN	4.6	1[1]	14.7	1[1]	19.4	1[1]
Nashville, TN	2.6	19	9.7	27	12.3	27
Nassau/Suffolk Counties, NY	1.4	42	10.5	19	12.0	30
New Orleans, LA	1.8	37	4.9	46	6.7	46
New York, NY	0.9	47	3.1	50	4.0	50
Newark, NJ	1.6	39	9.3	33	10.9	35
Norfolk/VA Beach/Newport News, VA	1.8	35	7.6	42	9.4	41
Oakland, CA	1.4	43	7.1	43	8.5	43
Orange County, CA	1.3	44	8.4	37	9.5	40
Orlando, FL	2.4	27	8.8	35	11.2	33

(continued)

Table 3.7 *(continued)* Percentage of Loan Dollars to Low- and Moderate-Income Tracts%*

	Low Income	Rank	Moderate Income	Rank	Low and Moderate Income	Rank
Philadelphia, PA	2.8	14[5]	9.7	28[11]	12.5	24[10]
Phoenix, AZ	2.5	22	9.6	29	12.1	29
Pittsburgh, PA	1.8	38[14]	7.9	40[14]	9.6	39[14]
Portland, OR	1.4	41	9.3	32	10.8	36
Providence, RI	2.6	21	12.5	5	15.1	8
Riverside/San Bernadino, CA	1.8	34	6.2	44	8.0	44
Rochester, NY	2.7	17	10.9	18	13.6	15
Sacramento, CA	2.0	32	7.7	41	9.7	38
Salt Lake City, UT	2.2	31	13.7	3	15.9	5
San Antonio, TX	2.5	25	7.9	39	10.4	37
San Diego, CA	1.1	45	4.7	48	5.8	47
San Francisco, CA	0.7	49	4.8	47	5.5	48
San Jose, CA	1.0	46	8.3	38	9.3	42
Seattle, WA	1.9	33	11.1	16	13.0	19
St. Louis, MO	4.1	2[2]	12.1	7[3]	16.2	4[3]
Tampa/St. Petersburg, FL	2.9	12	10.1	23	12.4	26
Washington, DC	3.0	10	12.2	6	15.2	7

Note:
%The FFIEC has defined income categories as follows: Low Income = Less than 50% of MSA Median Income, Moderate Income = 50–79% of MSA Median Income, Middle Income = 80–119% of MSA Median Income, and Upper Income = 120% or more of MSA Median Income.
*For example, of the $1,894,669 loan dollars in the Milwaukee MSA, $47,495 or 2.5% went to low income tracts.
#Rank among the fourteen frostbelt cities.
&MSAs are ranked from 1 to 50 where the lowest number indicates the highest percent of loan dollars to low- and moderate-income tracts. What may appear to be ties are numbers that have been rounded to the nearest tenth.
SOURCE: 1997 HMDA

white denial rate of 2.2 ranks forty-seventh, higher than all areas except Minneapolis, Newark, and Buffalo. Consequently, Milwaukee ranks last (fourteenth) among frostbelt communities in terms of the black/white ratio and twelfth in terms of the Hispanic/white ratio.

The denial rate for conventional home purchase loan applications from low- and moderate-income areas is lower in Milwaukee than in any of the other communities (see table 3.9). But this is also true for

Table 3.8 Denial Rates and Ratios by Race and Ethnicity*

	White	Black	Hispanic	B/W Ratio	Rank	H/W Rank	Rank
Atlanta, GA	14.5	24.2	24.8	1.7	16[&$]	1.7	23
Baltimore, MD	10.5	20.6	17.4	2.0	31[8#]	1.7	18[4]
Bergen/Passaic Counties, NJ	7.9	20.4	13.2	2.6	46	1.7	20
Boston, MA	7.5	18.5	13.1	2.5	43[10]	1.7	28[8]
Buffalo, NY	10.3	25.5	28.8	2.5	44[11]	2.8	50[14]
Charlotte, NC	26.6	49.1	45.7	1.8	27	1.7	26
Chicago, IL	7.4	22.2	14.1	3.0	48[13]	1.9	39[10]
Cincinnati, OH	16.1	19.5	27.8	1.2	1[1]	1.7	27[7]
Cleveland, OH	10.1	21.6	16.7	2.1	37[9]	1.7	19[5]
Columbus, OH	13.0	19.7	22.2	1.5	11[5]	1.7	25[6]
Denver, CO	15.5	25.9	34.1	1.7	18	2.2	46
Detroit, MI	18.4	23.0	34.4	1.3	2[2]	1.9	37[8]
Fort Worth/Arlington, TX	36.2	46.4	43.6	1.3	3	1.2	2
Ft. Lauderdale, FL	12.7	21.9	17.0	1.7	22	1.3	7
Greensboro, NC	32.5	52.2	50.1	1.6	14	1.5	11
Hartford, CT	7.3	16.3	15.0	2.2	39	2.1	42
Houston, TX	28.6	43.4	36.0	1.5	10	1.3	4
Indianapolis, IN	15.9	20.4	25.7	1.3	4[3]	1.6	13[3]
Kansas City, MO	14.2	29.6	25.7	2.1	35	1.8	33
Las Vegas, NV	21.3	28.7	32.1	1.4	5	1.5	10
Los Angeles, CA	14.5	24.5	21.8	1.7	19	1.5	9
Miami, FL	14.2	24.3	17.7	1.7	21	1.2	3
Milwaukee, WI	6.0	19.2	13.3	3.2	49[14]	2.2	47[13]
Minneapolis, MN	11.3	20.1	25.8	1.8	24[7]	2.3	48[13]
Nashville, TN	20.8	34.7	37.3	1.7	17	1.8	29
Nassau/Suffolk Counties, NY	9.6	19.6	16.3	2.0	32	1.7	22
New Orleans, LA	17.9	46.4	19.0	2.6	47	1.1	1
New York, NY	11.2	24.9	18.8	2.2	38	1.7	21
Newark, NJ	6.9	22.6	17.9	3.3	50	2.6	49
Norfolk/VA Beach/ Newport News, VA	20.9	37.6	38.2	1.8	26	1.8	34
Oakland, CA	9.7	22.9	17.4	2.4	42	1.8	30
Orange County, CA	12.8	24.7	23.0	1.9	29	1.8	32
Orlando, FL	16.8	27.5	27.7	1.6	15	1.7	17
Philadelphia, PA	8.5	21.1	18.0	2.5	45[12]	2.1	43[11]
Phoenix, AZ	15.0	25.7	33.0	1.7	20	2.2	45

(continued)

Table 3.8 *(continued)*   Denial Rates and Ratios by Race and Ethnicity*

	White	Black	Hispanic	B/W Ratio	Rank	H/W Rank	Rank
Pittsburgh, PA	17.3	26.6	22.6	1.5	12[6]	1.3	5[1]
Portland, OR	14.3	22.3	26.2	1.6	13	1.8	35
Providence, RI	8.9	18.4	16.4	2.1	34	1.8	36
Riverside/San Bernadino, CA	14.1	26.4	22.4	1.9	28	1.6	12
Rochester, NY	15.4	22.9	27.7	1.5	7	1.8	31
Sacramento, CA	11.3	21.9	18.5	1.9	30	1.6	16
Salt Lake City, UT	16.5	25.0	26.9	1.5	9	1.6	14
San Antonio, TX	32.8	57.0	53.7	1.7	23	1.6	15
San Diego, CA	12.0	25.1	20.4	2.1	36	1.7	24
San Francisco, CA	10.9	24.5	20.5	2.2	40	1.9	38
San Jose, CA	11.7	21.0	23.0	1.8	25	2.0	40
Seattle, WA	11.0	22.7	23.7	2.1	33	2.2	44
St. Louis, MO	20.9	31.5	27.7	1.5	8[4]	1.3	6[2]
Tampa/St. Petersburg, FL	19.1	27.2	28.2	1.4	6	1.5	8
Washington, DC	9.1	21.2	18.3	2.3	41	2.0	41

Note:
*The denial rate is calculated by dividing the number of applications that were denied by the total number of applications, which included those loans that were originated, approved but not accepted, denied, withdrawn, or closed for incompleteness. For example, in Milwaukee, 315 black applications were denied out of 1,637 received for a 19.2% denial rate. The B/W or H/W ratio is calculated by dividing the black or Hispanic denial rate by the white denial rate. For example, in Milwaukee, the black denial rate is 19.2 and the white denial rate is 6.0. Therefore the B/W denial rate is 19.2/6.0 = 3.2.
#Rank among the fourteen frostbelt cities.
&MSAs are ranked from 1 to 50 where the lowest number indicates the highest B/W or H/W denial rates. What may appear to be ties are numbers that have been rounded to the nearest tenth.
SOURCE: 1997 HMDA

upper-income communities. The ratio of denial rates in low- and moderate-income areas to upper-income areas of 2.8 is the twenty-first highest nationwide and third within the region.

Changes between 1992 and 1997

Perhaps more significant than a snapshot at any point in time is the extent to which lending has changed over a period of time. Milwaukee scores relatively well in terms of increasing shares of lending to black

Table 3.9 Denial Rates and Ratios by Income Tract Level*

	Low Income	Moderate Income	Low and Moderate Income	Low and Moderate/ Upper Ratio	Rank
Atlanta, GA	44.6	23.3	30.8	4.7	39[&]
Baltimore, MD	30.2	18.0	22.3	3.4	30[5#]
Bergen/Passaic Counties, NJ	20.7	11.3	13.1	1.8	8
Boston, MA	19.2	10.9	12.9	2.4	17[2]
Buffalo, NY	36.7	17.2	22.4	4.0	33[7]
Charlotte, NC	58.4	42.0	48.5	5.8	48
Chicago, IL	22.1	12.4	14.8	2.4	15[1]
Cincinnati, OH	40.4	23.4	29.7	5.3	44[11]
Cleveland, OH	28.0	16.1	19.9	3.8	32[6]
Columbus, OH	36.4	20.3	26.0	4.4	37[8]
Denver, CO	40.5	24.9	30.3	3.5	31
Detroit, MI	49.1	26.3	34.8	6.0	50[14]
Fort Worth/ Arlington, TX	63.8	51.4	56.7	4.7	40
Ft. Lauderdale, FL	25.5	18.9	20.6	1.9	10
Greensboro, NC	60.5	46.0	52.0	4.9	42
Hartford, CT	20.0	9.9	12.7	2.5	18
Houston, TX	56.6	43.7	48.6	4.1	34
Indianapolis, IN	42.3	26.5	32.2	5.5	45[12]
Kansas City, MO	37.5	23.2	28.6	5.1	43
Las Vegas, NV	41.6	35.4	37.3	2.8	23
Los Angeles, CA	30.3	20.9	22.6	1.6	1
Miami, FL	33.1	22.3	24.5	1.7	4
Milwaukee, WI	16.4	10.6	12.2	2.8	21[3]
Minneapolis, MN	29.7	15.0	20.5	4.5	38[9]
Nashville, TN	46.8	32.8	37.8	4.3	35
Nassau/Suffolk Counties, NY	23.5	12.7	14.8	1.7	3
New Orleans, LA	53.4	40.8	45.5	4.4	36
New York, NY	33.5	24.3	26.0	2.3	14
Newark, NJ	24.0	12.1	14.8	2.4	16
Norfolk/VA Beach/ Newport News, VA	57.5	39.3	45.7	5.9	49
Oakland, CA	19.6	15.4	16.4	1.8	6
Orange County, CA	26.4	17.6	19.7	1.7	2
Orlando, FL	41.4	28.5	32.6	3.1	27

(continued)

Table 3.9 *(continued)* Denial Rates and Ratios by Income Tract Level*

	Low Income	Moderate Income	Low and Moderate Income	Low and Moderate/ Upper Ratio	Rank
Philadelphia, PA	23.0	14.0	17.2	2.8	22[4]
Phoenix, AZ	36.0	25.6	28.9	3.1	26
Pittsburgh, PA	46.8	28.7	34.6	5.7	47[13]
Portland, OR	34.1	23.2	25.6	3.0	25
Providence, RI	18.9	11.6	13.3	2.2	13
Riverside/					
San Bernadino, CA	27.3	21.6	23.3	1.7	5
Rochester, NY	42.8	25.1	31.1	5.5	46
Sacramento, CA	25.8	15.0	18.2	1.9	12
Salt Lake City, UT	39.2	23.8	27.8	2.8	24
San Antonio, TX	67.5	57.2	60.7	3.3	29
San Diego, CA	26.3	17.3	19.8	1.8	7
San Francisco, CA	25.4	17.1	18.7	1.8	9
San Jose, CA	29.4	17.3	19.5	1.9	11
Seattle, WA	29.0	16.4	19.6	2.7	20
St. Louis, MO	44.1	30.6	36.1	4.9	41[10]
Tampa/St.					
Petersburg, FL	38.8	27.4	31.1	2.6	19
Washington, DC	32.6	14.2	20.9	3.2	28

Note:

*The denial rate is calculated by dividing the number of applications that were denied by the total number of applications which included those loans that were originated, approved but not accepted, denied, withdrawn, or closed for incompleteness. For example, in Milwaukee, 246 applications for property located in low income tracts were denied out of 1,497 received for a 16.4% denial rate. The low and moderate/upper ratio is calculated by dividing the low and moderate denial rate by the upper denial rate. For example, in Milwaukee, the low and moderate denial rate is 12.2 and the upper-income denial rate is 4.4. Therefore the low and moderate/ upper denial ratio is 12.2/4.4 = 2.8.

#Rank among the fourteen frostbelt cities.

&MSAs are ranked from 1 to 50 where the lowest number indicates the highest lower and moderate/upper denial rates. What may appear to be ties are numbers that have been rounded to the nearest tenth.

SOURCE: 1997 HMDA

and Hispanic borrowers and to borrowers from low- and moderate-income areas. However, this finding must be tempered by the small increases that have occurred nationwide.

In Milwaukee the share of conventional home purchase loans to blacks increased from 3.2 percent in 1992 to 6.0 percent in 1997, an increase of 2.8 percentage points. This was the fifth largest increase in the nation and second highest among frostbelt communities. For Hispanics these numbers increased from 1.1 percent to 2.5 percent, a change of 1.4 percentage points. On this measure Milwaukee ranked sixteenth nationwide and second within the region (see table 3.10).

Table 3.10 Percent Change in Loans by Race and Ethnicity, 1992–1997*

	Black	Rank	Hispanic	Rank
Atlanta, GA	3.5	2[&]	1.1	22
Baltimore, MD	2.6	6[3]	0.0	46[14]
Bergen/Passaic Counties, NJ	2.1	10	3.4	4
Boston, MA	1.5	15[7]	1.1	20[4]
Buffalo, NY	−1.8	50[14]	0.1	44[12]
Charlotte, NC	1.1	18	0.9	24
Chicago, IL	1.0	19[8]	0.5	33[6]
Cincinnati, OH	0.1	38[13]	0.1	41[10]
Cleveland, OH	1.5	13[5]	1.4	17[3]
Columbus, OH	0.6	24[10]	0.1	43[11]
Denver, CO	0.1	35	1.2	19
Detroit, MI	0.7	22[9]	0.1	40[9]
Fort Worth/Arlington, TX	−0.3	41	2.1	9
Ft. Lauderdale, FL	5.4	1	10.8	2
Greensboro, NC	2.8	3	1.6	12
Hartford, CT	2.3	8	1.6	13
Houston, TX	−0.4	45	2.2	8
Indianapolis, IN	0.5	25[11]	0.3	38[7]
Kansas City, MO	1.3	17	0.4	37
Las Vegas, NV	0.4	29	1.2	18
Los Angeles, CA	−0.4	43	−2.6	49
Miami, FL	0.8	21	18.0	1
Milwaukee, WI	2.8	5[2]	1.4	16[2]
Minneapolis, MN	1.5	14[5]	0.7	28[5]

(continued)

Table 3.10 *(continued)* Percent Change in Loans by Race and Ethnicity, 1992–1997*

	Black	Rank	Hispanic	Rank
Nashville, TN	−0.3	42	0.7	26
Nassau/Suffolk Counties, NY	2.2	9	1.6	11
New Orleans, LA	−0.7	49	0.5	36
New York, NY	1.8	11	3.2	5
Newark, NJ	2.4	7	2.4	7
Norfolk/VA Beach/Newport News, VA	0.0	39	0.1	42
Oakland, CA	−0.2	40	1.0	23
Orange County, CA	−0.4	44	−3.3	50
Orlando, FL	0.3	30	4.9	3
Philadelphia, PA	2.8	4[1]	1.5	14[1]
Phoenix, AZ	0.4	27	0.6	30
Pittsburgh, PA	0.2	3[12]	0.0	45[13]
Portland, OR	0.2	32	0.8	25
Providence, RI	0.2	33	1.1	21
Riverside/San Bernadino, CA	0.9	20	−0.4	48
Rochester, NY	1.3	16	0.5	34
Sacramento, CA	0.4	28	0.0	47
Salt Lake City, UT	0.2	34	1.9	10
San Antonio, TX	−0.5	46	2.5	6
San Diego, CA	−0.6	48	0.5	35
San Francisco, CA	−0.5	47	0.6	29
San Jose, CA	0.1	36	0.6	32
Seattle, WA	0.5	26	0.6	31
St. Louis, MO	1.6	12[4]	0.2	39[8]
Tampa/St. Petersburg, FL	0.6	23	1.4	15
Washington, DC	0.1	37	0.7	27

Note:
*The percent change is calculated by subtracting the percent of loans originated in 1992 from the equivalent 1997 percent. For example, in Milwaukee 3.2% of all loans went to blacks in 1992 and 6.0% in 1997. Therefore, the percent change is 6.0 − 3.2 = 2.8%.
#Rank among the fourteen frostbelt cities.
&MSAs are ranked from 1 to 50 where the lowest number indicates the highest percent change. What may appear to be ties are numbers that have been rounded to the nearest tenth.
SOURCE: 1997 and 1992 HMDA. However, 1992 data was not available for Orange County, therefore 1994 data was used.

Milwaukee fared almost as well in terms of changes in lending to low- and moderate-income areas. The share of loans to low- and moderate-income census tracts increased from 16.6 percent to 24.0 percent, up 7.4 points. On this measure Milwaukee ranked thirteenth among the fifty largest communities nationwide and fourth among frostbelt communities (see table 3.11).

Table 3.11 Percent Change in Loans by Income Tract Level, 1992–1997*

	Low Income	Rank	Moderate Income	Rank	Low and Moderate Income	Rank
Atlanta, GA	1.7	22[&]	3.7	24	5.4	24
Baltimore, MD	2.7	12[7#]	3.0	29[9]	5.7	21[7]
Bergen/Passaic Counties, NJ	−0.3	42	7.8	2	7.5	11
Boston, MA	1.3	28[11]	3.4	28[8]	4.7	27[10]
Buffalo, NY	0.6	33[12]	4.6	14[4]	5.2	25[9]
Charlotte, NC	−1.0	44	3.4	27	2.4	36
Chicago, IL	0.2	36[13]	2.8	30[10]	3.0	32[12]
Cincinnati, OH	3.0	10[5]	3.9	22[8]	6.9	15[5]
Cleveland, OH	3.6	6[3]	6.1	6[1]	9.7	6[1]
Columbus, OH	2.8	11[8]	2.7	31[11]	5.5	22[8]
Denver, CO	−0.2	40	2.6	32	2.4	35
Detroit, MI	2.5	14[9]	1.9	37[13]	4.4	28[11]
Fort Worth/Arlington, TX	5.5	2	6.1	7	11.6	1
Ft. Lauderdale, FL	0.0	38	4.1	20	4.1	30
Greensboro, NC	5.0	3	6.0	8	11.0	4
Hartford, CT	3.4	8	7.7	4	11.1	3
Houston, TX	3.8	4	7.7	3	11.5	2
Indianapolis, IN	2.7	13[8]	3.5	26[7]	6.2	18[6]
Kansas City, MO	2.4	15	0.5	44	2.9	34
Las Vegas, NV	3.4	7	4.2	19	7.6	10
Los Angeles, CA	−2.1	49	2.0	35	−0.1	44
Miami, FL	−2.0	46	0.8	43	−1.2	49
Milwaukee, WI	2.2	18[10]	5.2	10[3]	7.4	13[4]
Minneapolis, MN	3.1	9[4]	−1.3	49[14]	1.8	38[13]
Nashville, TN	1.5	26	3.6	25	5.1	26

(continued)

Table 3.11 *(continued)* Percent Change in Loans by Income Tract Level, 1992–1997*

	Low Income	Rank	Moderate Income	Rank	Low and Moderate Income	Rank
Nassau/Suffolk Counties, NY	1.0	29	6.9	5	7.9	9
New Orleans, LA	0.1	37	–0.6	47	–0.5	47
New York, NY	–0.3	41	2.4	33	2.1	37
Newark, NJ	0.7	30	9.2	1	9.9	5
Norfolk/VA Beach/ Newport News, VA	1.9	21	–0.9	48	1.0	42
Oakland, CA	0.6	34	3.7	23	4.3	29
Orange County, CA	–2.3	50	–3.6	50	–5.9	50
Orlando, FL	1.6	23	–0.4	46	1.2	40
Philadelphia, PA	3.7	5[2]	5.0	12[3]	8.7	8[3]
Phoenix, AZ	1.9	20	1.8	39	3.7	31
Pittsburgh, PA	–1.3	45[14]	1.9	36[12]	0.6	43[14]
Portland, OR	0.7	32	0.9	42	1.6	39
Providence, RI	1.5	25	4.3	18	5.8	19
Riverside/ San Bernadino, CA	1.5	24	5.3	9	6.8	16
Rochester, NY	2.4	16	4.5	15	6.9	14
Sacramento, CA	2.0	19	4.4	16	6.4	17
Salt Lake City, UT	0.5	35	4.9	13	5.4	23
San Antonio, TX	1.4	27	4.3	17	5.7	20
San Diego, CA	–0.2	39	1.4	40	1.2	41
San Francisco, CA	–2.0	47	1.8	38	–0.2	45
San Jose, CA	–2.1	48	1.3	41	–0.8	48
Seattle, WA	2.3	17	5.1	11	7.4	12
St. Louis, MO	5.0	2[1]	4.0	21[5]	9.0	7[2]
Tampa/St. Petersburg, FL	0.7	31	2.3	34	3.0	33
Washington, DC	–0.5	43	0.1	45	–0.4	46

Note:

*The percentage change is calculated by subtracting the percent of loans originated in 1992 from the equivalent 1997 percent. For example, in Milwaukee 3.9% of all loans went to low income tracts in 1992 and 6.1% in 1997. Therefore, the percent change is 6.1 – 3.9 = 2.2%.

#Rank among the fourteen frostbelt cities.

&MSAs are ranked from 1 to 50 where the lowest number indicates the highest percent change. What may appear to be ties are numbers that have been rounded to the nearest tenth.

SOURCE: 1997 and 1992 HMDA. However, 1992 data was not available for Orange County, therefore 1994 data was used.

Milwaukee's Ambiguous Community Reinvestment Record

Nationwide, community reinvestment efforts appear to be paying off. Lending to low- and moderate-income areas and to racial and ethnic minorities has increased—at least in part—because of community reinvestment and fair lending advocacy (Evanoff and Segal 1996; Gramlich 1998; Meyer 1998a). Milwaukee is no exception. On a majority of measures, Milwaukee is doing better than most communities, though its record among comparable frostbelt communities is more ambiguous. Milwaukee ranks better and has shown more progress in lending to minorities than in lending activity to low- and moderate-income areas, particularly compared to its counterparts in the frostbelt. Milwaukee's relatively low denial rates and its progress—relative to other communities—in the share of loans going to blacks and Hispanics is promising. Still unexplained and most troubling, however, is the persistently high denial ratio for blacks and Hispanics compared to whites. The progress that has been made must be viewed relative to the substantial gaps that remain as delineated in chapter 2.

Nationwide, homeownership reached a record high of 66.3 percent in 1998, but substantial disparities persist that are associated with income and race. Homeownership among whites reached 72.6 percent but just 46.1 percent among blacks and 44.7 percent among Hispanics (Morrison 1999). Among low- and moderate-income households 55.2 percent were homeowners in 1995 compared to 83.1 percent among upper income households (Joint Center for Housing Studies of Harvard University 1998: 35).

Precisely comparable data are not available at the local level, but mortgage lending patterns reflect homeownership rates. In Milwaukee 6 percent of conventional home purchase loans went to blacks in 1997 though they constituted 13.8 percent of the metropolitan area population according to the 1990 census. Hispanics received 2.5 percent of these loans and accounted for 3.4 percent of the population. (The next census will show that both the black and Hispanic populations have increased substantially since 1990 so these gaps are, in fact, larger than these numbers reflect.) Although mortgage lending and homeownership gaps may have closed somewhat in Milwaukee during recent years, much remains to be done.

Obviously, many factors account for the continuing gaps. Income and wealth disparities, of course, restrict housing choices for low- and moderate-income households and contribute to differences associated with race and ethnicity. Credit problems are more prevalent in low-income areas, and these differences reflect inequalities in education and job opportunities. Discrimination on the part of appraisers, real estate agents, property insurers, and others in housing and housing-related industries persist. But as indicated in chapter 1, discrimination and redlining have also been documented in the mortgage lending industry and several lenders have settled discrimination lawsuits with the U.S. Departments of Justice and Housing and Urban Development in recent years (Massey and Denton 1993; Yinger 1995; Munnell et al. 1996; U.S. Department of Justice 1998). Significant barriers persevere in housing and housing finance markets.

There is no single "bottom line." Some will view these indicators and conclude that the proverbial glass is half full while others will see it as half empty. It is important to take credit and acknowledge progress where it has occurred without losing sight of what remains to be accomplished. Understanding where success has been achieved and recognizing where results have been disappointing is essential for future development.

4

Mortgage Lending and Segregation in Milwaukee's Suburbs

ALTHOUGH MOST OF THE REDLINING DEBATE has focused on urban communities, the most segregated communities (or at least the most exclusionary) continue to be in the suburbs. Milwaukee is one of the most residentially segregated metropolitan areas in the United States. Two percent of all black households in the Milwaukee metropolitan area reside in the suburbs compared to 23 percent of Hispanics (many of whom are concentrated in a few Waukesha County neighborhoods) and 64 percent of white households (U.S. Bureau of the Census 1992), leading the Milwaukee Urban League to conclude that Milwaukee is *the* most segregated community in the nation (McNeely and Kinlow 1986).

In their pathbreaking study of residential segregation, *American Apartheid: Segregation and the Making of the Underclass*, Massey and Denton (1993) calculate five different indices of segregation for thirty large metropolitan areas. Milwaukee was the most segregated according to two measures and was among the five most segregated communities on two others, leading the authors to identify Milwaukee as one of the nation's hypersegregated communities.

Segregation is costly. Housing segregation leads directly to inferior schools for minorities. Employment opportunities are denied to minorities who are isolated, frequently in declining and dangerous neighborhoods (Massey and Denton 1993). Discriminatory housing practices and the consequent segregation of housing patterns reduces homeownership opportunities for minorities and depresses the market values of the homes they do own. Compared to the housing wealth that whites have accumulated, the costs of such discrimination to blacks and Hispanics has been estimated to reach $600 billion nationwide (Yinger 1995). In Milwaukee, the costs have been estimated to be $2.2 billion — $31,000 per black household and $26,000 per Hispanic household (Madison and Squires 1996).

Several factors contribute to the concentration of minority populations within the nation's central cities, including Milwaukee. Housing costs tend to be higher in the suburbs and minority income tends to be lower than that of the majority population. Some families choose to live in neighborhoods that are racially or ethnically homogeneous. More significant factors accounting for these segmented housing patterns, however, are a range of discriminatory government policies and private industry practices.

As examined in chapter 1, a range of government policies have contributed to the dual housing market including: enforcement of racially restrictive covenants, exclusionary zoning laws, subsidization of highways, and concentration of public housing in central cities (Bradford 1979; Bradford and Cincotta 1992; Massey and Denton 1993; Jackson 1985; Goering 1986). Many private housing industry practices have had similar effects including racial steering by real estate agents (Turner et al. 1991), discriminatory appraisal practices (Pittinger 1996), and redlining by lenders and property insurers policy (Munnell et al. 1996; Yinger 1996; Squires 1997). All of these practices have been prevalent in the Milwaukee metropolitan area (Tisdale 1989; City of Milwaukee [undated]).

But there has been substantial reaction against discriminatory lending and housing practices generally in recent years, as also discussed in chapter 1. The U.S. Departments of Justice and Housing and Urban Development have settled several mortgage lending discrimination complaints (Ritter 1995). Community groups in Milwaukee and around the nation have negotiated reinvestment agreements with lenders utilizing leverage provided by the Community Reinvestment Act (National Community Reinvestment Coalition 1995). Voluntary commitments from lenders and monitoring by local officials have also generated reinvestment activity (Morics 1998).

One key question that arises is the following: In light of the legislative, administrative, and community-based activity of recent years that has focused on mortgage lending practices, has the mortgage market changed for minority households attempting to purchase homes in the suburbs? This chapter is designed to address this question by analyzing the following factors in home purchase practices and their impact on the level of metropolitan segregation:

1. Are more minority households applying for loans to purchase suburban homes?

2. Are minority applicants receiving more loans?

3. Is the denial rate for minority households declining?

4. How, if at all, has the racial gap in the suburbs changed?

5. What are the implications of these developments in mortgage lending for segregated housing patterns?

The following pages examine these trends in the Milwaukee metropolitan area.

Data and Methodology

The data for this study are taken from Home Mortgage Disclosure Act (HMDA) statements, which most banks, credit unions, savings associations, and nondepository mortgage bankers that make mortgage loans in any metropolitan area are required to submit to the federal government and make available to the public annually (Federal Financial Institutions Examination Council 1996a).

Conventional and government insured home purchase loans are analyzed because these are the categories that relate most directly to homeownership. Trends in lending activity within the City of Milwaukee are compared to trends in lending activity within the suburbs which includes the four-county metropolitan area (Milwaukee, Waukesha, Ozaukee, and Washington) outside the Milwaukee city limits (see map 4.1)

The numbers of, and percentage increases for, loan applications, loan originations, and dollar volume of lending are reported for each year for Milwaukee and its suburban ring. These figures are also reported for whites, blacks, and Hispanics. Application rejection rates

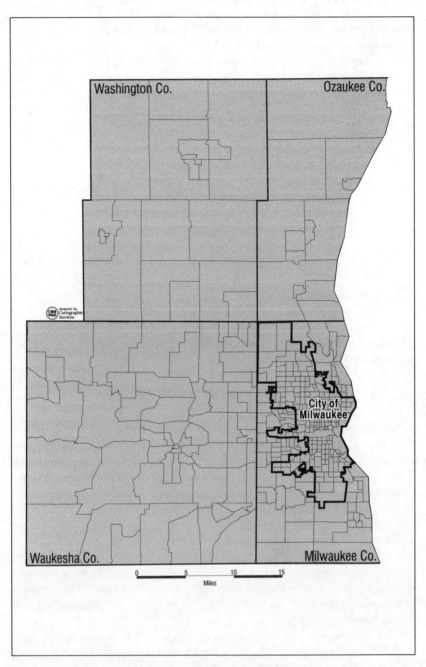

Washington Co.

Ozaukee Co.

City of
Milwaukee

Waukesha Co.

Milwaukee Co.

0   5   10   15
Miles

Map 4.1 Metropolitan Milwaukee: City and Suburbs

and the ratio of black to white and Hispanic to white rejection rates are also reported.

Findings

The basic conclusion is that lending activity to blacks and Hispanics in Milwaukee and the suburban ring has increased during the past seven years; and lending activity to both groups has increased at a greater rate in the suburbs than in the city. However, both black and

Table 4.1 Home Purchase Applications* in Milwaukee and Its Suburbs: 1990, 1994, and 1997

	1990	1994	1997	Percent Change between 1990 and 1997
City Applications				
Total	4,595	6,113	5,867	27.7
White	3,345	3,942	3,530	5.5
Percent White	72.8	64.5	60.2	−12.6
Black	1.017	1,642	1,803	77.3
Percent Black	22.1	26.9	30.7	8.6
Hispanic	233	529	534	129.0
Percent Hispanic	5.1	8.7	9.1	4.0
Suburban Applications				
Total	9,971	14,483	14,927	49.7
White	9,831	14,176	14,550	48.0
Percent White	98.6	97.9	97.5	−1.1
Black	67	142	188	180.6
Percent Black	0.7	1.0	1.3	0.6
Hispanic	73	165	189	158.9
Percent Hispanic	0.7	1.1	1.3	0.6

* Applications based on all categories of the "disposition" variable: approved, approved not accepted, denied, withdrawn, and closed due to incomplete file. Applications include only those in which race is known.
Percentages may not add up to 100 due to rounding.
SOURCE: 1990, 1994, and 1997 HMDA

Hispanic households are still receiving a tiny proportion of all suburban mortgage loans and loan dollars relative to their share of Milwaukee metropolitan area households. The number of minority households receiving mortgage loans to purchase suburban homes has been too small to significantly alter longstanding segregated housing patterns; and continuation of current trends will freeze the status quo for decades to come.

Applications

Between 1990 and 1997 the number of black applications increased from 1,017 to 1,803 (an increase of 77.3 percent) in the City of Milwaukee and from 67 to 188 (up 180.6 percent) in the suburbs. For Hispanics the increase went from 233 to 534 (129.0 percent) in the city and from 73 to 189 (158.9 percent) in the suburbs. For whites, city loan applications

Table 4.2 Home Purchase Loans in Milwaukee and Its Suburbs: 1990, 1994, and 1997

	1990	1994	1997	Percent Change between 1990 and 1997
City Loans				
Total	3,509	4,928	4,545	29.5
White	2,696	3,354	2,935	8.9
Percent White	76.8	68.1	64.6	−12.2
Black	642	1,155	1,216	89.4
Percent Black	18.3	23.4	26.8	8.5
Hispanic	171	419	394	130.4
Percent Hispanic	4.9	8.5	8.7	3.8
Suburban Loans				
Total	8,683	12,810	12,800	47.4
White	8,578	12,567	12,540	46.2
Percent White	98.8	98.1	98.0	−0.8
Black	48	110	122	154.2
Percent Black	0.6	0.9	1.0	0.4
Hispanic	57	133	138	142.1
Percent Hispanic	0.7	1.0	1.1	0.4

Percentages may not add up to 100 due to rounding.
SOURCE: 1990, 1994, and 1997 HMDA

went from 3,345 to 3,530 (up 5.5 percent) and loan applications for the suburbs went from 9,831 to 14,550 (up 48.0 percent) (see table 4.1).

Loans

Growth in the number of loans changed accordingly. For blacks the number of loans in the city increased from 642 to 1,216 (89.4 percent) and the suburban increase went from 48 to 122 (154.2 percent). For Hispanics, loan totals went from 171 to 394 (130.4 percent) in the city and from 57 to 138 (142.1 percent) in the suburbs. For whites, loans granted in the city went from 2,696 to 2,935 (up 8.9 percent) and loans granted for suburban purchases increased from 8,578 to 12,540 (up 46.2 percent) (see table 4.2).

Table 4.3 Home Purchase Loan Dollars* in Milwaukee and Its Suburbs: 1990, 1994, and 1997

	1990	1994	1997	Percent Change between 1990 and 1997
City Loan Dollars				
Total	$178,251	$299,389	$313,214	75.7
White	$145,780	$224,545	$225,643	54.8
Percent White	81.8	75.0	72.0	–9.8
Black	$25,965	$55,355	$66,312	155.4
Percent Black	14.6	18.5	21.2	6.6
Hispanic	$6,506	$19,489	$21,259	226.8
Percent Hispanic	3.6	6.5	6.8	3.2
Suburban Loan Dollars				
Total	$747,272	$1,466,061	$1,629,806	118.1
White	$737,201	$1,437,185	$1,596,712	116.6
Percent White	98.7	98.0	98.0	–0.7
Black	$5,200	$15,080	$16,868	224.4
Percent Black	0.7	1.0	1.0	0.3
Hispanic	$4,871	$13,796	$16,226	223.1
Percent Hispanic	0.7	0.9	1.0	0.3

*Dollars are in thousands.
Percentages may not add up to 100 due to rounding.
SOURCE: 1990, 1994, and 1997 HMDA

Loan Dollars

Increases in the dollar amount of home purchase loans increased in the same direction. For blacks, the amount of lending increased from $26.0 million to $66.3 million in the city (155.4 percent) and from $5.2 million to $16.9 million in the suburbs (224.4 percent). For Hispanics the increase within Milwaukee was from $6.5 million to $21.3 million (226.8 percent) while in the suburban ring the increase was from $4.9 million to $16.2 million (223.1 percent). Lending to whites increased from $146 million to $226 million (up 54.8 percent) in the city and from $737 million to about $1.6 billion in the suburbs (up 116.6 percent) (see table 4.3).

Denial Rates and Ratios

Application denial rates declined for all groups with one major exception; denial rates for blacks in the suburban ring increased 4.0 percent between 1990 and 1997. In the city denial rates for blacks decreased 9.2 percent. For Hispanics denial rates dropped by 3.0 percent in the city and 0.9 percent in the suburbs. Denial rates declined for whites 2.6 percent in the city and about 1 percent in the suburbs (see table 4.4).

Table 4.4 Denial Rates* in Milwaukee and Its Suburbs: 1990, 1994, and 1997

	1990	1994	1997	Percent Change between 1990 and 1997
City and Suburban				
Percent White	7.1	4.5	6.2	–0.9
Percent Black	27.0	19.2	18.7	–8.3
Percent Hispanic	14.8	10.4	12.3	–2.5
City				
Percent White	11.2	7.6	8.6	–2.6
Percent Black	27.7	19.9	18.4	–9.2
Percent Hispanic	15.6	12.0	12.6	–3.0
Suburban				
Percent White	5.7	3.7	5.6	–0.1
Percent Black	17.0	10.6	20.9	4.0
Percent Hispanic	12.3	4.9	11.5	–0.9

*Denial rates are computed by dividing number of applications denied by total number of applications where applications are: approved, approved not accepted, and denied.
SOURCE: 1990, 1994, and 1997 HMDA

Consequently, the ratio of black/white denial rates declined in the city during these years but increased in the suburban area. On average, blacks were rejected two and a half times as often as whites in the city and over three times as often in the suburbs. Hispanics were rejected about one and a half times as frequently as whites in the city and twice as often in the suburbs (see table 4.5).

Denial rates are particularly difficult to interpret. High denial rates for a given group may reflect a lender's aggressive efforts to attract more applications from members of that group, including many marginal and unqualified applicants. At the same time a low denial rate may reflect pre-screening where members of a particular group are rarely offered the opportunity to submit a formal application. Therefore, it is critical to examine denial rates in conjunction with lending activity reported above.

Conclusion

Although there has been a substantial increase in the percentage of black and Hispanic suburban home purchase loans, the real impact on metropolitan segregation has been minimal given the small base that minority loans represented at the beginning of this time period. Changes in the raw numbers reflect this phenomenon. The number of loans to blacks in the suburbs actually increased by just 74 (from 48 to

Table 4.5 Denial Ratios* in Milwaukee and Its Suburbs: 1990, 1994, and 1997

	1990	*1994*	*1997*
City and Suburban			
Black/White	3.8:1	4.2:1	3.0:1
Hispanic/White	2.1:1	2.3:1	2.0:1
City			
Black/White	2.5:1	2.6:1	2.2:1
Hispanic/White	1.4:1	1.6:1	1.5:1
Suburban			
Black/White	3.0:1	2.9:1	3.7:1
Hispanic/White	2.2:1	1.3:1	2.0:1

*Denial rates are computed by dividing percent black or Hispanic denial by percent white denial.
Source: 1990, 1994, and 1997 HMDA

122, with at least some of these loans going to blacks who currently live in the suburbs but who are seeking another suburban home). For Hispanics the increase was 81 (from 57 to 138). At the same time the number of loans to whites in the suburbs increased by 3,962 (from 8,578 to 12,540). Despite the relative gains that blacks and Hispanics have made in the Milwaukee area mortgage market, they still receive a minute proportion of all suburban loans and loan dollars given their share of all metropolitan area households. No doubt the concentration of black and Hispanic loans within the city reflects their current spatial location in Milwaukee's housing market. But this fact begs the critical question: Why are racial minorities excluded from Milwaukee's suburban ring?

Assuming the absence of discrimination (in the nation's housing and housing finance markets as well as in schools, labor markets, and elsewhere) and assuming similar housing choices among all racial groups, approximately the same proportion of each group would probably live in the city and the suburbs and each group would receive about the same share of all mortgage loans and loan dollars within each area. But that is clearly not the case in Milwaukee.

Blacks account for 11.5 percent of all households in the Milwaukee metropolitan area. But in 1997 they accounted for only 1.3 percent of all suburban home purchase mortgage loan applications, they received 1.0 percent of all suburban loans, and 1.0 percent of all suburban loan dollars. Hispanics accounted for 2.3 percent of area households but submitted just 1.3 percent of all suburban home purchase mortgage loan applications and received 1.1 percent of all loans and 1.0 percent of loan dollars.

One way of viewing the changes that have occurred toward closing the suburban racial gap is to determine how long it will take to reach parity (that is for the proportion of black and Hispanic loans in the suburbs to equal the proportion of black and Hispanic households in the metropolitan area) given the rate of progress over the previous seven years. For example, how long will it take for blacks to receive 11.5 percent of all suburban home purchase mortgage loans given the increasing share of such loans they received in the past seven years? Between 1990 and 1997 the share of all such loans going to blacks increased from 0.6 percent to 1.0 percent, an increase of 0.4 percent *(that is four tenths of one percent, not four percent).* At this rate, in order to close the remaining gap of 10.5 percent (11.5 percent–1.0 percent) it will take more than 184 years. For Hispanics the remaining gap is 1.2 percent (2.3 percent–1.1 percent) and it will take twenty-one years to close it.

These figures were calculated in the following way. First, progress in closing this gap over the past seven years is identified in table 4.2. In 1990 blacks received 0.6 percent of all suburban home purchase loans. In 1997 they received 1.0 percent. So 0.4 percent of the gap was closed during these years. Second, the remaining gap to be closed was derived by subtracting the current proportion of suburban loans going to blacks (1.0 percent) from the proportion of black households in the metropolitan area (11.5 percent). The remaining gap, therefore, is 10.5 percent. Finally, the number of years it would take to close this gap was calculating by determining how long it would take for black loans to reach 11.5 percent of the total if 0.4 percent of the gap were closed every seven years. The current gap—10.5 percent—was divided by 0.4 percent (for a total of 26.3) and then multiplied by seven; a total of 184.1 years.

Lenders alone, of course, cannot close the racial gap in mortgage lending. Racial and ethnic groups differ on several characteristics including financial capacity and other factors that affect their credit-worthiness. Under any conditions, precisely the same proportion of each group would not choose to live in the city, suburbs, or elsewhere, but in the absence of discrimination, housing and lending patterns would be quite different. As indicated earlier, the weight of social science evidence clearly establishes that discriminatory practices by various actors in the housing industry—not choice or economic capacity—account for the dual housing markets in virtually every metropolitan area. It remains evident that significant racial gaps persist in the spatial location of racial minorities in the Milwaukee metropolitan area and in the distribution of home purchase mortgage loans that is intricately connected to that broader housing pattern.

Hypersegregation in Milwaukee has not been resolved or even significantly reduced in recent years. The destructive impact of segregated housing is felt in a variety of social and economic arenas including education, employment, and the legacy of intense racial conflict among Milwaukee residents. However, this malignant condition whereby blacks and, to a lesser extent, Hispanics are separated in everyday residential life from their white counterparts and deprived of the most basic choices related to establishing a home and community base will not be cured without serious and sustained attention by all levels of government, private industry, and community organizations.

5

Milwaukee's Best (and Worst?) Mortgage Lenders

M ORE STRIKING THAN THE GRADUAL CHANGES among financial institutions generally are dramatic differences in the community reinvestment profile among individual lenders. This chapter compares the lending records of major mortgage lending institutions in the Milwaukee metropolitan area on several key measures of community reinvestment and fair lending. From these specific measures, an overall index is created that ranks each of these lenders, from best to worst, in terms of their community reinvestment record.

Data and Methodology

Information for this report is taken from the 1996 Home Mortgage Disclosure Act (HMDA) reports of Milwaukee metropolitan area commercial banks and savings institutions which made more than 300 loans in 1996. It includes conventional and government insured (by the Federal Housing Administration, Veterans Administration, and

Table 5.1 Lending Activity in the Milwaukee Metropolitan Area, 1996

Lender	Total Applications	Total Loans	Total Dollars (Thousands)
Associated Bank Milwaukee	1,096	959	90,487
Bank One, Wisconsin	10,710	6,364	176,671
First Financial Bank	2,526	2,118	155,419
Firstar Bank Milwaukee, N.A.	2,997	2,395	209,820
Guaranty Bank	2,149	1,686	144,038
M & I Marshall and Ilsley	3,284	2,553	225,491
Mutual Savings Bank	947	893	85,577
North Shore Bank, FSB	1,205	1,046	137,046
Norwest Bank Wisconsin, N.A.	2,089	1,481	122,534
Security Bank, S.S.B.	5,527	3,097	203,120
St. Francis Bank, FSB	1,918	1,589	115,524
TCF Bank Wisconsin FSB	650	438	26,167
The Equitable Bank, S.S.B.	941	782	79,517
Tri City National Bank	636	526	26,956
Universal Savings Bank, F.A.	501	470	49,731
Wauwatosa Savings Bank	804	754	121,417
AVERAGE	2,374	1,697	123,095

SOURCE: 1996 HMDA

Farmers Home Administration) single-family and multidwelling home purchase, home improvement, and refinancing loans. Loan purchases are not included. Only those lenders that contain the entire city of Milwaukee in their assessment area under the federal Community Reinvestment Act (CRA) are included.

The sixteen institutions included in this report accounted for more than 55 percent of all HMDA reported loans in 1996 in the Milwaukee metropolitan area. On average they accounted for 2,374 applications, 1,697 loans, and $123 million mortgage loan dollars (see table 5.1). Though larger and perhaps more focused on the City of Milwaukee, these sixteen lenders are fairly representative of all reporting institutions in several key respects. For example, blacks accounted for 9.4 percent of the applications submitted to these sixteen lenders and 9.3 percent for all HMDA reporting institutions. Hispanics accounted for 2.6 percent of the loans made by this sample and 2.3 percent of loans made by all Milwaukee area lenders. Applicants from the city's Target Area accounted for 3.4 percent of loans provided by this sample and 3.5 percent for all lenders.

The following indicators are created for these sixteen lenders: percent of applications from, and percent of loans and loan dollars to, blacks, Hispanics, and residents of the Target Area; Black/White denial ratios; Hispanic/White denial ratios; and Target Area/Nontarget Area denial ratios. Each lender is ranked from first to sixteenth on each of these twelve measures. The average of these twelve rankings serves as the final ranking for individual lenders in terms of their relative overall community reinvestment performance based on available HMDA data.[1]

Although there is no ideal single measure that captures every dimension of community reinvestment, this approach reflects the key process and performance aspects. Marketing is captured by the application data. Lending, perhaps the most significant indicator, is revealed in the data on loans and loan dollars. Denial rates can be more difficult to interpret but they provide an approximate measure of equitable treatment. However, high denial rates can result from effective advertising and marketing while low denial rates might indicate prescreening or the absence of marketing.

By utilizing percentages rather than absolute numbers, this methodology avoids unfairly rewarding or punishing an institution due to size. A very large lender might report more loans to blacks, Hispanics, or residents of the Target Area, but that could simply reflect its size. A smaller lender that makes a much higher percentage of its loans in such areas should be credited for, and not punished by, its lending record. By focusing on depository institutions in one metropolitan area, lenders are evaluated against their peers who are competing for basically the same type of business. The level of risk in the pool of potential borrowers is essentially the same for each of these lenders.

These findings, in and of themselves, cannot confirm or deny compliance or noncompliance with the Community Reinvestment Act or other fair lending requirements, but they clearly reveal which lenders are doing more and less effective jobs in responding to the credit needs of the Milwaukee metropolitan area.[2]

Findings

Two key findings emerge. First, lenders vary substantially in the levels of service they provide to different communities. For example, the proportion of an institution's loans to black borrowers ranges from 1.9 percent to 18.7 percent (see table 5.2). Second, there is consistency in performance across the various measures. That is, an institution that

Table 5.2 Lending Activity to Blacks in the Milwaukee Metropolitan Area by Lender, 1996

Lender	Percent Black Apps.	Lender	Percent Black Loans	Lender	Percent Black Dollars	Lender	Black/White Denial Ratio
TCF Bank Wisconsin, FSB	24.0	TCF Bank Wisconsin, FSB	18.7	TCF Bank Wisconsin FSB	10.6	Universal Savings Bank, F.A.	1.1
Guaranty Bank	13.6	Guaranty Bank	11.9	Guaranty Bank	7.1	TCF Bank Wisconsin, FSB	2.0
Security Bank, S.S.B.	12.8	Mutual Savings Bank	7.1	Mutual Savings Bank	4.4	Associated Bank Milwaukee	2.4
Bank One, Wisconsin	11.1	Firstar Bank Milwaukee, N.A.	7.0	Norwest Bank Wisconsin, NA	3.6	Norwest Bank Wisconsin, N.A.	2.8
Firstar Bank Milwaukee, N.A.	9.2	Security Bank, S.S.B	6.7	Bank One, Wisconsin	3.5	Bank One, Wisconsin	2.8
M & I Marshall and Ilsley	7.5	Northwest Bank Wisconsin, N.A.	5.9	Universal Savings Bank, F.A.	3.2	Tri City National Bank	3.1
St. Francis Bank, FSB	7.2	Bank One, Wisconsin	5.6	Firstar Bank Milwaukee, N.A.	3.0	Security Bank, S.S.B.	3.2
Mutual Savings Bank	7.2	St. Francis Bank, FSB	5.3	Security Bank S.S.B.	2.8	Mutual Savings Bank	3.5
First Financial Bank	6.6	M & I Marshall and Ilsley	5.0	First Financial Bank	2.8	St. Francis Bank, FSB	3.6

(continued)

Table 5.2 (*continued*) Lending Activity to Blacks in the Milwaukee Metropolitan Area by Lender, 1996

Lender	Percent Black Apps.	Lender	Percent Black Loans	Lender	Percent Black Dollars	Lender	Black/White Denial Ratio
Norwest Bank Wisconsin, N.A.	6.2	Universal Savings Bank, F.A.	4.5	M & I Marshall and Ilsley	2.6	The Equitable Bank, S.S.B.	3.7
The Equitable Bank, S.S.B.	5.6	First Financial Bank	4.3	St. Francis Bank, FSB	2.6	M & I Marshall and Ilsley	4.4
North Shore Bank, FSB	5.4	North Shore Bank, FSB	4.1	The Equitable Bank, S.S.B.	2.1	Guaranty Bank	5.0
Universal Savings Bank, F.A.	4.8	The Equitable Bank, S.S.B.	4.0	North Shore Bank, FSB	2.1	North Shore Bank, FSB	5.2
Wauwatosa Savings Bank	3.7	Wauwatosa Savings Bank	3.2	Associated Bank Milwaukee	1.5	Firstar Bank Milwaukee, N.A.	6.8
Tri City National Bank	3.0	Tri City National Bank	2.5	Wauwatosa Savings Bank	1.4	Wauwatosa Savings Bank	8.1
Associated Bank Milwaukee	2.0	Associated Bank Milwaukee	1.9	Tri City National Bank	1.1	First Financial Bank	8.5
Average	9.4	Average	5.9	Average	3.1	Average	3.8

SOURCE: 1996 HMDA

Table 5.3   Lender by Average Rank: Metropolitan Milwaukee, 1996

Lender	Rank
TCF Bank Wisconsin, FSB	3.3
Security Bank, S.S.B.	5.4
St. Francis Bank, FSB	5.5
The Equitable Bank, S.S.B.	6.1
Bank One, Wisconsin	6.4
Firstar Bank Milwaukee, N.A.	7.5
First Financial Bank	7.8
Mutual Savings Bank	8.7
Norwest Bank Wisconsin, N.A.	8.8
Tri City National Bank	8.8
Guaranty Bank	9.3
Universal Savings Bank, F.A.	9.3
M & I Marshall and Ilsley	10.9
Wauwatosa Savings Bank	11.3
North Shore Bank, FSB	12.3
Associated Bank Milwaukee	13.4
Average	8.4

SOURCE: 1996 HMDA

scores well on one measure or set of indicators tends to do well on others.[3] For example, TCF Bank (the highest ranked lender overall [see table 5.3] had the best score on four indicators and was among the top five institutions on nine of the twelve different measures. On the other hand Associated Bank Milwaukee (the lowest ranked lender overall) had the worst score on five indicators and was among the bottom five on nine of the twelve measures.

Lending Activity to Blacks

Black households accounted for 11.5 percent of all households in the Milwaukee metropolitan area according to the 1990 census, but on average accounted for 9.4 percent of mortgage applications, 5.9 percent of loans, and 3.1 percent of loan dollars. Black applications, loans, and loan dollars ranged from 1.1 percent to 24.0 percent among these sixteen mortgage lenders. For at least 75 percent of these institutions, blacks accounted for 10 percent or less of applications, loans, and loan dollars (see table 5.3 and table 5.4).

Table 5.4 Lending Activity to Blacks as a Proportion of Lending Activity in the Milwaukee Metropolitan Area, 1996

	Applications	Loans	Loan Dollars		Black/White Denial Ratio
Greater Than 10%	4 (25.0%)	2 (12.5%)	1 (6.3%)	2/1 or Less	2 (12.5%)
Between 5% and 10%	8 (50.0%)	7 (43.8%)	1 (6.3%)	Greater Than 2/1 and Less Than 3/1	3 (13.8%)
Greater Than 2% and Less Than 5%	3 (18.8%)	6 (37.5%)	11 (68.8%)	Between 3/1 and 5/1	7 (43.8%)
2% or Less	1 (6.3%)	1 (6.3%)	3 (18.8%)	Greater Than 5/1	4 (25.0%)

Black households account for 11.5% of all households in the Milwaukee metropolitan area.

SOURCE: 1996 HMDA

Table 5.5 Lending Activity to Hispanics as a Proportion of Lending Activity in the Milwaukee Metropolitan Area, 1996

	Applications	Loans	Loan Dollars		Hispanic/White Denial Ratio
Greater Than 4%	3 (18.8%)	2 (12.5%)	1 (6.3%)	1/1 or Less	3 (18.8%)
Between 2% and 4%	7 (43.8%)	6 (37.5%)	3 (18.8%)	Greater Than 1/1 and Less Than 2/1	4 (25.0%)
Greater Than 1% and Less than 2%	5 (31.3%)	6 (37.5%)	7 (43.8%)	Between 2/1 and 5/1	6 (37.5%)
1% or Less	1 (6.3%)	2 (12.5%)	5 (31.3%)	Greater Than 5/1	3 (18.8%)

Hispanic households account for 2.4% of all households in the Milwaukee metropolitan area.

SOURCE: 1996 HMDA

Black applicants were rejected almost four times as often as whites; the black/white denial ratio was 3.8/1. Again, this varied widely. One lender denied black and white applicants at virtually the same rate. On the other hand, two lenders denied black applicants at least eight times as often as white applicants.

Lending Activity to Hispanics

Hispanic households accounted for 2.4 percent of Milwaukee area households. They submitted 3.0 percent of all applications and received 2.6 percent of all loans and 1.5 percent of loan dollars (see table 5.5 and table 5.6). Applications and loans ranged from 0.9 percent to approximately 9 percent while loan dollars peaked at 5.1 percent. More than one-third of these lenders received fewer than two percent of their applications from Hispanics, more than half made fewer than two percent of their loans to Hispanics and more than three-quarters of them provided less than two percent of loan dollars to Hispanics.

Hispanic applications were rejected more than twice as often as whites. Two lenders denied no applications from Hispanics and another lender turned down Hispanics less frequently than whites. At the other end, one lender denied Hispanic applications more than fourteen times as often as white applications.

Lending Activity in the Target Area

Households in the Target Area accounted for 11.6 percent of all metropolitan area households. They submitted 5.5 percent of all applications and received 3.4 percent of all loans and 2.3 percent of loan dollars (see table 5.7 and table 5.8). Target Area applications ranged from 0.7 percent to 8.6 percent, loans varied from 0.7 percent to 5.3 percent, and loan dollars went from 0.4 percent to 6.7 percent. Almost two-thirds of the lenders received less than six percent of their applications from the Target Area, while more than 85 percent of the lenders provided less than six percent of all loans and loan dollars to this community.

Target Area applications were denied three times as often as applications from other parts of the metropolitan area. Two lenders denied no applications from the Target Area while three lenders rejected Target Area applicants at least five times as often as others.

Milwaukee's Highest and Lowest Ranked Mortgage Lenders

Lenders vary substantially in the level of services they provide Milwaukee's Black, Hispanic, and Target Area communities according

Table 5.6 Lending Activity to Hispanics in the Milwaukee Metropolitan Area by Lender, 1996

Lender	Percent Hispanic Apps.	Lender	Percent Hispanic Loans	Lender	Percent Hispanic Dollars	Lender	Hispanic/White Denial Ratio
St. Francis Bank, FSB	9.2	St. Francis Bank, FSB	8.9	St. Francis Bank, FSB	5.1	North Shore Bank, FSB	0.0
First Financial Bank	4.8	The Equitable Bank, S.S.B.	4.6	TCF Bank Wisconsin, FSB	2.6	Universal Savings Bank, F.A.	0.0
The Equitable Bank, S.S.B.	4.3	First Financial Bank	3.7	The Equitable Bank, S.S.B.	2.5	The Equitable Bank, S.S.B.	0.8
Firstar Bank Milwaukee, N.A.	3.9	Firstar Bank Milwaukee, N.A.	3.5	First Financial Bank	2.2	Tri City National Bank	1.4
Security Bank, S.S.B.	2.9	TCF Bank Wisconsin, FSB	2.7	Firstar Bank Milwaukee, N.A.	1.8	TCF Bank Wisconsin, FSB	1.5
Bank One, Wisconsin	2.7	Security Bank, S.S.B.	2.4	Tri City National Bank	1.6	St. Francis Bank, FSB	1.5
TCF Bank Wisconsin, FSB	2.6	Tri City National Bank	2.3	Security Bank, S.S.B.	1.5	Bank One, Wisconsin	1.9
Tri City National Bank	2.4	Bank One, Wisconsin	2.0	Bank One, Wisconsin	1.5	Security Bank, S.S.B.	2.1
M & I Marsall and Ilsley	2.3	M & I Marsall and Ilsley	1.8	Universal Savings Bank, F.A.	1.3	Norwest Bank Wisconsin, N.A.	2.7
Mutual Savings Bank	2.2	Mutual Savings Bank	1.8	Mutual Savings Bank	1.2	M & I Marshall and Ilsley	3.0

(continued)

Table 5.6 (continued) Lending Activity to Hispanics in the Milwaukee Metropolitan Area by Lender, 1996

Lender	Percent Hispanic Apps.	Lender	Percent Hispanic Loans	Lender	Percent Hispanic Dollars	Lender	Hispanic/White Denial Ratio
Norwest Bank Wisconsin, NA	1.7	Norwest Bank Wisconsin, N.A.	1.6	Norwest Bank Wisconsin, NA	1.1	Associated Bank Milwaukee	3.1
Guaranty Bank	1.7	Universal Savings Bank, F.A.	1.5	Guaranty Bank	0.9	First Bank Milwaukee, N.A.	3.4
Universal Savings Bank, F.A.	1.6	Guaranty Bank	1.4	M & I Marshall and Ilsley	0.9	First Financial Bank	4.5
Wauwatosa Savings Bank	1.2	Wauwatosa Savings Bank	1.1	Associated Bank Milwaukee	0.7	Guaranty Bank	7.9
Associated Bank Milwaukee	1.2	North Shore Bank, FSB	1.0	North Shore Bank, FSB	0.6	Mutual Savings Bank	8.3
North Shore Bank, FSB	0.9	Associated Bank Milwaukee	1.2	Wauwatosa Savings Bank	0.4	Wauwatosa Savings Bank	14.6
Average	3.0	Average	2.6	Average	1.5	Average	2.2

SOURCE: 1996 HMDA

Table 5.7 Lending Activity in Milwaukee's Target Area as a Proportion of Lending Activity in the Milwaukee Metropolitan Area, 1996

	Applicants	Loans	Loan Dollars	TA/Non TA Denial Ratio	
Greater Than 5%	6 (37.5%)	2 (12.5%)	3 (18.8%)	1/1 or Less	2 (12.5%)
Between 3% and 5%	6 (37.5%)	6 (37.5%)	1 (6.3%)	Greater Than 1/1 and Less than 2/1	5 (31.3%)
Greater Than 1.5% and Less than 3%	3 (18.8%)	6 (37.5%)	4 (25.0%)	Between 2/1 and 5/1	7 (43.8%)
1.5% or Less	1 (6.3%)	2 (12.5%)	8 (50.0%)	Greater Than 5/1	2 (12.5%)

Households in the Target Area account for 11.6% of all households in the Milwaukee metropolitan area.

SOURCE: 1996 HMDA

Table 5.8 Lending Activity to the Target Area in the Milwaukee Metropolitan Area by Lender, 1996

Lender	Percent Target Area Apps.	Lender	Percent Target Area Loans	Lender	Percent Target Area Dollars	Lender	TA/ Non-TA Denial Ratio
Security Bank, S.S.B.	8.6	TCF Bank Wisconsin, FSB	5.3	The Equitable Bank, S.S.B.	6.7	Mutual Savings Bank	0.0
TCF Bank Wisconsin, FSB	7.5	Security Bank, S.S.B.	5.1	Security Bank, S.S.B.	5.9	Universal Savings Bank, F.A.	0.0
First Financial Bank	6.4	St. Francis Bank, FSB	4.5	Wauwatosa Savings Bank	5.2	The Equitable Bank, S.S.B.	1.5
Bank One, Wisconsin	6.1	Wauwatosa Savings Bank	4.5	First Financial Bank	4.5	Wauwatosa Savings Bank	1.6
Firstar Bank Milwaukee, N.A.	5.8	The Equitable Bank, S.S.B.	4.2	Tri City National Bank	2.4	Tri City National Bank	1.6
St. Francis Bank, FSB	5.2	First Financial Bank	4.1	TCF Bank Wisconsin, FSB	2.0	TCF Bank Wisconsin, FSB	1.8
Wauwatosa Savings Bank	4.5	Firstar Bank Milwaukee, N.A.	4.0	Bank One, Wisconsin	1.9	St. Francis Bank, FSB	1.9
The Equitable Bank, S.S.B.	4.5	Bank One, Wisconsin	3.4	St. Francis Bank, FSB	1.8	Norwest Bank Wisconsin, N.A.	2.0

(continued)

Table 5.8 (*continued*) Lending Activity to the Target Area in the Milwaukee Metropolitan Area by Lender, 1996

Lender	Percent Target Area Apps.	Lender	Percent Target Area Loans	Lender	Percent Target Area Dollars	Lender	TA/ Non-TA Denial Ratio
Norwest Bank Wisconsin, N.A.	4.2	Tri City National Bank	2.9	Firstar Bank Milwaukee, N.A.	1.3	Associated Bank Milwaukee	2.0
Guaranty Bank	4.2	Guaranty Bank	2.7	Guaranty Bank	1.3	Bank One, Wisconsin	2.2
Tri City National Bank	3.6	Norwest Bank Wisconsin, N.A.	2.6	Norwest Bank Wisconsin, N.A.	1.1	Security Bank, S.S.B.	2.4
M & I Marshall and Ilsley	3.4	Mutual Savings Bank	2.2	Associated Bank Milwaukee	0.7	North Shore Bank, FSB	4.0
North Shore Bank, FSB	2.8	North Shore Bank, FSB	2.1	Mutual Savings Bank	0.7	M & I Marshall and Ilsley	4.4
Mutual Savings Bank	2.2	M & I Marshall and Ilsley	1.9	North Shore Bank, FSB	0.6	Firstar Bank Milwaukee, N.A.	5.0
Universal Savings Bank, F.A.	1.8	Universal Savings Bank, F.A.	1.5	M & I Marshall and Ilsley	0.4	First Financial Bank	5.5
Associated Bank Milwaukee	0.7	Associated Bank Milwaukee	0.7	Universal Savings Bank, F.A.	0.4	Guaranty Bank	6.3
Average	5.5	Average	3.4	Average	2.3	Average	3.0

SOURCE: 1996 HMDA

Table 5.9　Lending Activity of the Highest and Lowest Ranked Lender in the Milwaukee Metropolitan Area, 1996

	Highest Ranked	Lowest Ranked
	TCF Bank Wisconsin	Associated Bank Milwaukee
Black Applications %	24.0	2.0
Black Loans %	18.7	1.9
Black Dollars %	10.6	1.5
Black/White Denial Ratio	2.0	2.4
Hispanic Applications %	2.6	1.2
Hispanic Loans %	2.7	0.9
Hispanic Dollars %	2.6	0.7
Hispanic/White Denial Ratio	1.5	3.1
Target Area Applications %	7.5	0.7
Target Area Loans %	5.3	0.7
Target Area Dollars %	2.0	0.7
Target Area/Non-Target Area Denial Ratio	1.8	2.0

SOURCE: 1996 HMDA

to HMDA reported mortgage loans. And those which do well in one area tend to do well in others. In averaging their rank on each of the twelve measures, it is possible to capture lenders' overall relative reinvestment record. On this scale, the best record was achieved by TCF Bank with an average rank of 3.3. Associated Bank Milwaukee achieved the worst record with an average rank of 13.4 (see table 5.9 and table 5.10).

These scores reflect real, concrete differences in levels of service provided. For example, TCF provided ten times the level of service to blacks as did Associated. TCF received 24 percent of its applications from, and provided 18.7 percent of its loans and 10.6 percent of its loan dollars to blacks compared to two percent or less for Associated. TCF provided more than twice the level of service to Hispanics as did Associated. Hispanics accounted for at least 2.6 percent of TCF's applications, loans, and loan dollars compared to approximately 1.0 percent at Associated. Disparities were even larger in the Target Area. For TCF Bank the Target Area accounted for 7.5 percent of applications, 5.3 percent of loans, and 2.0 percent of loan dollars compared to 0.7 percent for Associated in each category. And TCFs black/white,

Table 5.10 Lender by Rank for Each Indicator: Metropolitan Milwaukee, 1996

Lender	Black Apps.	Black Loans	Black Dollars	Black/ White Denial Ratio	Hispanic Apps.	Hispanic Loans	Hispanic Dollars	Hispanic/ White Denial Ratio	Target Area Apps.	Target Area Loans	Target Area Dollars	TA/ Non-TA Denial Ratio	Average
Associated Bank Milwaukee	16	16	14	3	14	16	14	11	16	16	12	8	13.0
Bank One, Wisconsin	4	7	5	4	6	8	7	7	4	8	7	10	6.4
First Financial Bank	9	11	8	16	2	3	4	13	3	6	4	15	7.8
Firstar Bank Milwaukee, N.A.	5	4	7	14	4	4	5	12	5	7	9	14	7.5
Guaranty Bank	2	2	2	12	11	13	12	14	9	10	9	16	9.3
M & I Marshall and Ilsley	6	9	10	11	9	9	13	10	12	14	15	13	10.9
Mutual Savings Bank	7	3	3	8	10	9	10	15	14	12	12	1	8.7
North Shore Bank, FSB	12	12	12	13	16	15	15	1	13	13	14	12	12.3

(continued)

Table 5.10 (*continued*) Lender by Rank for Each Indicator: Metropolitan Milwaukee, 1996

Lender	Black Apps.	Black Loans	Black Dollars	Black/White Denial Ratio	Hispanic Apps.	Hispanic Loans	Hispanic Dollars	Hispanic/White Denial Ratio	Target Area Apps.	Target Area Loans	Target Area Dollars	TA/Non-TA Denial Ratio	Average
Norwest Bank Wisconsin, N.A.	10	6	4	4	11	11	11	9	9	11	11	8	8.8
Security Bank S.S.B.	3	5	8	7	5	6	7	8	1	2	2	11	5.4
St. Francis Bank, FSB	7	8	10	9	1	1	1	5	6	3	8	7	5.5
TCF Bank Wisconsin, FSB	1	1	1	2	7	5	2	5	2	1	6	6	3.3
The Equitable Bank, S.S.B.	11	13	12	10	3	2	3	3	7	5	1	3	6.1
Tri City National Bank	15	15	16	6	8	7	6	4	11	9	5	4	8.8
Universal Savings Bank, F.A.	13	10	6	1	13	12	9	1	15	15	15	1	9.3
Wauwatosa Savings Bank	14	14	15	15	14	14	16	16	7	3	3	4	11.3

NOTE: When two or more lenders tied for a given rank, each was assigned that same rank. The subsequently ranked lender was assigned the numerical rank it would have received had there been no ties. For example, North Shore and Universal Savings tied for the top rank on the Hispanic/White Denial variable. Each was assigned a rank of "1"; the subsequent lender, Equitable, was ranked "3."

SOURCE: 1996 HMDA

Hispanic/white, and Target Area/Nontarget area denial ratios were lower than Associated in each case.

Conclusions

Some Milwaukee area lenders are clearly outperforming their peers in community reinvestment. As stated earlier, these data cannot confirm or deny compliance or noncompliance with the Community Reinvestment Act and other fair lending requirements. More information on borrower qualifications, property characteristics, and market conditions, would be required to make such specific judgments. But this information provides useful guidance for lenders, regulators, and community groups. For lenders, they indicate both potential trouble spots in their current lending profiles and market opportunities they can exploit in the future. For regulators, they suggest areas where enforcement resources might be allocated. And for community groups they indicate potential community reinvestment partners and targets for possible CRA challenges and other organizing activity.

These findings clearly demonstrate wide variations in community reinvestment lending. But they do not reveal what policies or practices account for these disparities. Among the issues that need to be researched are the home loan products offered by lenders (e.g., mix of conventional and government insured loans), other types of financial services that are offered (e.g., business loans, which is the subject of the following chapter), counseling services provided, marketing strategies, practices of opening and closing branches, use of technology in providing banking services, relationships (or lack thereof) with community-based organizations, and aggressiveness of regulatory agencies. Further research is necessary to determine what distinguishes these lenders and to identify tactics that will result in even greater progress in Milwaukee's ongoing community reinvestment efforts. Chapter 7 examines one potential factor; the extent to which lenders employ racial and ethnic minorities. But far more remains to be learned about the cultural and structural characteristics of financial institutions, as well as the environment in which they operate, in order to identify precisely what accounts for their wide ranging records and what can be done to enhance industry-wide efforts.

6

Small Business
Lending Gaps

S MALL BUSINESSES—PARTICULARLY SMALL minority-owned businesses
in urban communities—often experience difficulty in obtaining
small business loans. Recent evidence indicates that minority-
owned firms receive fewer and smaller loans than white-owned firms
with identical traits (Cavalluzzo, Cavalluzzo, and Wolken 1999;
Blanchflower, Levine, and Zimmerman 1998; Ando 1988; Bates 1989,
1997; Conta and Associates 1990). Under the federal Community Reinvestment Act (CRA) depository institutions are required to affirmatively ascertain and be responsive to the credit needs of their entire
service areas, including low- and moderate-income communities. The
new Community Reinvestment Act (CRA) regulations (12 C.F.R.
R25.42(a)) promulgated in 1995 require large commercial banks and
thrift institutions to report small business and small farm lending by
geographic location to their regulators (Marsico 1996). Lending activity for the 1996 calendar year was reported to federal financial regulatory agencies and in October 1997 small business and small farm
lending data were released to the public for the first time by the Federal Financial Institutions Examination Council (FFIEC).

93

Researchers with the Federal Reserve Board conducted a preliminary nationwide analysis of the small business lending data and concluded that the distribution of loans and loan dollars in low-, moderate-, middle-, and upper-income areas reflected the distribution of the population and number of businesses in those areas (Bostic and Canner 1998). However, researchers with the Woodstock Institute responded that when loans-per-business were calculated there were substantial gaps between lending activity in low- and upper-income areas (Immergluck 1998). In a study documenting such gaps in the Chicago metropolitan area, Woodstock researchers asserted the importance of examining individual markets as well as national trends (Immergluck and Mullen 1997).

Researchers with the Federal Reserve Bank of Chicago (1998) published a preliminary analysis of small business lending in five midwestern communities (Chicago, Des Moines, Detroit, Indianapolis, and Milwaukee), which compared lending among these communities and lenders nationwide. They found that the percentage of all loans and ratio of loans per businesses were lower in low- and moderate-income tracts than in middle- and upper-income tracts in each geographic location, with the largest gaps occurring in Milwaukee. The *Milwaukee Journal Sentinel* found that among the fifty largest metropolitan areas in the nation, Milwaukee had the lowest proportion of small business loans going to low- and moderate-income areas (Norman 1998).

This chapter provides a more detailed review of small business lending in Milwaukee.

Data and Methodology

Under the new CRA rules issued in 1995, banks with assets totaling more than $250 million or affiliated with a holding company totaling more than $1 billion in assets are required to report small business and small farm loan information to their regulatory agency beginning with the 1996 calendar year. This information includes the number, dollar volume, and census tract of business loans for less than $1 million and farm loans up to $500,000. Lenders are also required to report lending activity to businesses and farms with annual revenues below $1 million, an approximation of lending to small businesses. In other words, not all small business loans go to small businesses.

Data made available by the FFIEC report aggregate lending (i.e., loans made by all lenders combined) by census tract by county. However, individual lender disclosure reports do not provide data at the tract level. For individual lenders, data are reported by aggregations of census tracts according to median family income levels of those tracts. The categories used in this analysis are the following:

1. low income (median family income in the tract is less than 50 percent of the metropolitan area median family income);

2. moderate income (50 to 79 percent);

3. middle income (80 to 120 percent); and

4. upper income (more than 120 percent).

This chapter examines small business loans in the four-county-metropolitan-Milwaukee statistical area (MSA). The four counties are Milwaukee, Ozaukee, Washington, and Waukesha. Small business loans are defined as those whose original amounts were $1 million or less and were secured by nonfarm or nonresidential real estate. Generally this includes loans that meet the definition of "loans to small business" that are reported in Call Reports and Thrift Financial Reports (Federal Financial Institutions Examination Council 1996c: 13).

Nationwide for 1996 2,078 lenders reported 2,414,805 small business loans totaling $147 billion (see table 6.1). Since smaller institutions are not covered by these reporting requirements, not all small business lending is included. But among depository institutions, these reports account for approximately two-thirds of all small business lending. These loans included originations and purchases with originations accounting for more than 98 percent of the total. A slight majority of these loans went to businesses with annual revenues below $1 million (Federal Financial Institutions Examination Council 1997: 5, 6; Greenspan 1998: 3). In Milwaukee there were 15,181 small business loans totaling $1.5 billion with originations accounting for more than 98 percent.

There are several limitations to these data. First, the location reported for the borrower may not be the same location that is supported with the borrowed funds. A business may have several locations and some or all of the borrowed funds may be invested in neighborhoods other than the one that is reported to the federal regulator as the main address of the organization. Most businesses, however, have only one location so the extent of misclassification is minimal. Second, in some cases the borrower reported post office addresses where correspondence is sent which can be different from where the business is actually located. This problem will be rectified in future reports where lenders will be asked to solicit a street address and then report the appropriate census tract (*Federal Register* 1997: 52125). Third, no information is pro-

Table 6.1 Small Business Lending (Totals) by Neighborhood Income Level: Milwaukee MSA and United States, 1996

	Total Loans	Total Dollars (Thousands)	Total Loans to Firms with Assets of Less Than $1 Million	Total Dollars to Firms with Assets of Less Than $1 Million
Low Income <50%				
Milwaukee	834	81,729	314	21,597
United States	113,098	8,164,017	52,957	2,885,809
Moderate Income 50–79%				
Milwaukee	1,037	87,757	568	34,073
United States	384,949	23,480,138	203,238	9,357,294
Middle Income 80–119%				
Milwaukee	7,597	743,557	3,969	275,912
United States	1,193,181	68,758,922	694,871	30,427,882
Upper Income =>120%				
Milwaukee	5,697	546,113	3,060	212,016
United States	711,273	45,482,023	394,097	19,638,266
Not Reported				
Milwaukee	16	3,004	8	578
United States	12,304	1,095,384	4,661	274,087
Total				
Milwaukee	15,181	1,462,160	7,919	544,176
United States	2,414,805	146,980,484	1,349,824	62,583,338

[1]Neighborhood income level based on Milwaukee MSA and U.S. median income, U.S. Census Bureau 1990.
SOURCE: FFIEC CRA Aggregate & Disclosure 1996

vided on credit demand. That is, unlike mortgage loans reported under Home Mortgage Disclosure Act (HMDA), there is no information on the number or types of businesses that applied for a loan. Consequently, there is no information on the disposition (e.g., approval or denial, reasons for denial) of applications for small business loans. Fourth, again unlike the HMDA data, there is no information on the race, gender, or income of those receiving business loans. Fifth, only loan originations and purchases made in 1996 are reported. Outstanding loans made in previous years are not included so total lending activity in a given area by a particular institution may not be fully accounted for in these reports. Finally, business lending activity is reported by census tract. Once again unlike HMDA data, individual small business loan data are not reported. Given the limited information about the characteristics of borrowers and the nature of demand for small business loans as well as the limited information on the disposition of the loan and the nature of the supply for such credit, it is important to cautiously interpret any reported differences in the distribution of small business loans (Bostic and Canner 1998).

The following section examines aggregate small business loans and loan dollars by census tract income level for financial institutions doing business in the Milwaukee metropolitan area and compares those patterns to all reporting institutions nationwide. Loans and loan dollars to businesses with annual revenues of less than $1 million by tract income level are then presented. The ratio of loans and loan dollars per person and per business are also presented by tract income level. Business counts were generated by Dun and Bradstreet and provided by the Board of Governors of the Federal Reserve System. Aggregate lending activity on the part of financial institutions serving the Milwaukee area is then examined by racial composition of neighborhoods. Finally, comparative data are provided for each lender that made more than one hundred business loans in Milwaukee. This sample includes twenty lenders which accounted for approximately 90 percent of all reported small business loans and loan dollars in the metropolitan area. Comparative information is presented on small business loans and loan dollars as well as loans and loan dollars to businesses with revenues of less than $1 million by tract income level.

Findings

Four basic findings emerge from this analysis. First, lending activity in Milwaukee is concentrated in middle- and upper-income areas, and is more concentrated in such communities than is the case nationwide. Second, lending to small businesses (i.e., the proportion of all small business loans and loan dollars that went to firms with assets below $1 million) in Milwaukee is below nationwide levels, particularly in low-income areas. Third, small business lending and lending to small firms is concentrated in predominantly white communities with black and Hispanic communities receiving relatively small shares of such

loans and loan dollars. Fourth, Milwaukee area lenders vary substantially in their distribution of small business loans by neighborhood
income level.

Small Business Lending by Neighborhood Income Level

In Milwaukee, small business lending was concentrated among higher
income census tracts. Upper-income tracts received over 37 percent of
all loans and loan dollars (see tables 6.1 and 6.2) but accounted for just
27.1 percent of the population (see table 6.3) and 32.2 percent of all
businesses (see table 6.4). Low-income tracts received approximately
5.5 percent of all loans and loan dollars while accounting for 12.7
percent of the population and 8.8 percent of all businesses. Loans per
one thousand persons ranged from five in low-income tracts to fifteen

Table 6.2 Small Business Lending by Neighborhood Income Level:
Milwaukee MSA and the United States, 1996

	Percent of All Loans	Percent of All Loan Dollars
Low Income		
Milwaukee	5.5	5.6
United States	4.7	5.6
Moderate Income		
Milwaukee	6.8	6.0
United States	15.9	16
Middle Income		
Milwaukee	50.0	50.8
United States	49.4	46.8
Upper Income		
Milwaukee	37.5	37.3
United States	29.5	30.9
Income Not Reported		
Milwaukee	0.1	0.2
United States	0.5	0.7
Total		
Milwaukee	99.9[1]	99.9[1]
United States	100.0	100.0

[1]Percentage does not add up to 100% due to rounding.
SOURCE: FFIEC CRA Aggregate & Disclosure 1996

in upper-income tracts while loans per one hundred businesses varied from twenty to thirty-seven in these two areas (see figure 6.1 and map 6.1). Loan dollars varied in a similar manner. Loan dollars per one thousand persons ranged from $449 in low-income areas to $1,407 in upper-income areas. Loan dollars per one hundred businesses reached $1,950 in low-income tracts and $3,561 in upper-income tracts. The lowest loan dollar per one hundred businesses ratio, $1,675, occurred in moderate-income tracts.

The percentage of small business loans in low-income tracts was actually higher in Milwaukee (5.5 percent) than nationwide (4.7 percent). This reflects the fact that the proportion of the total population and of all small businesses in low-income areas is substantially higher

Table 6.3 Small Business Lending per Person by Neighborhood Income Level: Milwaukee MSA and the United States, 1996

Population	Population	Percent of Total Population	Number of Loans per 1,000 Persons	Loan Dollars per 1,000 Persons
Low Income				
Milwaukee	181,883	12.7	5	449
United States	12,358,000	4.9	9	661
Moderate Income				
Milwaukee	193,340	13.5	5	454
United States	46,657,000	18.5	8	503
Middle Income				
Milwaukee	667,381	46.6	11	1,114
United States	134,170,000	53.2	9	512
Upper Income				
Milwaukee	388,112	27.1	15	1,407
United States	58,736,000	23.2	12	774
Income Not Reported				
Milwaukee	1,432	0.1	11	2,098
United States	504,000	0.2	24	2,173
Total				
Milwaukee	1,432,148	100.0	11	1,020
United States	252,425,000	100.0	10	582

SOURCE: FFIEC CRA Aggregate & Disclosure 1996, and 1990 U.S. Census Bureau

Table 6.4 Small Business Lending per Business by Neighborhood Income Level: Milwaukee MSA and the United States, 1996

	Number of Businesses	Percent of Total Businesses	Number of Loans per 100 Businesses	Loan Dollars per 100 Businesses
Low Income				
Milwaukee	4,191	8.8	20	1,950
United States	453,600	5.6	25	1,800
Moderate Income				
Milwaukee	5,239	11.0	20	1,675
United States	1,522,800	18.8	25	1,542
Middle Income				
Milwaukee	22,669	47.6	34	3,280
United States	4,001,400	49.4	30	1,718
Upper Income				
Milwaukee	15,335	32.2	37	3,561
United States	2,081,700	25.7	34	2,185
Income Not Reported				
Milwaukee	191	0.4	8	1,573
United States	32,400	0.4	38	3,381
Total				
Milwaukee	47,625	100.0	31.9	3,070
United States	8,091,900	99.9[1]	29.8	1,816

[1]Percentage does not add up to 100 due to rounding.
SOURCE: FFIEC CRA Aggregate & Disclosure 1996, and Federal Reserve System, Division of Research and Statistics 1996

in Milwaukee than elsewhere. Low-income tracts accounted for 12.7 percent of the population in Milwaukee compared to 4.9 percent nationwide and 8.8 percent of all businesses in Milwaukee compared to 5.6 percent nationwide. Consequently, loans per population and per number of businesses in low-income tracts were lower in Milwaukee than elsewhere. In low-income areas, the number of loans per one thousand people was five in Milwaukee and nine nationwide, whereas

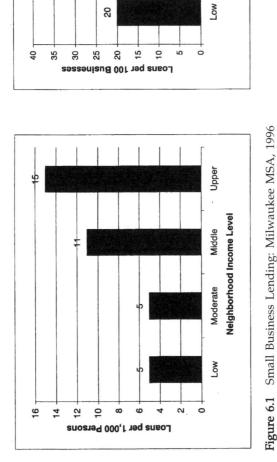

Figure 6.1 Small Business Lending: Milwaukee MSA, 1996

SOURCE: FFIEC CRA Aggregate & Disclosure 1996, 1990 U.S. Census Bureau, and Federal Reserve System, Division of Research and Statistics 1996

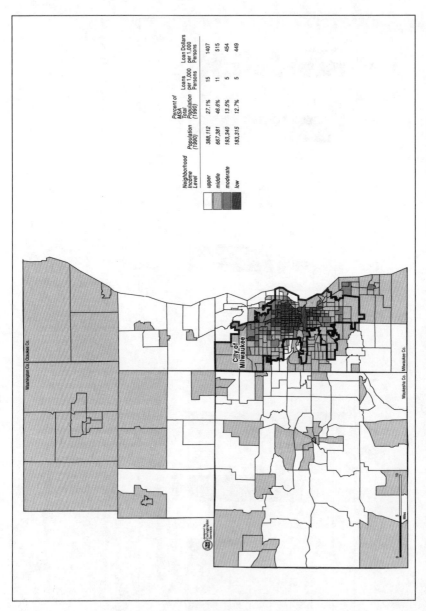

Neighborhood Income Level	Population (1990)	Percent of MSA Total Population (1990)	Loans per 1,000 Persons	Loan Dollars per 1,000 Persons
upper	388,112	27.1%	15	1407
middle	667,381	46.6%	11	515
moderate	193,340	13.5%	5	454
low	183,315	12.7%	5	449

Map 6.1 Small Business Lending by Neighborhood Income Level: Milwaukee MSA, 1996

SOURCE: FFIEC CRA Aggregate & Disclosure 1996, and 1990 U.S. Census Bureau

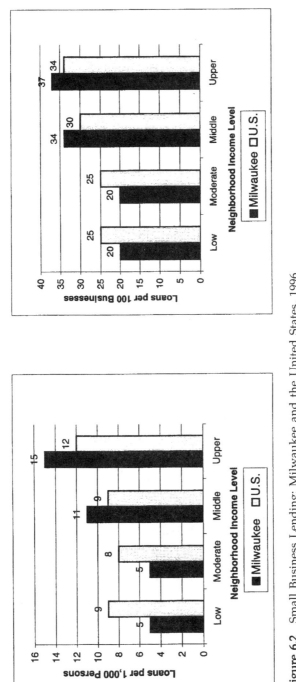

Figure 6.2 Small Business Lending: Milwaukee and the United States, 1996

SOURCE: FFIEC CRA Aggregate & Disclosure 1996, 1990 U.S. Census Bureau, and Federal Reserve System, Division of Research and Statistics 1996

the number of loans per one hundred businesses was twenty in Milwaukee and twenty-five nationwide (see figure 6.2). Similar gaps were found in moderate-income areas. The number of loans per one thousand persons was five in Milwaukee and eight nationwide, whereas the number of loans per one hundred businesses was twenty in Milwaukee and twenty-five nationwide in moderate-income areas.

The percent of loan dollars in low-income areas was the same in Milwaukee and the nation: 5.6 percent. Loan dollars per one thousand persons reached $449 in Milwaukee and $661 throughout the nation. However, loan dollars per one hundred businesses were slightly higher in Milwaukee ($1,950) compared to the nation generally ($1,800).

Conversely, lending activity in upper-income tracts was greater in Milwaukee than elsewhere. The proportion of all loans in such neighborhoods was 37.5 percent in Milwaukee compared to 29.5 percent nationwide. Loans per population and per business were also higher in Milwaukee. And loan dollars were similarly distributed. In Milwaukee the number of loans per one thousand persons in upper-income tracts was fifteen compared to twelve nationwide while loans per one hundred businesses was thirty-seven in Milwaukee and thirty-four nationwide. Loan dollars per one thousand persons was $1,407 in Milwaukee and $774 nationwide while loan dollars per 100 businesses was $3,561 in Milwaukee and $2,185 nationwide.

Loans to Small Businesses

The share of small business lending going to small businesses (i.e., firms with assets of less than $1 million) was approximately the same in all areas except low-income tracts in Milwaukee. Approximately 54 percent of these loans and 38 percent of loan dollars went to small firms in moderate-, middle-, and upper-income areas compared to just 37.6 percent of loans and 26.4 percent of loan dollars in lower-income tracts (see table 6.5).

The proportion of small business loans and loan dollars going to small businesses was substantially lower in Milwaukee than the nation generally. In Milwaukee 52.2 percent of all loans and 37.2 percent of loan dollars went to such businesses compared to 55.9 percent of loans and 42.6 percent of loan dollars nationwide. (Percentages are derived from the last two rows of table 6.1. Also see figure 6.3.)

These differences are accounted for primarily by lending activity in low-income tracts. In moderate-, middle-, and upper-income tracts the proportion of small business loans going to small businesses in Milwaukee was approximately the same as for the nation generally though

Table 6.5 Small Business Lending to Firms with Revenues of $1 Million or Less by Neighborhood Income Level: Milwaukee MSA and the United States, 1996

	Percent of All Loans to Firms with Assets of Less Than $1 Million	*Percent of All Loan Dollars to Firms with Assets of Less Than $1 Million*
Low Income		
Milwaukee	37.6	26.4
United States	46.8	35.3
Moderate Income		
Milwaukee	54.8	38.8
United States	52.8	39.9
Middle Income		
Milwaukee	52.2	37.1
United States	58.2	44.3
Upper Income		
Milwaukee	53.7	38.8
United States	55.4	43.2
Income Not Reported		
Milwaukee	50.0	19.2
United States	37.9	25.0
Total		
Milwaukee	52.2	37.2
United States	55.9	42.6

SOURCE: FFIEC CRA Aggregate & Disclosure 1996

the proportion of loan dollars going to such firms was slightly lower in Milwaukee (see table 6.5). But in lower-income tracts the differences were substantial. The proportion of loans going to small businesses was 37.6 percent in Milwaukee and 46.8 percent nationwide while comparable figures for loan dollars were 26.4 percent and 35.3 percent (see figure 6.3).

Lending Activity by Neighborhood Racial Composition in Milwaukee

Small business lending activity is concentrated in predominantly white communities with approximately 90 percent of loans and loan dollars

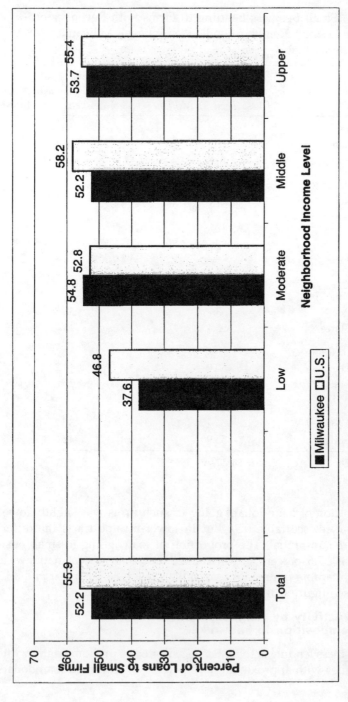

Figure 6.3 Small Business Lending to Firms with Revenues of $1 Million or Less by Neighborhood Income Level: Milwaukee MSA and the United States, 1996

SOURCE: FFIEC CRA Aggregate and Disclosure 1996

Table 6.6 Small Business Lending (Totals) by Neighborhood Racial
Composition: Milwaukee MSA, 1996

	Total Loans	Total Dollars (Thousands)	Total Loans to Firms with Assets of Less Than $1 Million	Total Dollars (Thousands) to Firms with Assets of Less Than $1 Million
<10% Black[1]	13,600	1,289,091	7,214	497,630
10–70% Black	1,256	143,934	268	39,082
>70% Black	325	29,135	137	7,464
Total	15,181	1,462,160	7,919	544,176
<5% Hispanic[1]	13,907	1,338,920	7,296	506,006
5–25% Hispanic	1,134	111,733	560	34,436
>25% Hispanic	140	11,507	63	3,734
Total	15,181	1,462,160	7,919	544,176

[1]There is minimal double counting on tables 6.6–6.9 due to the fact that some
individuals identify themselves as both black and Hispanic to the Census Bureau.
SOURCE: FFIEC CRA Aggregate & Disclosure 1996, and 1990 U.S. Census Bureau

Table 6.7 Small Business Lending by Neighborhood Racial
Composition: Milwaukee MSA, 1996

	Percent of All Loans	Percent of All Loan Dollars
<10% Black	89.6	88.2
10–70% Black	8.3	9.8
>70% Black	2.1	2.0
Total	100.0	100.0
<5% Hispanic	91.6	91.6
5–25% Hispanic	7.5	7.6
>25% Hispanic	0.9	0.8
Total	100.0	100.0

SOURCE: FFIEC CRA Aggregate & Disclosure 1996, and 1990 U.S. Census Bureau

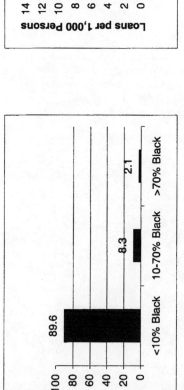
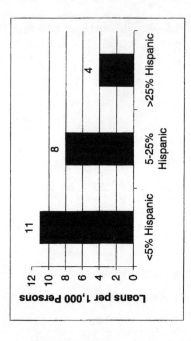
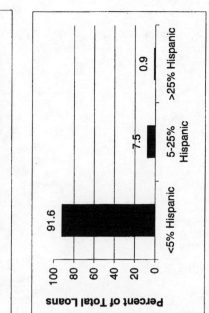

Figure 6.4 Small Business Lending by Neighborhood Racial Composition: Milwaukee MSA, 1996

SOURCE: FFIEC CRA Aggregate & Disclosure 1996, and 1990 U.S. Census Bureau

going to firms in these areas. In the Milwaukee metropolitan area blacks account for 13.8 percent and Hispanics account for 3.4 percent of the total population according to the 1990 census. Approximately 2 percent of loans and loan dollars went to the area's predominantly black neighborhoods and less than 1 percent went to Hispanic areas (see table 6.6 and 6.7 and figure 6.4).

The number of loans per one thousand persons varied from a high of thirteen in neighborhoods where the population was at least 90 percent white to a low of two in neighborhoods where the population was more than 70 percent black. Loans per one thousand persons also varied from eleven in areas that were less than 5 percent Hispanic to four in areas that were more than 25 percent Hispanic (see table 6.8, figure 6.4, and maps 6.2 and 6.3). Loan dollars varied similarly. That is, the number of loan dollars per one thousand persons decreased as the proportion of nonwhites in the population increased.

Lending activity per business by racial composition could not be calculated because the data on the number of small businesses were not available at the·individual census tract level. This information was made available only by aggregate census tracts based on income level. That is, the number of businesses was provided in each of the

Table 6.8 Small Business Lending per Person by Neighborhood Racial Composition: Milwaukee MSA, 1996

	Population	Number of Loans per 1000 Persons	Loan Dollars per 1000 Persons
<10% Black	1,081,231	13	1,192
10–70% Black	215,470	6	668
>70% Black	135,447	2	215
Total	1,432,148	11	1,020
<5% Hispanic	1,267,762	11	1,056
5–25% Hispanic	129,545	8	863
>25% Hispanic	34,841	4	330
Total	1,432,148	11	1,020

SOURCE: FFIEC CRA Aggregate and Disclosure 1996, and 1990 U.S. Census Bureau

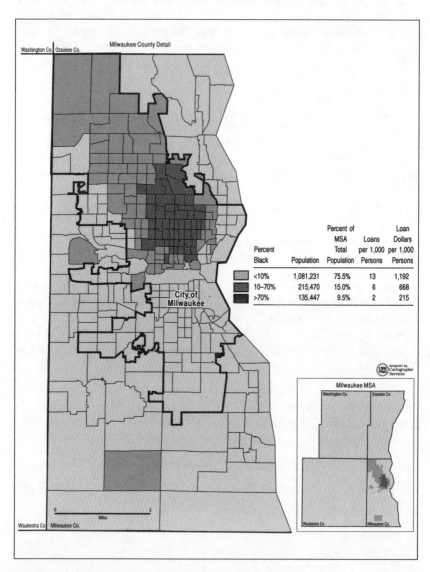

Map 6.2 Small Business Lending by Black Population Concentration: Milwaukee MSA, 1996

SOURCE: FFIEC CRA Aggregate & Disclosure 1996, and 1990 U.S. Census Bureau

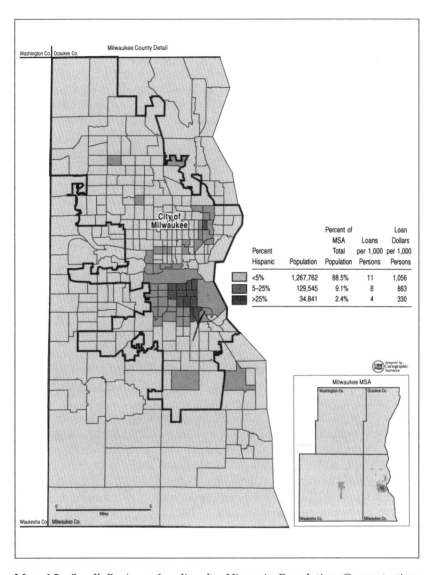

Map 6.3 Small Business Lending by Hispanic Population Concentration: Milwaukee MSA, 1996
SOURCE: FFIEC CRA Aggregate & Disclosure 1996, and 1990 U.S. Census Bureau

Table 6.9 Small Business Lending to Firms with Revenues of
$1 Million or Less by Neighborhood Racial Composition:
Milwaukee MSA, 1996

	Percent of All Loans to Firms with Assets of Less Than $1 Million	Percent of All Loan Dollars to Firms with Assets of Less Than $1 Million
<10% Black	53.0	38.6
10–70% Black	45.2	27.2
>70% Black	42.2	25.6
<5% Hispanic	52.5	37.8
5–25% Hispanic	49.4	30.8
>25% Hispanic	45.0	32.4

SOURCE: FFIEC CRA Aggregate and Disclosure 1996, and 1990 U.S. Census Bureau

following four categories (low, moderate, middle, and upper income)
of census tracts. From the available data, it is impossible to determine
the number of businesses in a group of census tracts characterized by
their racial composition.

The proportion of loans to small businesses also decreased as the
nonwhite population increased. The share of all small business loans
that went to firms with assets of less than $1 million varied from a
high of 53.0 percent in predominantly white areas to 42.2 percent in
predominantly black areas. The share of loans to small firms also varied
from 52.5 percent in areas where the Hispanic population was less
than 5 percent to 45.0 percent where Hispanics accounted for more
than 25 percent of the population (see table 6.9).

Variations among Milwaukee Area Lenders

Perhaps more revealing than the differences between Milwaukee area
lenders and those nationwide are the disparities among financial
institutions within the Milwaukee metropolitan area. Just as some
mortgage lenders have far surpassed their colleagues in levels of
service provided to lower-income communities (see chapter 5) business lending in these communities also varied dramatically among
lenders.

Although 5.5 percent of all loans went to low-income tracts, among the twenty institutions included in this sample two of them made fewer than one percent of their small business loans in low-income areas and one of these lenders provided no loans in low- or moderate-income areas. However, one lender did 14.0 percent of its lending while three others provided 9 percent or more of their loans in low-income areas (see table 6.10). While 5.6 percent of all loan dollars went to low-income areas, three lenders provided less than one percent of their small business loan dollars, whereas one lender provided 14.4 percent of its loan dollars in these areas (see table 6.11).

Approximately 37 percent of loans and loan dollars went to upper-income areas, but six lenders made more than 40 percent of their loans and nine provided more than 40 percent of their loan dollars to borrowers in these neighborhoods. One lender made only 5.8 percent of its loans and 7.6 percent of its loan dollars in the upper-income tracts.

Loans to small businesses varied dramatically as well. Over half of all small business loans went to small firms, but two lenders made less than 1 percent of their small business loans to small firms, one made 85 percent of these loans to small firms, and in four other cases this number exceeded 75 percent. Overall, 37.2 percent of loan dollars went to small firms, but loan dollars to such firms varied from zero to 86.8 percent (see table 6.12).

Patterns varied by neighborhood income level as well. Of all loans made in lower-income tracts, four lenders provided no loans to small firms while four institutions made 75 percent or more of their loans and three provided more than 75 percent of their loan dollars to such businesses (see tables 6.13 and 6.14). In upper-income areas, however, only one lender reported none of its loans to small businesses while five made more than 75 percent of their loans and three provided more than 75 percent of their loan dollars to these firms.

Although aggregate data for all lenders reporting loan activity in the Milwaukee area are available at the individual census tract level, data for individual lenders are available only by the four income levels reported above. Therefore, it is not possible to determine lending activity for an individual institution by racial composition of neighborhood.

But lending by income level and to small firms varies substantially among lenders. Given the association between income and race, it is likely that lending patterns also vary substantially by the racial composition of neighborhoods as well. In Milwaukee, access to small business loans appears to be at least in part a function of the institution to which a borrower applies. Characteristics of those institutions,

Table 6.10 Small Business Lending (Loans) by Neighborhood Income Level and Individual Lenders: Milwaukee MSA, 1996

Lender	Total Loans	Lower % of Total[1]	Moderate % of Total	Middle % of Total	Upper % of Total	Unknown % of Total
Advantage Financial	320	5.9	14.1	46.3	33.8	0.0
American Express	1,369	5.3	9.2	43.3	42.0	0.1
Associated Bank, Milwaukee	944	7.7	4.4	36.5	51.1	0.2
Bank One, Wisconsin	1,580	6.8	3.6	60.0	29.5	0.0
Bank Wisconsin	334	9.0	0.0	81.1	9.9	0.0
First Bank	357	14.0	7.6	40.1	38.4	0.0
First Bank of South Dakota	219	5.0	8.7	46.6	39.7	0.0
Firstar Bank, Wisconsin	280	1.4	8.9	56.8	32.9	0.0
Firstar, Milwaukee	1,040	6.5	8.8	44.9	39.8	0.0
M & I Bank, Menomonee Falls	541	3.7	2.2	48.1	46.0	0.0
M & I First National Bank	618	0.0	0.0	94.2	5.8	0.0
M & I Lake Country	658	1.2	1.2	50.6	46.8	0.2
M & I Marshall & Ilsley	1,609	6.8	11.4	46.5	35.1	0.2
M & I Northern	1,098	4.4	6.3	42.2	47.2	0.0
Mountain West	1,032	8.1	8.3	48.4	35.0	0.1
Norwest Bank	233	9.4	11.2	42.1	36.9	0.4
Park Bank	492	9.3	10.0	45.1	35.0	0.6
Tri City National Bank	340	3.5	10.3	48.2	37.9	0.0
Waukesha Bank	712	0.1	5.3	45.3	49.2	0.0
Wells Fargo Bank	176	5.1	11.9	45.5	36.4	1.1
Percent of MSA Population		12.7	13.5	46.6	27.1	0.1
Percent of Businesses		8.8	11.0	47.6	32.2	0.4

[1]The percentages in each of these columns refer to the percentage of total loans shown in the first column. For example, 5.9% of Advantage Financial's 320 small business loans were originated to businesses located in low income level neighborhoods.

SOURCE: FFIEC CRA Aggregate & Disclosure 1996, 1990 U.S. Census Bureau, and Federal Reserve System, Division of Research and Statistics 1996

Table 6.11 Small Business Lending (Loan Dollars) by Neighborhood Income Level and Individual Lenders: Milwaukee MSA, 1996

Lender	Total Dollars (Thousands)	Lower % of Total[1]	Moderate % of Total	Middle % of Total	Upper % of Total	Unknown % of Total
Advantage Financial	3,413	6.1	13.6	46.5	33.9	0.0
American Express	9,235	4.6	8.2	41.3	45.7	0.2
Associated Bank, Milwaukee	109,384	7.8	4.4	41.7	45.8	0.3
Bank One, Wisconsin	118,775	4.7	3.7	65.2	26.4	0.0
Bank Wisconsin	26,625	6.9	0.0	81.4	11.7	0.0
First Bank	74,188	14.4	4.7	46.1	34.8	0.0
First Bank of South Dakota	3,674	2.7	3.9	35.9	57.5	0.0
Firstar Bank, Wisconsin	40,348	1.3	7.1	56.7	34.9	0.0
Firstar, Milwaukee	123,657	8.1	7.0	40.6	44.3	0.0
M & I Bank, Menomonee Falls	64,024	4.0	2.3	48.4	45.3	0.0
M & I First National Bank	59,007	0.0	0.0	92.4	7.6	0.0
M & I Lake Country	57,832	0.6	1.7	52.7	44.8	0.2
M & I Marshall & Ilsley	238,950	7.8	9.6	47.1	34.5	0.9
M & I Northern	178,265	3.3	6.1	44.8	45.8	0.0
Mountain West	3,278	7.2	6.9	53.7	32.2	0.1
Norwest Bank	36,977	5.4	8.6	41.1	44.8	0.1
Park Bank	86,723	7.5	7.5	46.6	38.3	0.2
Tri City National Bank	18,593	2.4	10.0	57.2	30.4	0.0
Waukesha Bank	31,625	0.1	4.5	41.1	54.4	0.0
Wells Fargo Bank	4,563	5.7	12.8	43.7	35.9	2.0
Percent of MSA Population		12.7	13.5	46.6	27.1	0.1
Percent of Businesses		8.8	11.0	47.6	32.2	0.4

[1]The percentages in each of these columns refer to the percentage of total loans shown in the first column. For example, 6.1% of Advantage Financial's $3,413 small business loans were originated to businesses located in low income level neighborhoods.

SOURCE: FFIEC CRA Aggregate & Disclosure 1996, 1990 U.S. Census Bureau, and Federal Reserve System, Division of Research and Statistics 1996

Table 6.12 Small Business Lending to Firms with Revenues of $1 Million or Less by Individual Lenders: Milwaukee MSA, 1996

Lender	Total Loans	Loans to Small Firms	Percent of Loans to Small Firms	Total Dollars (Thousands)	Dollars to Small Firms	Percent of Total Dollars to Small Firms
Advantage Financial	320	0	0.0	3,413	0	0.0
American Express	1,369	1,172	85.6	9,235	8,015	86.8
Associated Bank, Milwaukee	944	681	72.1	109,384	65,843	60.2
Bank One, Wisconsin	1,580	468	29.6	118,775	31,772	26.7
Bank Wisconsin	334	110	32.9	26,625	10,733	40.3
First Bank	357	45	12.6	74,188	5,713	7.7
First Bank of South Dakota	219	2	0.9	3,674	1,130	30.8
Firstar Bank, Wisconsin	280	178	63.6	40,348	19,944	49.4
Firstar, Milwaukee	1,040	659	63.4	123,657	57,872	46.8
M & I Bank, Menomonee Falls	541	327	60.4	64,024	23,585	36.8
M & I First National Bank	618	470	76.1	59,007	32,848	55.7
M & I Lake Country	658	518	78.7	57,832	38,531	66.6
M & I Marshall & Ilsley	1,609	998	62.0	238,950	77,198	32.3
M & I Northern	1,098	474	43.2	178,265	40,619	22.8
Mountain West	1,032	112	10.9	3,278	217	6.6
Norwest Bank	233	131	56.2	36,977	13,412	36.3
Park Bank	492	161	32.7	86,723	14,422	16.6
Tri City National Bank	340	266	78.2	18,593	13,832	74.4
Waukesha Bank	712	554	77.8	31,625	23,521	74.4
Wells Fargo Bank	176	102	58.0	4,563	2,319	50.8

SOURCE: FFIEC CRA Aggregate & Disclosure 1996

Table 6.13 Small Business Lending (Loans) to Firms with Revenues of $1 Million or Less by Neighborhood Income Level and Individual Lenders: Milwaukee MSA, 1996

Lender	Lower		Moderate		Middle		Upper		Unknown	
	Total Loans	Percent of Total[1]	Total Loans	Percent of Total	Total Loans	Percent of Total	Total Loans	Percent of Total	Total Loans	Percent of Total
Advantage Financial	19	0.0	45	0.0	148	0.0	108	0.0	0	0.0
American Express	73	82.2	126	90.5	593	85.0	575	85.6	2	100
Associated Bank, Milwaukee	73	54.8	42	61.9	345	67.2	482	79.0	2	100
Bank One, Wisconsin	108	15.7	58	29.3	948	38.2	466	15.5	0	0.0
Bank Wisconsin	30	0.0	0	0.0	271	31.0	33	78.8	0	0.0
First Bank	50	14.0	27	18.5	143	16.8	137	6.6	0	0.0
First Bank of South Dakota	11	0.0	19	0.0	102	0.0	87	2.3	0	0.0
Firstar Bank, Wisconsin	4	75.0	25	88.0	159	59.7	92	63.0	0	0.0
Firstar, Milwaukee	68	58.9	91	74.7	467	58.7	414	66.9	0	0.0
M & I Bank, Menomonee Falls	20	25.0	12	33.3	260	61.5	249	63.5	0	0.0
M & I First National Bank	0	0.0	0	0.0	582	76.5	36	69.4	0	0.0
M & I Lake Country	8	62.5	8	87.5	333	79.0	308	78.6	1	100
M & I Marshall & Ilsley	109	43.1	69	63.6	748	63.9	564	63.1	4	0.0
M & I Northern	48	52.1	69	43.5	463	39.5	518	45.6	0	0.0
Mountain West	84	6.0	86	8.1	500	11.8	361	11.4	1	0.0
Norwest Bank	22	45.5	26	80.8	98	53.1	86	54.7	1	100
Park Bank	46	32.6	49	26.5	222	36.0	172	30.2	3	33.3
Tri City National Bank	12	75.0	35	82.9	164	76.8	129	79.1	0	0.0
Waukesha Bank	1	100.0	38	97.4	323	79.6	350	74.0	0	0.0
Wells Fargo Bank	9	55.6	21	52.4	80	58.8	64	59.4	2	50.0
Percent of MSA Population	13		14		47		27		0.1	
Percent of MSA Businesses	8.8		11		48		32		0.4	

[1]The percentages for each neighborhood income level refer to the percentage of loans in the corresponding neighborhood. For example, 54.8% of Associated's 73 loans in lower income neighborhoods went to firms with revenues of $1 million or less.

SOURCE: FFIEC CRA Aggregate & Disclosure 1996, 1990 U.S. Census Bureau, and Federal Reserve System, Division of Research and Statistics 1996

Table 6.14 Small Business Lending (Loan Dollars) to Firms with Revenues of $1 Million or Less by Neighborhood Income Level and Individual Lenders: Milwaukee MSA, 1996

Lender	Lower Total Dollars (Thousands)	Lower Percent of Total[1]	Moderate Total Dollars (Thousands)	Moderate Percent of Total	Middle Total Dollars (Thousands)	Middle Percent of Total	Upper Total Dollars (Thousands)	Upper Percent of Total	Unknown Total Dollars (Thousands)	Unknown Percent of Total
Advantage Financial	207	0.0	463	0.0	1,586	0.0	1,157	0.0	0	0.0
American Express	426	81.2	758	90.1	3,815	85.9	4,216	87.5	20	100.0
Associated Bank, Milwaukee	8,529	47.5	4,768	43.3	45,656	57.4	50,114	66.2	317	100.0
Bank One, Wisconsin	5,624	7.1	4,395	29.0	77,454	29.7	31,302	22.7	0	0.0
Bank Wisconsin	1,835	0.0	0	0.0	21,672	41.8	3,118	53.5	0	0.0
First Bank	10,666	6.5	3,500	25.0	34,223	10.9	25,799	1.7	0	0.0
First Bank of South Dakota	99	0.0	143	0.0	1,319	0.0	2,113	53.5	0	0.0
Firstar Bank, Wisconsin	510	28.4	2,854	92.3	22,884	50.3	14,100	40.1	0	0.0
Firstar, Milwaukee	9,977	49.9	8,658	63.7	50,243	41.4	54,779	48.5	0	0.0
M & I Bank, Menomonee Falls	2,537	25.0	1,446	20.7	31,009	38.9	29,032	36.5	0	0.0
M & I First National Bank	0	0.0	0	0.0	54,542	56.3	4,465	47.8	0	0.0
M & I Lake Country	368	32.1	1,004	90.0	30,450	64.5	25,910	68.6	100	100.0
M & I Marshall & Ilsley	18,685	11.9	22,891	35.5	112,626	33.5	82,498	35.3	2,250	0.0
M & I Northern	5,827	16.5	10,929	25.8	79,907	22.5	81,602	23.1	0	0.0
Mountain West	235	5.1	227	4.4	1,759	6.9	1,055	6.9	0	0.0
Norwest Bank	2,008	42.6	3,170	34.2	15,210	37.6	16,564	34.6	2	100.0
Park Bank	6,499	25.1	6,462	11.4	40,381	17.6	33,180	14.8	201	28.4
Tri City National Bank	440	75.9	1,865	72.3	10,640	71.1	5,648	81.1	0	0.0
Waukesha Bank	16	100.0	1,415	89.4	12,994	67.8	17,200	78.1	0	0.0
Wells Fargo Bank	258	38.0	586	33.4	1,992	51.5	1,638	57.4	89	66.3
Percent of MSA Population	12.7		13.5		46.6		27.1		0.1	
Percent of MSA Businesses	8.8		11.0		47.6		32.2		0.4	

[1] The percentages for each neighborhood income level refer to the percentage of loans in the corresponding neighborhood. For example, 47.5% of Associated's $8,529 in low income neighborhoods went to firms with revenues of $1 million or less.

SOURCE: FFIEC CRA Aggregate & Disclosure 1996, 1990 U.S. Census Bureau, and Federal Reserve System, Division of Research and Statistics 1996

along with the credit worthiness of borrowers, likely affect the distribution of small business loans.

The Woodstock Institute recently found that banks with branch offices in low- or moderate-income areas make a greater proportion of their loans in those areas (Immergluck and Mullen 1997). This appears to be the case in Milwaukee as well. Those lenders with branches located within the city's economically distressed census tracts, referred to previously as the Target Area (City of Milwaukee 1996: 21), made 6.6 percent of their loans in low-income tracts compared to 5.1 percent for lenders without a Target Area branch (see table 6.15). Figures for loan dollars were 6.8 percent and 5.5 percent. However, lenders without Target Area branches provided a slightly higher proportion of their loans and loan dollars to small firms. As is the case with mortgage lending, a range of lender characteristics may well be influencing the allocation of small business loans. Size of lender, whether it is independently owned or part of a regional or national holding company, working relationships with community organizations, and racial composition of the workforce are just some of the factors that might affect the distribution of small business loans.

Research and Policy Implications

In the Milwaukee metropolitan area small business lending is concentrated in upper-income and predominantly white communities. These patterns may reflect differences in demand, credit-worthiness of borrowers, unfamiliarity on the part of potential borrowers and lenders about prevailing opportunities, unlawful discrimination, Milwaukee's low rate of minority business ownership and representation in corporate management compared to other metropolitan areas (Norman 1998) and a range of other factors. These are clearly not random fluctuations.

These findings also reveal substantial differences between Milwaukee area lenders and financial institutions nationwide in the distribution of loans and loan dollars by neighborhood income levels. Compared to their counterparts nationwide, Milwaukee area lenders provide a lower concentration of their lending activity in lower-income neighborhoods and among small businesses. This pattern may reflect differences in the industrial composition of the Milwaukee economy, variations in the demand for business credit, more conservative lending practices by Milwaukee area financial institutions, or some combination of these and other factors.

The findings also indicate widespread disparities among lenders in the distribution of small business loans throughout Milwaukee area

Table 6.15 Small Business Lending by Branch Location, Neighborhood Income Level, and Individual Lenders: Milwaukee MSA, 1996

	Target Area Branch Bank Location	Percent of Loans in Low Income Tracts	Percent of Dollars in Low Income Tracts	Percent of Loans to Firms with Revenues of $1 Million or Less	Percent of Dollars to Firms with Revenues of $1 Million or Less
Advantage Financial	No	5.9	6.1	0.0	0.0
American Express	No	5.3	4.6	85.6	86.8
Associated Bank, Milwaukee	No[1]	7.7	7.8	72.1	60.2
Bank One, Wisconsin	Yes	6.8	4.7	29.6	26.7
Bank Wisconsin	No	9.0	6.9	32.9	40.3
First Bank	No[1]	14.0	14.4	12.6	7.7
First Bank of South Dakota	No	5.0	2.7	0.9	30.8
Firstar Bank, Wisconsin	No	1.4	1.3	63.6	49.4
Firstar, Milwaukee	Yes	6.5	8.1	63.4	46.8
M & I Bank, Menomonee Falls	No	3.7	4.0	60.4	36.8
M & I First National Bank	No	0.0	0.0	76.1	55.7
M & I Lake Country	No	1.2	0.6	78.7	66.6
M & I Marshall & Ilsley	Yes	6.8	7.8	62.0	32.3
M & I Northern	No	4.4	3.3	43.2	22.8
Mountain West	No	8.1	7.2	10.9	6.6
Norwest Bank	Yes	9.4	5.4	56.2	36.3
Park Bank	No	9.3	7.5	32.7	16.6
Tri City National Bank	Yes	3.5	2.4	78.2	74.4
Waukesha Bank	No	0.1	0.1	77.8	74.4
Wells Fargo Bank	No	5.1	5.7	58.0	50.8
Percent of MSA Population		6.6	6.8	53	36
Percent of Businesses		5.1	5.5	56	38

[1]This bank's only branch in the Target Area is in a downtown location which has few residential areas. Therefore, this bank is coded as outside the Target Area.

SOURCE: FFIEC CRA Aggregate & Disclosure 1996, and Ameritech Milwaukee Yellow Pages 1996.

neighborhoods. These patterns may reflect legitimate differences in marketing strategies among lenders, illegal discrimination against low-income areas and minority communities, business opportunities overlooked by some institutions, size or structure of financial institutions, relationships (or lack thereof) with community organizations, or a combination of these and other factors. The broad disparities suggest that something other than the quantity and quality of the demand for credit accounted for current lending patterns since all of these reporting institutions are serving the same metropolitan area.

Clearly, far more research is essential to fully understand the underlying causes and policy implications, if any, of these findings. But recent disclosure of small business lending provides additional insight into the lending behavior of financial institutions covered by the CRA. Three minor changes in current small business disclosure requirements would enhance the value of this information.

First, covered lenders should be required to report the number of applications for small business loans they receive along with the disposition of those applications. This would provide at least one measure of demand for such credit and further insight into the response of lenders to that demand.

Second, the Federal Reserve Board should act on a proposal it is currently considering that would allow lenders to solicit information on the race of small business loan applicants. Currently, requesting such information violates the Equal Credit Opportunity Act. The U.S. Departments of Justice and the Treasury, the Comptroller of the Currency, and the Office of Thrift Supervision support the proposed these regulatory changes which would facilitate collection of this information (Reno 1998).

Anecdotal and econometric evidence suggests that minority-owned businesses have more difficulty accessing small business loans than majority-owned firms. Although disclosure of this information alone would not confirm or deny the existence of unlawful discrimination, it would enhance current understanding of racial disparities in access to small business loans. Many businesses, of course, are owned by more than one person. In those cases where there is multiple ownership, if more than 50 percent of the business is owned by members of a particular race, that would be the one which is reported. A multirace option could also be utilized where no single group is controlling.

Such additional reporting could increase the chances that the identity of a particular business would be revealed. The FFIEC could establish a threshold for a minimum number of loans (e.g., at least three loans in a tract) that must be reported before the individual loan data would be revealed in order to preserve confidentiality where it might otherwise be breached.

Third, the FFIEC should release tract level data for individual lenders and make available tables that display lending activity by racial composition of tracts. While users could locate the racial composition of each tract and then aggregate them in order to examine the distribution of loans for all reporting institutions by neighborhood racial make-up, as we have done here, data currently available do not permit such analysis at the individual bank level. FFIEC should provide this information in a similar manner as mortgage lending is provided in HMDA reports. Selected aggregate HMDA reports display lending activity (e.g., applications, originations, etc.) in tracts that are less than 10 percent minority, those between 10 and 19 percent, 20 to 49 percent, 50 to 79 percent, and 80 to 100 percent. These reports are available for individual lenders and for all lenders combined by metropolitan area. Similar tables reporting business loan activity should be prepared and disseminated by FFIEC. Again, where confidentiality might be breached, the information could be suppressed.

The data examined in this study and called for in these recommendations, alone, would not be sufficient to confirm or deny the existence or prevalence of compliance or noncompliance with the CRA or other fair lending rules. Comparative analysis of individual loan files or paired testing by "mystery shoppers" posing as small business credit applicants would be required for that purpose. The patterns that are revealed, however, can provide guidance to regulators, lenders, and others concerned with problems and potential opportunities in small business lending. The information provided by the small business data can assist regulators in targeting and conducting their examinations, reveal potential trouble spots for lenders, and identify missed opportunities for financial institutions and their community reinvestment partners. The minimally expanded reporting and disclosure recommended here can enhance the value of that guidance.

HMDA and CRA have changed the way many mortgage lenders do business and increased the supply of funds for community reinvestment as indicated in chapter 1. Hopefully, the new CRA regulations calling for disclosure of small business loans can extend those effects by nurturing an increase in the availability of small business loans in previously underserved communities.

7

Does Anybody Look Like Me?

Minority Employment and Minority Lending

THE CHARGE OF RACIAL DISCRIMINATION and redlining by lenders has generated contentious debate for decades. In recent years, the debate has intensified and become more complex. At least part of the debate is shifting to the question of why racial lending patterns are manifested and what can be done to reduce the significance of race in mortgage lending. One issue that is frequently raised, but on which there is little systematic information, is the impact of employment patterns of mortgage lending institutions on their lending practices. This chapter addresses the question of whether or not there is a relationship between minority employment and approval of minority loan applications.

Many factors are identified as causes of racial disparities in mortgage lending. Income and related financial differences explain part of the racial gap. But it is also recognized that some underwriting practices on the part of lenders, private mortgage insurers, and the secondary mortgage market often adversely affect racial minorities. Subjective and arbitrary implementation of those rules, including selective utilization of race-neutral standards, frequently results in discriminatory loan patterns. Location of branch offices can also have adverse racial effects ("Discrimination in the Housing and Mortgage Markets 1992"; Squires 1992).

The relatively low number of racial minorities employed in decisionmaking positions in banks in some communities is often pointed to as one of the reasons for the low levels of lending to minorities. From data supplied by the U.S. Equal Employment Opportunity Commission for 1989 nonwhites (blacks, Hispanics, Asians, and American Indians) accounted for approximately 23 percent of bank employees nationwide but less than 12 percent of those in professional, official and administrative positions. In Milwaukee nonwhite representation was 13 percent of all employees and 4 percent among official and administrative workers. For thrifts (i.e., savings and loans or mutual savings banks), the numbers were even lower. Nonwhites accounted for 20 percent of all employees nationwide but just 12 percent of professionals, officials and administrators. In Milwaukee, comparable figures were 8 percent and 3 percent. There is anecdotal evidence that racial minorities often feel intimidated when they walk into a financial institution and do not see anyone working there "who looks like me." In addition to the research evidence that minority loan applications are treated differently, there is anecdotal evidence that applications brought in by nonwhite loan officers are scrutinized more carefully by underwriters (Squires 1992). Consequently, in recent years, reinvestment agreements signed by lenders with community organizations frequently included affirmative action commitments to increase the representation of minority employees (National Training and Information Center 1991; National Community Reinvestment Coalition 1994).

This chapter systematically explores the relationship between minority employment and lending to minority borrowers. The key questions are the following. Do lenders who employ more racial minorities approve a larger proportion of applications they receive from minority borrowers and are those lenders more likely to approve an application from an individual minority borrower than do institutions that employ relatively few racial minorities? If so, do these relationships hold after taking into consideration relevant risk factors and structural characteristics of financial institutions.

Because housing and mortgage markets are primarily local markets (Shlay et al. 1992), this research focuses on one metropolitan area;

Milwaukee, Wisconsin. Lenders are regulated primarily by federal agencies and they do operate in an increasingly global economic environment. Also, secondary mortgage market institutions that operate nationally are assuming greater importance each year. But the formulation of underwriting policies, decisions to accept or reject an application, and marketing and outreach efforts, are conducted primarily at the local level in response to local conditions.

Data and Methodology

Three data sets are utilized. First, 1990 EEO-1 reports for Milwaukee area commercial banks and thrifts will provide detailed data on the total number of employees and the racial composition of employees in each of eight major occupational classifications. Private sector employers with 100 or more employees, employers with fifty or more employees who are government contractors or a depository of government funds, and institutions that issue U.S. Savings Bonds are required to submit an EEO-1 form each year to the U.S. Equal Employment Opportunity Commission. The data were obtained for twenty-one banks and thirteen thrifts providing home mortgages in the Milwaukee metropolitan area. The lenders in this data set accounted for 68.4 percent of all publicly reported mortgage loans in the Milwaukee metropolitan area in 1990. All reports and information from individual reports is confidential.

EEO data do not distinguish officials, professionals, managers, sales positions, and technicians by specific job title. This precluded, therefore, an analysis of the relationship between minority loan approvals and the racial composition of specific occupational groups, like "loan officer" or "underwriter." As a proxy, officials, managers, professionals, and technicians were grouped together as "professionals/administrators" and used to estimate the impact of the racial composition of employees on the loan approval process. Statistics generated from the EEO data included percent of total black employees and the percent of black professional/administrators at each individual institution.

The second data set is the Home Mortgage Disclosure Act (HMDA) report which commercial banks, savings and loan association, mutual savings bank, credit unions, and mortgage banks are required to submit annually to their federal financial regulatory agency (i.e., Federal Reserve Board, Federal Deposit Insurance Corporation, Office of the Comptroller of the Currency, or Office of Thrift Supervision) and make available to the general public. As indicated in previous chapters, this report provides several pieces of information for each mortgage application filed with the institution including the type (e.g., home purchase, home improvement, multifamily, FHA/VA) and the dollar amount of the loan; the income, race (American Indian or Alaskan Native, Asian or Pacific Islander, Black, Hispanic, White, Other, Information not provided, and Not applicable) and gender of the applicant; the census tract of the property; and the disposition of the application (approved, approved but not accepted by the applicant, denied, withdrawn by the applicant, closed for incompleteness, or purchased by the financial institution).

The 1990 HMDA data set for the Milwaukee metropolitan area comprised 35,422 loan applications. Applications for owner-occupied home purchases numbered 22,691, 64.1 percent of the total. Altogether 14,473 of these applications were either approved or denied with 13,919 of them being from either blacks or whites. For simplicity, this research was limited to those applications by blacks and whites for owner-occupied home purchases that were either approved or denied. The thirty-four lenders generated 9,338 mortgage loan applications from blacks and whites for owner-occupied home purchases for which there was an approval or denial. This is 67.1 percent of all such loan applications in the Milwaukee metropolitan area in 1990.

Finally, as the HMDA data include the census tract in which the property is located, we are able to merge information from the 1990 Census of Population and Housing into the dataset. The census data provide useful information on the neighborhood characteristics in which the property is located. Given the importance of neighborhood quality in home values, it would be an important determinant for mortgage loan approval.

In order to examine the effect of minority employment on minority mortgage loans, we conduct two sets of analysis. First, simple correlations and other descriptive statistics are presented that reveal an association between minority employment and the dependent variables. Second, logit analysis using the disposition of the individual loan application as a dependent variable is used to examine the relation between the likelihood of an individual applicant receiving mortgage loan approval and black employment controlling for applicant's socio-economic characteristics, loan amount, neighborhood quality, and lender characteristics.

Findings

As a group, banks had a higher black employment level than thrifts; but black application rates for mortgage loans and black approval rates for mortgages were higher at the thrifts. Black employment ratios ranged from 0 percent to 18.1 percent with a mean of 6.8 percent. For black professional/administrator ratios, the range was 0 percent to 6.0 percent with an average of 1.6 percent. Black employment rates at the twenty-one banks in the sample varied from 0 percent to 18.1 percent, with the industry-wide average being 6.2 percent. Aggregating employment among all banks in the sample, the banking industry had a workforce that was 10.3 percent black. Black employment at the thirteen thrifts ranged from 0 percent to 15.0 percent, with an average black employment rate of 5.9 percent. The combined industry-wide average of all blacks in the thrift workforce was 6.2 percent. Four banks and one thrift had no black employees. Five banks and one thrift had only one black employee each.

The proportion of all mortgage loan applications from blacks among all lenders varied from 0 percent to 20.8 percent with an average of 6.3 percent. Among home mortgage applications from only blacks and whites that were approved or denied, 6.3 percent of the applicants at banks were black, whereas 8.8 percent of the applicants at thrifts were black. Black borrowers at thrifts received mortgage loans at a 73.4 percent rate, but blacks applying at banks were approved only 65.5 percent of the time. The loan approval rate for whites was virtually identical for both types of lenders; banks approved mortgage applications from whites at a 92.3 percent rate, while thrifts approved mortgage applications from whites at a 92.9 percent rate.

On average, blacks and whites have quite different characteristics in terms of income, amount of the loan, and the neighborhood in which the property is located. In 1990 the average white household had an annual income of $52,674, applied for a mortgage loan of $77,841, and bought a house in a census tract which had the average single family home value of $85,575. The average black household had an annual income of $33,496, applied for a mortgage loan of $43,271, and bought a house in a census tract which had an average single family home value of $46,533.

Similarly, banks and thrifts also have different characteristics. In general, thrifts have a higher concentration of their business in home mortgage loans, while banks employ more workers. The average number of applications submitted to a thrift institution was 688.38 compared to 332.54 for a bank. Banks, on average, employed 664.77 workers, out of which 2.62 percent of administrative/professional and 9.08 percent of total positions were held by blacks. Thrifts, on average, employed 364.33 workers, out of which 1.8 percent of administrative/professional and 6.15 percent of total positions were held by blacks.

Table 7.1 Racial Composition of Mortgage Loan Applications to Banks and Thrifts in 1990

| | Banks | | | |
	Applications	Percent of all Applications	Approved	Percent Approved
Blacks	226	6.4	148	65.5
Whites	3,292	93.6	3,045	92.5
Total	3,518	100.6	3,193	90.9
	Thrifts			
	Applications	Percentage of all Applications	Approved	Percent Approved
Blacks	512	8.8	376	73.4
Whites	5,303	91.2	4,926	92.9
Total	5,815	100.2	5,302	91.2

SOURCE: 1990 HMDA

Black application rates and total black employment ratios were positively correlated [$\rho = 0.55$]. A positive correlation also existed between black application rates and a lender's approval rate for blacks [$\rho = 0.49$]. More significantly, minority employment appears to be associated with lending to minority borrowers. There is a positive correlation between levels of black employment and a lender's loan approval rate for blacks [$\rho = 0.39$]. Further, the lenders in the sample with above average levels of black employment average a 68.6 percent approval rate for mortgage loan applications received from blacks compared to 40.4 percent for those with below average black employment. The question that arises, therefore, is whether or not this relationship holds after controlling on key applicant, neighborhood, and institutional characteristics.

Binary choice model of logit analysis is utilized in order to examine the effect of lender employment on the disposition of individual mortgage loan applications. The dependent variable of the logit model is whether or not the mortgage application is approved by the lender (APPROVE = 1 when the loan application is approved and 0 when it is rejected). The independent variables include characteristics of the financial institution including the minority employment variables, characteristics of the applicant, and characteristics of the property.

The key minority employment variables for lenders were the ratio of black employees in the total workforce at the institution (BLKRATIO), and the ratio of blacks in professional or administrative positions (BLADRAT). Other lending institution characteristics included size measured in terms of number of employees (EMP), the number of home mortgage applications (HOMELOAN), and type of institution (INST). Institution type referred to whether the lender is a commercial bank or thrift (INST = 0 for commercial banks and 1 for thrifts). For applicant characteristics, applicant race (RACE = 1 for black and 0 for white), annual income of the applicant (INCOME) and mortgage loan amount (LOANAMT) were considered. As a control for the neighborhood characteristics, median home value of the census tract in which the property is located (CTVALUE) was also included in the model as an independent variable.

The results of the logit estimation are reported in table 7.2. Various interaction terms with race were included in the estimated model to test the hypothesis that black applicants are treated differently from white applicants. Also due to several structural distinctions between commercial banks and thrifts, several interaction terms with institution type are included.

The results generally confirm the hypothesis that institutional characteristics as well as the characteristics of the applicant and the property are important determinants of the loan approval. All the variables that represent applicant characteristics turned out to be significant. Applicant income is statistically significant at .001 level, and has the expected sign. In other words, the higher the income, the more likely the loan will be approved. The amount of the loan is significant at the .05 level, and also has the expected sign meaning that applications for smaller amounts are more likely to be approved. The race of the applicant turned out to be significant at the .001 level indicating that minority applicants have a lower likelihood of getting the loan approved. The interaction term between race and income is significant with a positive coefficient indicating that higher income for blacks increases the approval rate more than it does for whites. The neighborhood characteristic also turned out to be significant at the .001 level indicating that applications for loans on properties in higher valued neighborhoods are more likely to be approved. The type of institution turned out to be significant at the .001 level. This result suggests that mortgage loans are more likely to be approved by a thrift than by a bank, everything else being equal.

It is important to note that many interaction terms with institution type were significant. The interaction term between institution type

Table 7.2 Estimated Logit Model of Home Mortgage Application Approval[#]

Variable	Coefficient	t-ratio	Mean
Constant	2.00	9.451***	
Number of Employees (EMP)	0.657E-03	4.616***	477.58
Number of Mortgage Applications (HOMELOAN)	-0.245E-02	-2.949***	554.25
Ratio of Blacks in Professional or Administrative Positions (BLADRAT)	0.249E-01	0.481	2.1107
Ratio of Black Employees in Total Workforce (BLKRATIO)	-0.406E-01	-1.799	7.255
Type of Institution (INST)	-0.784	-3.575***	0.62306
Annual Income of Applicant (INCOME)	0.110E-01	4.908***	51.158
Mortgage Loan Amount (LOANAMT)	-0.196E-02	-1.957*	75.107
Race of Applicant (RACE)	-2.02	-6.273***	0.0791
Median Home Value in Census Tract (CTVALUE)	0.105E-04	5.941***	82488
Interaction between Race of Applicant and Ratio of Blacks in Professional or Administrative Positions (RACE*BLADRAT)	-0.100	-1.119	
Interaction between Race of Applicant and Ratio of Blacks in Total Workforce (BLKRATIO)	0.501E-02	1.345	
Interaction between Race and Annual Income of Applicant (RACE*INCOME)	0.127E-01	2.098*	
Interaction between Type of Institution and Number of Employees (INST*EMP)	-0.185E-02	-5.153***	
Interaction between Type of Institution and Number of Mortgage Applications (INST*HOMELOAN)	0.354E-02	4.109***	
Interaction between Type of Institution and Ratio of Blacks in Professional or Administrative Positions (INST*BLADRAT)	0.201	3.137***	

Table 7.2 *(continued)*   Estimated Logit Model of Home Mortgage Application Approval[#]

Variable	Coefficient	t-ratio	Mean
Interaction between Type of Institution and Ratio of Black Employees in Total Workforce (INST*BLKRATIO)	-0.282E-01	-1.080	
Interaction between Race of Applicant, Type of Institution, and Ratio of Blacks in Professional or Administrative Positions (RACE*INST*BLADRAT)	0.242	2.041*	
Interaction between Race of Applicant, Type of Institution, and Ratio of Black Employees in Total Workforce (RACE*INST*BLKRATIO)	-0.206E-02	-0.053	

[#]The dependent variable is APPROVE (= 1 if loan was approved, 0 if not approved; mean = .909).

*** Significant at .001
** .01
* .05 with two-tail t-test

Number of Observations, 9,333
Log-Likelihood, -2523.5
Constrained Log-Likelihood, -2590.5 (with no RACE effect)
Constrained Log-Likelihood, -2560.6 (with no INST effect)

SOURCE: EEO-1 Reports provided by the U.S. Equal Employment Opportunity Commission 1990, and 1990 HMDA, and 1990 U.S. Census Bureau

and number of employees and the term between institution type and number of mortgage applications are significant at the .001 level indicating that banks and thrifts behave very differently in the mortgage lending market. More specifically, holding everything else constant the loan approval rate of a larger bank is higher than a smaller bank, whereas it is higher for a smaller thrift. Similarly, a bank with a smaller number of mortgage loan applications has a higher approval rate, whereas a thrift with a larger number of applications has a higher approval rate.

The interaction terms between institution type and the racial composition of lenders also reveal substantial differences between the types of lenders. The interaction term between institution type and the proportion of black administrative and professional employees turned out to be significant at the .001 level indicating that the effect of the proportion on the approval rate is stronger with thrifts than with banks. Moreover, the interaction term with race, institution type, and the proportion was significant at the 5 percent significance level indicating that the effect is stronger for blacks than whites. In other words the likelihood that a loan application will be approved is higher in those institutions where black professional employment is relatively larger, and this relationship holds after controlling on several socio-economic characteristics of borrowers and neighborhoods in which properties are located. The relationship is stronger with thrifts than with banks. Most importantly, it is stronger for blacks than for whites. Given the larger role of thrifts than commercial banks in mortgage lending, the findings pertaining to thrifts may be the most significant.

An intriguing finding is the fact that increasing minority employment increases the likelihood of loan approval for whites as well as blacks. Although we do not explore this relationship here, we suspect that several interrelated factors contribute to this finding. Lenders with higher levels of minority employment may be taking several steps to increase lending to groups that have been previously underserved. They may have developed more flexible underwriting guidelines, new branch offices in low income communities, and other marketing and outreach efforts to reach low-income borrowers. Marginal white as well as marginal black applicants who previously may have been rejected, or who are still rejected by more "conventional" lenders, therefore may be more successful with those institutions that employ a greater number of minority workers.

Contrary to the strong results relating to the proportion of black administrative and professional employees, the proportion of all black employees including all its interaction terms with institution type and/or race turned out to be insignificant. Given the fact that the latter includes all employees such as clerical, janitorial and other low level positions, it is not surprising to find out that it does not affect the likelihood of loan approval.

Using the base model, we conducted two nested hypotheses using likelihood ratio tests. The first null hypothesis is that blacks and whites have the same likelihood of mortgage loan approval. The hypothesis is rejected at the significance level of 1 percent, as the test statistic, $2*(2{,}590.5 - 2{,}523.5) = 134$, is greater than the critical value of χ^2 (6 degrees of freedom) = 16.81. The constrained log-likelihood value is obtained by estimating the constrained model that does not included RACE and race interaction variables. The second null hypothesis is that banks and thrifts have the same likelihood of approving an application. This hypothesis is also rejected as the test statistic, 2*(2,560.6 – 2,523.5) = 74.2 is greater than the critical value of χ^2 (7 degrees of freedom) = 18.48.

The estimated model is used to calculate the likelihood of approval of a mortgage loan submitted to two types of lenders. In order to highlight the difference, we chose two different sets of applicant characteristics: those of an average white applicant (i.e., an applicant with the mean value for whites on each variable) and an average black applicant. These calculations are shown in table 7.3. The base case refers to our data set. The model predicts that the average white will have 93.4 percent approval rate when submitting an application to an average bank (i.e., a bank with mean values for each variable), and 94.5 percent when applying to an average thrift. The average black, has a substantially lower approval rate. The average black approval rate is 66.6 percent for the average bank and 77.6 percent for the average thrift. However, part of these discrepancies can be accounted for by the socioeconomic differences of the two racial groups. The bottom four figures in table 7.3 control for these differences. If a black applicant has the same income, applies for the same amount of the loan, for a home in the same neighborhood as the average white applicant, the approval rate would be 81.6 percent for the average bank and 88.5 percent for the average thrift. These rates are substantially lower than 93.4 percent and 94.5 percent for the average white. On the other hand, if a white applicant has the same characteristics as the average black, the approval rate will be 89.0 percent for the average bank and 90.8 percent for the average thrift. These figures are substantially greater than the comparable numbers of 66.6 percent and 77.6 percent for blacks.

The next columns in table 7.3 represent the estimated approval rates if the percentage of the black administrative/professional employment (BLADRAT) and black employment (BLKRATIO) were to increase by one percentage point. The first observation of this thought experiment is that the increase in the latter will not yield any significant changes, whereas the increase in the former will. The second result is that the change is much larger for thrifts. For example, if the former increases from the current average of 1.8 percent to 2.8 percent in the thrift industry, the approval rate of the average black will increase from 77.6 percent to 83.4 percent.

In this sample 70.0 percent of mortgage loan applications from blacks and 62.3 percent of applications from blacks and whites were made at thrift institutions. Thrifts, of course, focus more exclusively on mortgage

Table 7.3 Estimated Probabilities of the Approval Rate (in Percent)

	Base Case	1 Percent Point Increase in BLADRAT	1 Percent Point Increase in BLKRATIO
Avg. white at avg. bank	93.4	93.5	93.1
Avg. white at avg. thrift	94.5	95.4	94.1
Avg. black at avg. bank	66.6	64.9	66.8
Avg. black at avg. thrift	77.6	83.4	77.3
Black equal to avg. white at avg. bank	81.6	80.4	81.7
Black equal to avg. white at avg. thrift	88.5	91.7	88.3
White equal to avg. black at avg. bank	89.0	89.2	88.6
White equal to avg. black at avg. thirft	90.8	92.5	90.2

SOURCE: EEO-1 Reports provided by the U.S. Equal Employment Opportunity Commission 1990, and 1990 HMDA

lending than do commercial banks that are involved in a variety of commercial, consumer, and residential lending and investment activities. Therefore, a higher proportion of thrift employees and particularly professional employees, are involved in the mortgage lending process than is the case with commercial banks. The evidence from this chapter strongly suggests that the proportion of black professional/ administrators in thrift institutions significantly affects the probability of loan approval for black applicants.

A couple of caveats are in order. First, several other important applicant characteristics are missing in our model. Although applicant's wealth, loan-to-value ratio, credit and employment history are important determinants for a mortgage application approval decision, these data are not publicly available. The missing variables may create biases in the estimates of our model. The study that includes the most comprehensive list of applicant characteristic variables, the Boston Federal Reserve Bank study by Munnell et al. (1996), reports that though the effect of race is less than indicated by the original HMDA data when loan-to-value ratio and credit history variables are included, minority applicants still have substantially lower probabilities of loan approval than comparable white applicants. Based on the experience of the Boston study, if these variable were added in the estimation of this research, the effect of race would likely be lower than reported. However, it is not clear how the effect of lender employment characteristics, size, or type would change, if these variables were added.

Second, the model presented here does not address the possibility of selection bias in the initial application process. For example, African Americans may be discouraged from even applying for a mortgage loan from lenders who employee few African American employees. Such applicants may find it intimidating to deal with predominantly white lenders so they may be hesitant to initiate or pursue an application. Whatever the reason, if there exists such selection bias, the estimates of lender employment characteristics would be biased downwards as the lenders with a low African American employment ratio would have relatively fewer applications submitted by African Americans to reject.

Research and Policy Implications

In summary, the basic finding of this research is that racial composition of the workforce matters. As the proportion of black employees of a mortgage lender increases the likelihood that an application from a black borrower will be approved also increases. Particularly significant is the ratio of black professionals with thrift institutions. This relationship persists even after controlling on several applicant and lender characteristics that influence the loan review process. These preliminary findings indicate the need for further research but they also reveal directions for public policy.

A critical research question is the impact of minority employment in more detailed occupational classifications. Loan officers and underwriters are in particularly important positions to determine lending patterns, but top management and boards of directors may also have significant influence. Analysis of minority representation in these positions would be particularly useful. This research, of course, would require voluntary cooperation of lenders themselves or the assistance of financial regulatory agencies. Such information is not available in any public data source.

Another clear research need is replication of this study for additional cities. Cities where the racial composition or levels of segregation differ may exhibit different relationships between employment and lending patterns. City size, region of the country, number of financial institutions, and other factors may change the association between employment and lending. Perhaps more important, where similar patterns are found the responses by lenders, public officials, community groups, and others will be more substantial in those communities than is likely to be the case if only one city is examined. It is simply too easy to dismiss as irrelevant for a given city, the research findings from a case study of another community. Elsewhere we have examined this relationship in Boston, Atlanta, Denver, and San Francisco and similar patterns prevailed. Similar research of more communities would shed more light on this issue (Kim and Squires 1998).

The impact of the employment of other protected groups also needs to be examined. Employment levels for Hispanics, Asians, and other minorities, for women, and minority women may influence lending to these groups. These issues need to be subject to empirical investigation. We have preliminarily explored these effects in the same four communities noted above as well as Milwaukee. The basic pattern held for Hispanics but not for Asians (Kim and Squires 1998).

A related research need is employment practices of other financial institutions that directly impact on mortgage lending. Real estate agents, property insurers, private mortgage insurers, and secondary mortgage market institutions which purchase most of the loans originated by lenders are some of those actors for whom little is known about employment practices.

One proffered explanation for the racial gap in mortgage lending in general and the significance of minority employment in particular is what has been referred to as the "cultural affinity" hypothesis (Calomiris et al. 1994; Hunter and Walker 1996). According to this perspective, white loan officers will give the benefit of the doubt to marginal white applicants, but not to similar nonwhite applicants, because these lenders are more familiar with the white applicants (e.g., the types of jobs they hold, the communities where they live) and, consequently, are more aware of compensating factors in their overall financial situations.

In addition, some of these loan officers may use an observed characteristic—the race of the applicant—as a proxy for unobserved characteristics, which relate to the likelihood that a potential borrower will be able to repay the loan, even though such a practice would constitute "statistical discrimination" in violation of federal fair lending laws including the Fair Housing Act and Equal Credit Opportunity Act. Given the costs involved in collecting additional information, loan officers will make decisions based on what they "know" and such knowledge often works against minority borrowers even though no racial animus may be intended.

Assuming that cultural affinity affects mortgage loan decisions, presumably where there is a presence of minority loan officers minority loan applicants would benefit from that affinity. Personal relationships between bankers and their customers often provide an efficient means for overcoming information cost problems (Meyer 1997: 2). But this can work both ways. Personal knowledge of, as well as sympathy with, the characteristics of minority borrowers and the barriers they confront might enable some loan officers to readily justify a marginal application from a minority loan applicant (Hamilton and Cogswell 1997: 121). But such cultural affinity might also result in minority loan officers having personal knowledge of particular minority applicants that would result in a denial where the information supplied in the loan application alone might suggest another outcome (Longhofer 1996). Similarly, there is some evidence that, in fact, black rejection rates are higher at black-owned banks than at white-owned institutions (Black, Collins, and Cyree 1997).

Even assuming a positive statistical association between the proportion of workers from a particular minority group and the approval rate for that group does not directly reveal whether or not members of that group in fact have any additional information about any particular community. Other plausible explanations may account for the link between employment and approval rates in particular and the racial gap in mortgage lending generally.

Minority loan officers may be more informed about fair lending rules. They may be more sympathetic to applicants from their communities. The presence of a critical mass of minority workers, particularly high ranking employees, may encourage white employees to reexamine their own biases perhaps treating potential minority customers more politely and reviewing loan applications differently. The presence of many minority employees may result in a self-selection process whereby qualified minority borrowers seek out such institutions when they decide to buy a home.

The findings reported here are consistent with the cultural affinity hypothesis. When more people within a financial institution are from a given community it is plausible that they may be more familiar with applicants from that community. Consequently, they may be better situated to more efficiently obtain information from marginal applicants that would enable them to approve applications which do not clearly meet all the objective indicators. But the cultural affinity hypothesis remains just that; a hypothesis. Again, other explanations might account for this relationship. Why the racial composition of a lender's work force matters remains unclear. That such employment patterns do matter, however, increasingly appears to be the case.

Further research can tease out these relationships. In addition to the quantitative research on more detailed occupational classifications in more markets, more qualitative research may be essential. Ethnographic case studies may be required to understand why employment and lending patterns are related. It remains unclear the extent to which loan officers and bank officials have or rely on informal knowledge of selected communities, understand fair lending rules, empathize with particular types of applicants, influence their colleagues, or otherwise affect the loan disposition process. By interviewing, talking to, working with, and observing loan officers and bank officials in their daily routines, reviewing internal company documents (e.g., underwriting guidelines, training manuals), and utilizing other qualitative techniques, much more can be learned about how the racial composition of the work force affects mortgage lending decisions.

Another direction for future research is the effect of variables not included in this study. For example, the number of branch offices and whether any are located in the central city, the types of loans (e.g., conventional or government insured, single family or multifamily, home purchase or home improvement), local economic conditions (e.g., unemployment rates, number of housing starts), relationships among lenders and other providers of housing services (e.g., real estate agents, insurers, mortgage investors), and other factors which affect lending practices may also affect the relationship between employment and lending.

But there are policy implications that need not await further research. First, these findings reinforce the wisdom of those community groups that have negotiated affirmative action commitments in CRA agreements with local lenders. Second, and more importantly, these findings suggest the need to revise the regulations federal financial regulatory agencies have developed to enforce the Community Reinvestment Act (CRA). Under the CRA federally regulated lenders have a continuing and affirmative obligation to assess and be responsive to the credit needs of their entire service areas, including low- and moderate-income neighborhoods. Regulated financial institutions are evaluated in terms of their lending, investment, and related services. Based on this evaluation lenders receive one of four ratings:

1. outstanding;

2. satisfactory;

3. needs improvement;

4. substantial noncompliance.

Minority employment and affirmative action should be included as an additional assessment factor in these evaluations and ratings. And data on minority employment by occupational classifications should be included among the information lenders are required to make available to the public.

Many lenders are depositories of federal and other public funds. Most if not all lenders offer credit products and savings accounts that are federally insured. Several of these institutions are federal contractors and subject to Executive Order 11246 (1965) which requires affirmative action by most private businesses that contract with federal agencies to provide goods and services. Given the significance of credit availability for urban redevelopment and the linkage between employment and lending, the U.S. Equal Employment Opportunity Commission (EEOC—a federal agency charged with enforcing Title VII of the Civil Rights Act of 1964 prohibiting employment discrimination) and the Office of Federal Contract Compliance Programs (OFCCP—a division of the U.S. Department of Labor, which enforces Executive Order 11246), should give greater priority to lending institutions in their monitoring and enforcement activities.

Finally many lenders stand to gain by voluntarily implementing more effective affirmative action plans to increase their employment of racial minorities. Good business that is missed today, either because of bias by a predominantly white workforce or the hesitancy of qualified borrowers to enter an institution where nobody looks like them, can become profitable loans tomorrow if more minority employees (particularly at the professional level) are successfully recruited and retained. As the *ABA Banking Journal* editor concluded, "banks may take some comfort from the fact that sincere efforts to eliminate bias are the right thing to do. Further, done properly they will prove to be good for business" (Streeter 1993: 19).

More lenders might recognize an enlightened self-interest attached to stepped-up efforts to recruit, hire, and train more minority loan officers and professional staff generally. Michael Porter has observed that the nation's inner cities represent major marketing opportunities for businesses that take creative, entrepreneurial approaches to tapping that market (Porter 1995). Accessing and utilizing business professionals who understand these communities (its people, culture, buying power) can facilitate profiting from that market.

Employment strategies constitute only one set of tools for simultaneously achieving fair lending and legitimate business objectives. They should complement but not supplant credit counseling for first time homebuyers, development of new products, partnerships with community groups, and other steps many lenders are already taking to expand market share in previously underserved communities. An observation offered by American Family Insurance Company officials following its 1995 settlement of a fair housing complaint has clear implications for the mortgage lending industry:

> We must recruit more women and minorities to achieve a diverse employee and agent mix so that we can maintain a high level of customer service and retention . . . Not only will it enable us to provide better service to a wider range of customers, it will help us tap into new and changing markets that result from a population that contains an increasingly large minority component. Companies that understand this and take action now will have the competitive edge in the next century. (American Family Insurance undated, 3)

These actions would constitute a significant beginning in efforts to positively address the linkage between minority employment and minority lending. Further research, no doubt, would reveal additional steps that could be taken. If discriminatory credit practices have become less explicit and overt in recent decades, they clearly have not disappeared. One dimension of this complex discriminatory process that has received little attention is the employment practices of lenders and their implications for lending in urban communities.

8

Fringe Banking in Milwaukee

The Rise of Check-Cashing Businesses and the Emergence of a Two-Tiered Banking System

> Despite their bare-bones decor, check cashing establishments are steadily becoming the financial centers for many communities in America's lower-income neighborhoods.
>
> —Moskowitz, 1995

REDLINING OF URBAN COMMUNITIES and the exodus of conventional banking services from those neighborhoods has created a market opportunity for many "fringe banking" institutions in those neighborhoods. Check-cashing businesses, pawn shops, rent-to-own stores and other high-cost credit related enterprises have emerged in recent years to offer services provided almost exclusively by banks and savings and loans just a few years ago. But this has not been an even trade. Fringe bankers charge considerably more for their services than do traditional banking institutions, even with the increase in bank fees of recent years.

This chapter examines the growth in fringe banking institutions in Milwaukee. It focuses on check-cashing businesses that have emerged as one of the fastest growing businesses within the nation's central cities. As indicated in previous chapters, Milwaukee has long been the site of contentious debates over the availability of banking services. Access to mortgage and small business loans, and basic "life line" banking services has been the subject of much policy debate and community organizing. In recent years innovative lending programs have been created by some lenders. More recently controversies have emerged over the expansion of check-cashing businesses in Milwaukee and the role of conventional institutions in creating a market for these fringe bankers (Governor's Committee on Minority Business 1988; Glabere 1992; Morics 1996; Norman 1997). The following pages examine the demographics of the areas served by check-cashing businesses, the fees they charge compared to the costs of conventional banking services, and why their customers use what is generally a more expensive service than traditional financial institutions. The impact of broader trends in urban economic development and restructuring, and some of the policy and research implications of the emergence of this two-tiered banking system are also explored.

Check-Cashing Businesses: A Leading Growth Industry

Check-cashing businesses have become a major growth industry, particularly (though not exclusively) in low-income neighborhoods, in recent years. These businesses provide several services but their principal business, as the name suggests, is cashing checks, usually paychecks or government benefits checks. Many also sell money orders, transportation passes and lottery tickets. Some also distribute welfare benefits and food stamps and provide income tax preparation services. Customers can pay their utility bills at some locations. Most of the revenues, however, are derived from the fees they charge for cashing checks (Caskey 1994).

Nationwide the number of yellow page telephone listings for check-cashing establishments grew from 2,151 in 1986 (the earliest year for which this information is available) to 4,843 in 1992 with most located in low-income communities. *Business Week* estimated that there are now 5,500 establishments in operation and concluded "the market is bifurcating—between private banking services and check-cashing outfits," with the former serving primarily middle- and upper-income households and the latter serving low-income households (Leonhardt 1997: 84–86).[1]

These are not simply small "Mom and Pop" businesses. According to one estimate the industry cashed 128 million checks in 1990 totaling $38 billion generating approximately $700 million in fees (Caskey 1994: 62–64). They are profitable businesses. A recent study found that average rates of return on equity between 1988 and 1991 were 9 percent for national banks, 12 percent for manufacturers, and 104 percent for Illinois currency exchanges (what check-cashing businesses are referred to in that state) (Binder 1992). There are at least six national chains with more than fifty outlets. Two of them, ACE America's Cash Express and Pay-O-Matic Corporation, have more than one hundred outlets each and are publicly traded on the over-the-counter market (Caskey 1994, 65).

Customers of check-cashing establishments generally are employed and work full time but have low or moderate incomes. They are a racially mixed group with blacks accounting for almost half and Hispanics making up about one-third of the clientele. Estimates of those with no bank account range from 12.5 percent to approximately one-third of all households. For at least some of these households the lack of a banking relationship is accounted for by the fact that they have insufficient funds to open a savings or checking account. Many live from paycheck to paycheck. Relying on check-cashing businesses as their banker means they pay more for services and do not benefit from the interest and financial services provided by traditional banking institutions, thus further reducing their opportunity to enter the economic mainstream or build a more secure future (Caskey 1994: 73; Lunt 1993: 51; Kennickell and Starr-McCluer 1994; Hellmer 1996; Ludwig 1996; Mullen, Bush, and Weinstein 1997).

Reasons for utilizing check-cashing businesses vary. Those with bank accounts often find it easier and faster to get their money at a check-cashing business. One of the reasons for this convenience is that their bank is often not open when they need the cash. Some are simply more comfortable in the check-cashing office while others do not have sufficient funds in their accounts to cover the checks they want to cash. As the distribution of income has become more polarized, the number of households with low incomes, and frequently no checking or savings account, has increased thus making the check-cashing business the only "banker" available to a growing number of people. Many communities served by fringe bankers do not have the same concentration of traditional branch banks as other communities. While branch

location is not a major impediment to accessing bank services nationwide, this is a problem in some communities (Caskey 1994: 107; 1997:
19–22; Lunt 1993: 51; Hudson 1996: 51–57; Hellmer 1996).

One feature of fringe banking and check-cashing businesses in
particular is that they are expensive. Customers pay far more for services provided by a check-cashing business than they pay for the same
services at a conventional bank. Fees for cashing payroll checks
nationwide generally range between 1 percent and 3 percent of the
face value of the checks. For personal checks the range was generally
between 1.7 percent and 20 percent, averaging around 8 percent (Caskey
1994: 58–60). In some instances, however, fees and interest rates have
been reported as high as 2000 percent (Hudson 1996: 1). A study by
the New York Office of the Public Advocate found that a check-
cashing customer with an annual income of $17,000 will pay almost
$250 a year at a check-cashing business for services that would cost
$60 at a bank (Moskowitz 1995: 9). The Federal Reserve Bank of Kan-
sas City reported that a family with a $24,000 annual income using a
check-cashing business will spend almost $400 in fees for services that
would cost under $110 at a bank (Lunt 1993: 52). The following pages
trace the concrete realities of these developments in the Milwaukee,
Wisconsin metropolitan area.

Check-Cashing Businesses in Milwaukee

In 1970 there were no check-cashing businesses listed in the Milwaukee Yellow Pages, in the 1996–1997 Yellow Pages there were thirty-
four listings. The Check Cashing Place had sixteen locations, Cashland
Checking, Check Express, and Milwaukee Check Cashers each had
four locations, Check 'n Go had three, Northstar Loans had two, and
Big Deal Check Cashers had one office. The following issues are addressed below:

1. the location of these offices, particularly in terms of the socio-
   economic status and racial composition of the neighborhoods;

2. the costs for typical services they provide and the costs charged
   by conventional banks for similar services;

3. the reasons customers report for using check-cashing businesses.

Location of Check-Cashing Businesses

Consistent with nationwide trends, check-cashing businesses in Milwaukee are concentrated in low-income and predominantly nonwhite

communities. Eleven (32 percent) of the thirty-four businesses listed in the 1996–97 Yellow Pages are located the city's Target Area (TA). While 32 percent of check-cashing businesses are located in the TA, just 9 percent of bank headquarters or branch offices (22 of 246) in the Milwaukee metropolitan area are located in this community. (Approximately 14 percent of all households reside in the TA.) This translates into 1.77 check-cashing businesses per 10,000 households in the TA compared to 0.74 per 10,000 households in the balance of the metropolitan area. Conversely there are 3.54 bank offices per 10,000 households in the TA compared to 7.19 per 10,000 households outside the TA (see maps 8.1 and 8.2).

The number of bank offices in the TA has grown in recent decades, but at a slower rate than in the balance of the metropolitan area. Between 1970 and 1996 the number of branch banks in this community increased from 11 to 22 for a 100 percent increase. Outside the TA the number of branches grew from 61 to 224, an increase of 267 percent. And, of course, since there were no check-cashing businesses in the TA or the metropolitan area in 1970, the rate of growth for these businesses has been much greater than that of banks in all communities. But, again, their growth and location are concentrated in Milwaukee's low-income communities.

Another way to view the concentration of these financial services is to compare the ratios of banks to check-cashing businesses. In the TA there were two banks for every check-cashing business whereas outside the TA there were almost ten banks for each check-cashing business (see table 8.1).

Check-cashing businesses are also concentrated in black and Hispanic communities, unlike banks that are concentrated in predominantly white areas. In areas that are 70 percent or more black there are 1.29 check-cashing businesses per 10,000 households and in areas that are between 10 and 70 percent black there are 1.87 per 10,000 households compared to just 0.52 per 10,000 households in areas that are less than 10 percent black. In the predominantly black communities there are just 1.29 banks per 10,000 households compared to 7.83 in white areas (see map 8.1). In the black communities there was one bank for every check-cashing business compared to fifteen banks for each check-cashing business in predominantly white areas.

A similar, though less distinct, pattern emerges in comparing Hispanic and white neighborhoods. In areas where Hispanics account for more than 25 percent of all households there are 2.77 check-cashing businesses per 10,000 households compared to 0.88 in communities where Hispanics are less than 5 percent of the total. There are 6.46

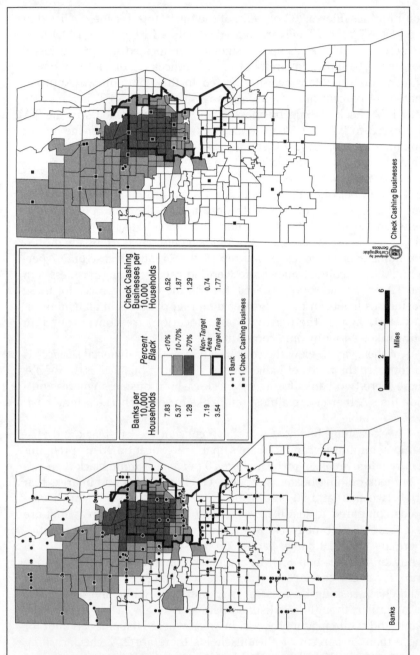

Map 8.1 Location of Banks and Check-Cashing Businesses by Black Population Concentration: Milwaukee County, 1996

SOURCE: 1990 U.S. Census Bureau, and Ameritech Milwaukee Yellow Pages 1996–1997

Check Cashing Businesses

Banks

	Banks per 10,000 Households		Check Cashing Businesses per 10,000 Households
Percent Black			
<10%	7.83		0.52
10-70%	5.37		1.87
>70%	1.29		1.29
Non-Target Area	7.19		0.74
Target Area	3.54		1.77

• = 1 Bank
■ = 1 Check Cashing Business

0   2   4   6
Miles

designed by
UWM
Cartographic
Services

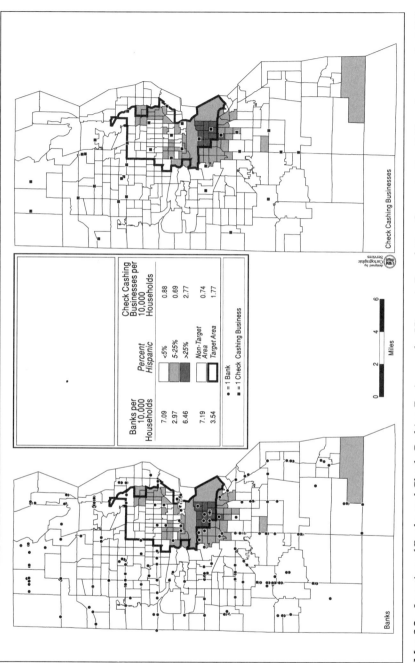

Map 8.2 Location of Banks and Check-Cashing Businesses by Hispanic Population Concentration: Milwaukee County, 1996

SOURCE: 1990 U.S. Census Bureau, and Ameritech Milwaukee Yellow Pages 1996–1997

The following text appears within the map figure:

Banks per 10,000 Households

Percent Hispanic	Banks per 10,000 Households	Check Cashing Businesses per 10,000 Households
<5%	7.09	0.88
5-25%	2.97	0.69
>25%	6.46	2.77
Non-Target Area	7.19	0.74
Target Area	3.54	1.77

● = 1 Bank
■ = 1 Check Cashing Business

0   2   4   6
Miles

designed by
UWM Cartographic Services

Banks

Check Cashing Businesses

Table 8.1   Ratio of Banks to Check-Cashing Businesses

Neighborhood Type	Number of Banks for Each Check-Cashing Business
Target Area	2
Nontarget Area	10
Greater Than 70% Black	1
Less Than 10% Black	15
Greater Than 25% Hispanic	2
Less Than 5% Hispanic	8

SOURCE: 1990 U.S. Census Bureau, and Ameritech Milwaukee Yellow Pages 1996–1997

banks per 10,000 households in Hispanic areas compared to 7.09 in white areas (see map 8.2). In the Hispanic communities there were just over two banks for each check-cashing business compared to more than eight banks for each check-cashing business in white communities.

Costs of Services at Check-Cashing Businesses

Although bank fees have increased in recent years, financial services remain considerably less expensive at traditional banks than at fringe banking institutions. As table 8.2 indicates, banking fees do vary, but five banks with branches in the TA offer checking accounts with no monthly fees, unlimited check-writing privileges, and no minimum balance requirement. These institutions include First Financial, St. Francis, Norwest, TCF, and Guaranty. Each of these banks requires an initial deposit ranging from $25 to $100. Guaranty does not include an automatic teller machine (ATM) card with its account, but the others offer at least four free transactions per month with an ATM card. Government checks and paychecks for bank customers are cashed for free at all locations. Fees for money orders for all banks including those with branches in the TA range from $.50 to $5.00 with most charging $2.00 or $3.00. This charge does not vary with the amount of the money order.[2]

Fees at check-cashing businesses are considerably higher. As table 8.3 indicates, fees for cashing paychecks and government checks are approximately one and one-half percent to three percent, precisely the range Caskey found nationwide (Caskey 1994: 5). For a $100 paycheck or government check the costs range from $1.75 to $2.90. For a $500 check fees vary from $7.15 to $8.75. As indicated above, there would be no fees for these services at banks where the customer has an account.

Table 8.2 Fees for Selected Services Charged by the Largest Banks in Milwaukee County[1]

Bank	Checking Account Name	Initial Deposit	Monthly Fee	Check Charge	Minimum Balance	ATM	Money Order
Firstar	Economy	$100.00	$2.95	First 10 free/$.75	0	First 10 free/$.75	$3.00 a
M & I	Basic	Any amount	$3.00	First 10 free/$.50	0	$.50 each	$3.00 c $5.00 nc
Bank One	Economy	$25.00	$2.95	First 12 free/$.95	0	Free in/$.60 out[2]	$3.00 c $5.00 nc
Security	Gold-Flex	$100.00	$6.95	Unlimited	0	First 5 free/$.50	$2.00 a
First Financial[3]	Absolutely Free	$50.00	0	Unlimited	0	First 4 free/$1.00	$1.50 c $3.00 nc
Mutual	Regular Free	$200.00	0	Unlimited	0	No Charge	$2.00 c $3.00 nc
St. Francis[3]	Totally Free	$25.00	0	Unlimited	0	First 4 free/$.75	$1.00 a
Wauwatosa	Diamond	$10.00	0	Unlimited	$100.00	Free in/$.75 out	$.50 a
Norwest[3]	Free Checking	$100.00	0	Unlimited	0	Free in/$.90 out	$2.00 c $4.00 nc
First Star	Chextra Value	$100.00	$6.00	Unlimited	0	No Charge	$3.00 a
TCF[3]	Totally Free	$100.00	0	Unlimited	0	Free in/$.75 out	$1.00 a
Tri-City	Regular	$100.00	$5.00	$.35 each	0	Free in/$.50 out	$2.00 a
Park Bank	Basic	$100.00	$2.50	First 8 free/$.50	0	First 4 free/$.50	$2.00 c $3.00 nc
North Shore	Free	$50.00	0	Unlimited	0	$.25 in/$.75 out	$2.00 a
Guaranty[3]	Totally Free	$50.00	0	Unlimited	0	No Tyme	$1.00 c
Equitable	No Minimum Balance	$100.00	0	Unlimited	0	$.50 each plus $5.00/ year	$.75 c $1.50 nc
Associated	Basic	$100.00	$3.00	First 5 free/$.30	0	First 5 free/$.50	$2.00 a
State Financial	Lifestyle	$100.00	$3.00	First 10 free/$.75	0	$1.00 each	$1.50 c $3.00 nc
Great Midwest	NOW	$200.00	$6.00	$.30 each	0	$.30 each	$1.00 c $2.00 nc
South Milwaukee	Traditional	$50.00	0	Unlimited	0	First 3 free/$.50	$2.00 a
Maritime	Flagship	Any amount	0	Unlimited	0	$.50 each	$1.00 c $3.00 nc

[1]Includes all banks with 1 percent or more of all deposits in Milwaukee County in 1994 according to data provided by the Federal Reserve Board and the Office of Thrift Supervision.

[2]Free = Free when using ATM inside bank. Out = Fee when using ATM outside of bank.

[3]These banks have branch offices in the Target Area.

a = Anyone

c = Customer

nc = Noncustomer

Table 8.3 Fees for Selected Services Charged by Check-Cashing Businesses in Milwaukee County

Check-Cashing Business[1]	Paycheck or Government Check for $100	Paycheck or Government Check for $500	Personal Check for $50	Money order for $25 and $100	
Check Cashing Place	$2.65	$7.90	NA	$1.55	$2.65
Cashland Checking	$2.70	$7.75	$5.00[2]	$1.65	$2.75
Big Deal Check Cashers	$2.70	$7.15	$5.00[2]	$1.88	$3.00[4]
Check Express	$1.75	$8.75	$2.49[3]	$1.74	$3.99[5]
Milwaukee Check Cashers	$2.90	$8.30	NA	$1.82	$2.90

[1]Check N Go and Northstar Loans are not reflected on this table because the only service they provide is payday loans.

[2]The fee for any personal check over $50 is 10% of the check amount.

[3]A flat fee of 3% of the check amount is charged plus a $.99 transaction fee.

[4]A flat fee of 3% is charged for money orders $100 and over.

[5]The charge for money orders is a flat 3% plus a $.99 transaction fee.

Cashing personal checks is also more costly at check-cashing businesses than at banks, at least for bank customers. At check-cashing businesses customers pay between 3 percent plus a $.99 transaction fee to a flat 10 percent to cash a $50 personal check. Several banks charge no fee for this service with the highest bank charge being $.95 and that is only after the customer has written twelve checks (for free) in a given month.

The comparative cost of money orders depends on the amount. For small money orders the fees at check-cashing businesses are slightly lower than those charged by banks. But money orders for larger amounts cost more at check-cashing businesses. For example, a $25 money order will cost around two or three dollars at most banks. At check-cashing businesses the fee ranges from $1.55 to $1.88. Although these charges do not vary by amount at banks, a $100 money order costs between $2.65 and $3.99 and the fees increase further as the amount of the money order increases at check-cashing businesses.

Significant fees are charged by check-cashing businesses for so-called "payday loans." A payday loan occurs when a check-cashing business agrees to cash a postdated personal check with the understanding that it will not be cleared through the banking system until the customer deposits his or her next paycheck. There are variations on this theme. For example, the check-cashing business may simply hold the personal check and provide the customer cash until the paycheck arrives and the customer repays the loan with funds provided by the paycheck or some other source of funds. In some cases the paycheck itself might be postdated but the customer is offered what amounts to a cash advance. Generally this service is provided only for those who have a record of stable employment and a checking account in good standing. The fees are generally quite high, but this is one service— basically a small and very short-term consumer loan—that banks do not offer.

Several Milwaukee area check-cashing businesses provide payday loans. The Check Cashing Place will provide such loans to customers who have had a checking account at a bank and have been employed at the same location for at least six months. Customers can receive $50 for a check written in the amount of $60 and dated fourteen days after the cash is provided. If the customer returns $55 within fourteen days he or she will get the personal check back. This, in effect, amounts to a $5.00 or 10 percent fee for the privilege of borrowing $50 for two weeks. The effective annual interest rate for this loan is 1,092 percent.[3] (The cost of a loan depends on the time period or frequency with which the interest is calculated as well as the interest rate itself.

Because loan products are frequently priced on the basis of an effective annual interest rate, that is an appropriate rate to use for the purpose of comparing the cost of various loan products.) If the customer fails to return with the $55, the check is cashed. The customer will then have paid $10 or 20 percent for the two-week loan for an effective annual interest rate of 11,348 percent.

Check Express offers a similar service at two of its four Milwaukee locations. The same sixth-month checking account and employment requirements apply. The fee is $15 for every $100 personal check postdated by fourteen days. This amounts to an effective annual interest rate of 3,686 percent.

Interest rates for similar products are much lower. For example, interest rates on unpaid balances of credit cards are frequently around 1.5 percent per month which translates to an effective annual rate of about 19.5 percent. Most consumer loans generally have even lower interest rates. However, as indicated above, banks do not provide small, short-term loans precisely comparable to the payday loans.

But checking accounts appear to be available and many who use check-cashing businesses have such accounts. (Again, having a checking account is a prerequisite for payday loans.) The question that arises, given these fee structures and requirements, is why check-cashing businesses have grown so rapidly in recent years.

Why Milwaukee Residents Use Check-Cashing Businesses

According to a recent survey of central city households, a substantial number of households in Milwaukee's central city neighborhoods use check-cashing businesses and do so in part because of the convenience provided by these services. A majority of these residents have a checking or savings account and most of them use their bank to cash checks, however, some of these residents use check-cashing businesses, at least on occasion. In order to obtain payday loans, the most expensive service check-cashing businesses offer, customers must have a checking account in good standing. The growth of this industry, however, is grounded in the exclusion of low-income and minority households. This exclusion results from both financial hardships that disqualify some residents for bank accounts as well as exclusionary practices by financial institutions that deny service to bankable segments of these communities.

Consumer Choices

Information on who uses check-cashing businesses and why was obtained through a telephone survey designed by the Employment and Training Institute at the University of Wisconsin-Milwaukee and conducted by the university's Social Science Research Facility (Quinn 1997: 16–17). A random sample of 518 Milwaukee households in the city's Community Development Block Grant neighborhoods was surveyed in December 1996. The Block Grant neighborhoods and the Target Area, referred to earlier, substantially overlap. The Target Area is slightly smaller and contained within the Block Grant community. Its population includes approximately three-quarters of Block Grant neighborhoods.

The focus of the survey was on work and training issues. The first two questions asked respondents if anyone in their household was interested in finding work or a new job or whether anyone was interested in training to upgrade their skills. If the respondent said "no" to both questions, the interview was concluded. Consequently, 309 of the initial 518 were asked questions about their banking practices. Therefore, these responses are based on a subset of the entire sample and do not necessarily constitute a random sample of central city residents. Given that these respondents are limited to households where at least one member was interested in seeking work or a new job or training that would provide skills enabling them to prepare for a new job, those residents with more severe financial problems may be underrepresented. The implications of such a sampling bias are discussed below.

Altogether 42.1 percent of those who responded to the banking questions of this survey said that they use check-cashing businesses to cash checks. Among the 309 people who responded to the banking questions 30.8 percent said they usually use check-cashing businesses to cash checks. Over half the respondents (53.7 percent) report having a checking or savings account at a bank and over one-quarter of these households (26.5 percent) said that they use check-cashing businesses. (Some of these may have meant that they used check-cashing businesses prior to opening their bank accounts.) A much higher proportion of those without bank accounts (62.0 percent compared to the 26.5 percent with an account) said they use check-cashing businesses. When asked where they usually cash checks just 1.8 percent of those with bank accounts compared to 26.3 percent of those without accounts identified check-cashing businesses as the place they generally go.

Of those who use these services 20.8 percent pointed to the hours they were open as the primary reason. The eleven check-cashing businesses in the Target Area are open an average of 68 hours per week compared to forty-four hours for banks located in these neighborhoods. Check-cashing businesses are open an average of 13.1 hours during the weekend compared to 2.7 hours for banks. During the week, check-cashing businesses are open approximately 2.5 hours in the evening (after 5:00 P.M.) compared to less than one-half hour for banks.

The biggest difference, of course, is weekend and evening hours. None of the banks are open after 7:00 P.M. on any day, but seven of the check-cashing businesses are open until 8:00 P.M. at least some days with the remaining four open at least that late six nights each week. Most of the banks close by noon on Saturday (although one is open until 2:00 and another until 3:00) and only one bank has Sunday hours (11:00–3:00), but all the check-cashing businesses are open at least until 5:00 P.M. on Saturdays and four are open until at least 6:00 P.M. on Sundays (see tables 8.4 and 8.5).

Location of the check-cashing businesses was mentioned by 14.6 percent as the principal reason they use these services. This is somewhat puzzling in light of the fact that there are twenty-two banks but just eleven check-cashing businesses in the Target Area. However, six of these banks are located in the western fringe of the downtown central business district and just inside the Target Area boundaries.

Almost one-quarter of the respondents referred generally to convenience or ease using terms like "convenient," "easy," "quick," or "fast" to explain their use of these services. Altogether 23.8 percent of responses fell into this general category and it is likely that hours and location constitute at least part of the convenience for them.

More than one-fifth of the respondents pointed to their relationship (or lack thereof) with banks as 13.8 percent reported they had no bank account and 8.5 percent referred to bank rules such as identification requirements that they could not meet. And 10 percent referred to services other than cashing paychecks including availability of money orders, income tax preparation service, and cashing of social security and Aid to Families with Dependent Children (AFDC) checks.

As indicated above, this sample excluded respondents where no household members were interested in finding work or a new job, or training that would upgrade their skills and lead to a new job. Consequently, those with relatively greater financial or credit problems, (and therefore facing greater difficulties in opening a conventional bank account, which would likely make them more dependent on check-cashing businesses) may have been underrepresented. Welfare recipients (particularly those with large families), mentally or physically disabled, teenagers, the elderly, and discouraged workers are among those who might not have been adequately represented. For these households, inability to open a bank account (because they did not meet bank requirements, bank employees were generally hostile

Table 8.4 Hours of Service for Banks Located in the Target Area

	Monday	Tuesday	Wednesday	Thursday	Friday	Saturday	Sunday
Bank One (3 locations)	9:00–5:00	9:00–5:00	9:00–5:00	9:00–5:00	9:00–5:00	9:00–12:00 (9:00–1:00 at one location)	CLOSED
First Bank (2 locations)	10:00–7:00 9:00–5:00	10:00–7:00 9:00–5:00	10:00–7:00 9:00–5:00	10:00–7:00 9:00–5:00	10:00–7:00 9:00–5:00	10:00–3:00 CLOSED	11:00–3:00 CLOSED
First Financial	9:00–5:00	9:00–5:00	9:00–5:00	9:00–5:00	9:00–6:00	9:00–12:00	CLOSED
Firstar (3 locations)	9:00–5:00	9:00–5:00	9:00–5:00	9:00–5:00	9:00–6:00 (9:00–5:00 at one location)	9:00–12:00	CLOSED
Guaranty	9:30–5:30	9:30–5:30	9:30–5:30	9:30–5:30	9:30–6:00	9:30–1:00	CLOSED
M & I (3 locations)	9:00–5:00	9:00–5:00	9:00–5:00	9:00–5:00	9:00–6:00 (9:00–5:00 at one location)	9:00–12:00	CLOSED
Mitchell	9:00–5:00	9:00–5:00	9:00–5:00	9:00–5:00	9:00–5:00	9:00–12:00	CLOSED
North Milwaukee	9:00–5:00	9:00–5:00	9:00–5:00	9:00–5:00	9:00–6:00	9:00–12:00	CLOSED
Norwest (2 locations)	9:00–5:00 9:00–6:00	9:00–5:00 9:00–6:00	9:00–5:00 9:00–6:00	9:00–5:00 9:00–6:00	9:00–5:30 9:00–6:00	CLOSED 10:00–3:00	CLOSED
St. Francis	8:00–5:00	8:00–5:00	8:00–5:00	8:00–5:00	8:00–5:00	CLOSED	CLOSED
Security (2 locations)	9:00–5:00 8:30–5:00	9:00–5:00 8:30–5:00	9:00–5:00 8:30–5:00	9:00–5:00 8:30–5:00	9:00–6:30 8:30–5:00	9:00–12:00 CLOSED	CLOSED
TCF	9:00–5:00	9:00–5:00	9:00–5:00	9:00–5:00	9:00–6:30	8:30–2:00	CLOSED
Universal	9:00–5:00	9:00–5:00	9:00–5:00	9:00–5:00	9:00–5:00	CLOSED	CLOSED
Avg. Number of Hours Opened by Day	8.2	8.2	8.2	8.2	8.2	2.7	0.2
Avg. Number of Hours Opened after 5:00 P.M.	.2	.2	.2	.2	.5	0	0
Avg. Number of Weekend Hours	2.7						
Avg. Number of Hours per Week	44.1						

Table 8.5 Hours of Service for Check-Cashing Businesses Located in the Target Area

	Monday	Tuesday	Wednesday	Thursday	Friday	Saturday	Sunday
Check Cashing Place (7 locations)	9:00–7:00	9:00–7:00	9:00–7:00	9:00–8:00	9:00–8:00	9:00–5:00	CLOSED
Cashland Checking (2 locations)	8:00–8:00	8:00–8:00	8:00–8:00	8:00–8:00	8:00–8:00	8:00–8:00	10:00–6:00
Milwaukee Check Cashers (2 locations)	8:00–8:00	8:00–8:00	8:00–8:00	8:00–8:00	8:00–8:00	8:00–8:00	8:00–8:00
Avg. Number of Hours Opened by Day	10.7	10.7	10.7	11.4	11.4	9.5	3.6
Avg. Number of Hours Opened after 5:00 P.M.	2.4	2.4	2.4	3	3	1.1	.7
Avg. Number of Weekend Hours	13.1						
Avg. Number of Hours per Week	68						

to them, other exclusionary practices, or any other reason) may be more salient than issues of convenience. Respondents generally, and these groups in particular, might also be hesitant to openly acknowledge personal financial problems or to admit discomfort with the treatment they have received or anticipate receiving at conventional financial institutions.

Exclusion and Financial Hardship
Check-cashing businesses do fill a niche in the market. Their fees are high and may be excessive. It must also be recognized that their fees are affected by the relatively high-risk markets they serve. These are small, for-profit businesses; not charitable organizations. They are generally smaller businesses than most banks with higher costs per transaction and, therefore, are under greater competitive pressure to assure that fees are adequate to cover each product and service they offer. Their longer hours add to their expenses, and they are often located in high-crime areas, which increases their business insurance and security costs (Caskey 1994: 112–114). The problem is not so much with the high fees they charge, but with the relative absence of conventional institutional services that creates market opportunities for these high-priced services. In Milwaukee, and elsewhere, these neighborhoods are not totally excluded by traditional banks, but clearly the concentration and current patterns of growth of banking services are away from these neighborhoods. Check-cashing businesses are simply responding to this void.

At least to some extent, this pattern reflects the polarization in Milwaukee's (and the nation's) economy generally. Caskey (1994 and 1997) attributes the declining use of banks among lower-income and minority households during the 1980s to their deteriorating economic condition that was exacerbated by rising bank fees. The closing of branch banks was not a significant factor nationally, though he acknowledged it could be in some local communities. Nationwide, the distribution of income has become more polarized over the past two decades and the buying power of the average wage has dropped. The number of middle-income families has declined while the number of low-income families has risen substantially and the number of high-income families has also increased (Harrison and Bluestone 1988; Mishel, Bernstein, and Schmitt 1997; Schafer and Faux 1996). This pattern holds true in Milwaukee.

Between 1970 and 1990 the share of low-wage jobs in Milwaukee County increased from 40.9 percent to 50.1 percent, high-wage jobs grew from 12.1 percent to 13.3 percent, but the share of middle-income jobs dropped from 47.0 percent to 36.5 percent (Levine 1994).

In a study of concentration of poverty in the one hundred largest metropolitan areas in 1990, Milwaukee was found to have the highest concentration of its poor population on one measure, it was ranked number two on a second measure, and was ranked number three on the third measure (Coulton et al. 1996). Milwaukee was also included among sixteen racially hypersegregated cities identified by Massey and Denton in their classic study, *American Apartheid* (1993).

These emerging economic and demographic trends may contribute to the decline of traditional banking services and the rise of alternative check-cashing businesses in Milwaukee. Some bankers may perceive distressed areas to be increasingly unbankable. Some residents in these communities may not have, or simply may not believe they have sufficient assets to open an account. As indicated above, five banks in the Target Area offer checking accounts with no monthly fee, unlimited check-cashing privileges, and no minimum balance requirement. The initial deposit requirement, however, may present a barrier for some. And, at least in part due to their strapped financial status, they may have written some checks in the past for which insufficient funds were available in their accounts, making them ineligible for conventional checking accounts. In other words, households in low-income areas and minority communities are excluded by a combination of legitimate considerations of risk due to financial hardship as well as exclusionary behavior of financial institutions that denies service to bankable consumers in these areas.

Banks are not simply innocent bystanders. Although there are many forces that shape the uneven development of metropolitan areas and the decline of central city neighborhoods, disinvestment and discrimination on the part of traditional financial institutions constitute key contributing factors (Bradford and Cincotta 1992; National Commission on Neighborhoods 1979). The distribution of branch banks throughout most metropolitan areas constitutes one indication of where they intend to do business. Even when they nominally provide basic-banking services, low-income residents are often directed to higher cost services or steered away altogether. For example, a staff member of the California Reinvestment Committee recently reported that when she visited several banks in Oakland she was consistently steered to the higher cost accounts they offered and away from the more affordable types. She also reported that in Los Angeles some residents were told by local banks that certain types of low-cost accounts were not available even though the banks' literature stated that such accounts were offered by them (Seward 1996). Some banks have begun to take actions to reverse these trends (Squires 1992). More can be done.

In general, check-cashing businesses are offering valued services that, apparently, are not as readily available at banks for many residents. If their fees are high, however, the principal problem is exclusion from conventional financial services, whether that exclusion is caused by undue riskiness of households or overly restrictive bank policies, which creates a market for fringe banks. Alleviating that exclusion, and bringing more households into primary, rather than fringe, banking institutions should be the focus of public policy.

Research and Policy Implications

This research raises a number of puzzling questions that should be the subject of future research. A detailed survey of actual customers of check-cashing businesses focusing on their banking practices would permit more definitive information about the demographics of users and the factors attracting them to these high cost services, or repelling them from conventional banks.

Some issues might be explored more effectively through in-depth personal interviews. For example, one question noted above is why so many residents point to the convenient location of check-cashing businesses when it appears there are as many, if not more, banks in their neighborhoods. Extended interviews with selected customers might be more revealing than a short answer as part of a telephone survey.

A second area of research pertains to customer banking practice and experience. It would be useful to know, for example, how many of those without current bank accounts actually want an account, how many of these households previously had accounts, and whether they closed their accounts after check-cashing businesses became more prevalent.

A third set of issues pertains to why those residents with bank accounts selected their banks. Some may bank near where they work. In other cases, the residents may have recently moved, but stayed with a bank in their former neighborhood and simply not bothered to shop for a new bank. But in others there may be specific services offered that were particularly attractive, or marketing efforts that made these residents aware of the services. Broader dissemination of this information might reward bankers and residents alike.

A fourth issue involves ownership of check-cashing businesses. In Milwaukee at least two of the major banks have provided loans to local check-cashing businesses (Schultze 1994; Zahn 1994). In New York, Chase Manhattan Bank operates several check-cashing businesses (Parry 1997). What is unclear is the impact of such financial arrangements. Do they constitute a financial underpinning of a two-tiered banking system that exploits low-income neighborhoods, or do they provide an opportunity for access to financial services that otherwise are generally not available in these neighborhoods?

A fifth set of issues pertains to the assets of the residents. An inventory of current assets, (e.g., savings, homeownership, business equity, employment) might reveal a market that is attractive to at least some lenders not serving this community (McKnight 1993). Banks often solicit new customers for relatively unprofitable lines of business, like savings or checking accounts, in hopes that they will soon be customers for other more profitable business like car, home, or business loans. Quantifying and publicizing the assets available in the central city may attract some bankers, again for the mutual benefit of local households and financial institutions.

If poor people and racial minorities are highly segregated and concentrated in Milwaukee, bankable customers still reside in the central city who are being missed by traditional financial institutions. Steps can be taken to bring these residents into the financial mainstream, even in the face of these broader economic trends. At the same time, equalizing access to traditional banking services (or in the short run, at least blunting the development of the two-tiered banking system) constitutes one step in reducing poverty and the economic bifurcation that has characterized the past two or three decades.

A key is more effective marketing on the part of banks. The overriding attraction of check-cashing businesses is the convenience they offer principally because of the hours they are open. The ability to cash a check on weekends and in the evening hours every day of the week is a major selling point of the check-cashing businesses. Traditional banks could readily compete with this feature. Expanded access to ATM machines coupled with reduced fees would be responsive, in part, to this concern. But customers cannot generally cash paychecks at ATM machines and some fear for their personal security at ATM machines, particularly during nonbusiness hours.

In addition to being open more hours, banks could advertise their services more effectively, particularly in those cases where free checking accounts are offered. Given the general increase in banking fees of recent years, many residents may simply not know that free or low-cost accounts are available.

More branch banks, or perhaps simply more visibility of those currently in operation might also attract more customers. Today there are actually more banks than check-cashing businesses in Milwaukee's central city so it is difficult to interpret the survey response that pointed to proximity of the latter as one reason for their attraction. Perhaps residents are simply not aware of the banks that are serving their communities. In some cases, they may have their accounts with those banks that do not have a branch that is conveniently located. In any case, as part of a broader marketing effort, opening more branches and better advertising existing offices would bring more conventional banking services to these neighborhoods.

Banks might also reconsider some of their current eligibility rules for checking accounts. Where they find, for example, that a name is listed with Check Systems (the service utilized by many banks to check the financial background of some applicants for checking account eligibility, referred to above in footnote one), they might consider the circumstances surrounding that action and offer greater flexibility in applying their normal rules. A related step would be elimination of any initial deposit requirement.

However, marketing is only part of the answer; continued enforcement of the Community Reinvestment Act (CRA) and related nondiscrimination rules is critical. Under the CRA federally regulated depository institutions have an affirmative obligation to ascertain and be responsive to the credit needs of their entire service areas, including low- and moderate-income communities. Although this statute is directed primarily at mortgage lending activities, there are service requirements (as well as lending and investment requirements) that apply to covered institutions. Location of branch banks is one service-related factor. Similarly, refusal to provide service to neighborhoods due to their racial composition would constitute a violation of the Federal Fair Housing Act. Access to bank facilities is critical in order to be able to obtain basic services, like checking and savings accounts, just as it is essential to have fair access to mortgage loans. Where branch banks are open to serve the mortgage credit needs of residents, access to these basic banking services increases as well.

Compliance with the CRA and aggressive enforcement of fair lending laws by the Justice Department in recent years have stimulated new lending, more branch offices, and broader availability of basic banking services in distressed urban communities (U.S. General Accounting Office 1996). As indicated in previous chapters, nationwide the CRA has led to one trillion dollars in new lending and investment commitments while in Milwaukee CRA agreements generated more than $110 million in new loan commitments and the opening of three new branch banks in distressed markets (see chapter 9). Property values in Milwaukee's central city increased between 1994 and 1996 for the first time in twenty years and Milwaukee Mayor John Norquist pointed to collaborative activities on the part of community groups and lenders, encouraged by the CRA, as an important factor contributing to that turnaround (Derus 1997). Again, while these rules are directed primarily at mortgage lending activities, effective enforcement can also enhance access to all basic banking services.

The advent of electronic banking poses additional and complex policy issues. As more financial institutions replace brick and mortar offices with electronic services and as government agencies increasingly distribute benefits (e.g., paychecks, grants, pensions) electronically, the poor risk being even further locked out. Many may have to go to check-cashing services to obtain the funds they now receive from checks that are mailed directly to them that they can cash at banks for no charge. Some conventional financial institutions are affiliating with check cashers in part for the precise purpose of arranging for the transfer of benefits in this manner. Financial regulatory agencies must assure that the efficiencies gained by the electronic transfer of benefits do not become another mechanism for increasing the cost of financial services for the poor (Stegman 1999b).

The Poor Still Pay More

The poor have long paid more for most products and services (Caplovitz 1963). It should come as no surprise that they pay more for banking services today. But this is no recipe for urban revitalization.

A two-tiered banking system, just like the dual housing market, segregated school systems, and segmented labor markets, constitute critical institutionalized barriers confronting cities in their efforts to bring hope to their most depressed areas and revitalize metropolitan economies. "Empowerment" is a popular theme among policymakers of various political persuasions. Part of that process involves the provision of conventional banking services where fringe banking institutions have become a dominant factor.

Residents of distressed communities deserve better. The health of the nation's cities depends on it.

9

Organizing Access
to Capital

The Fair Lending Coalition
and Community Advocacy

A PIT BULL FOR FAIR LENDING: Fair Lending Project uses attack dog tactics to change lending trends." That is how a weekly busi ness newspaper in Milwaukee characterized the Fair Lending Coalition in a 1992 front page headline (Cooper 1991). (The organization changed its name from "Project" to "Coalition" in 1993.) The article described how aggressive community organizing led to the success of this multiracial, inner city coalition which to date has negotiated eleven community reinvestment agreements totaling over $160 million in commitments for new loans in previously redlined neighborhoods (City of Milwaukee [undated]). Founded in 1991, the coalition has relied on its own credibility as a diverse organization and its ability to work with other institutions throughout the metropolitan area to increase access to capital for residents of Milwaukee's inner city and racial minorities throughout the metropolitan area.

The Fair Lending Coalition consists of representatives of local churches, labor unions, civil rights and community-based advocacy groups, and others. Its board is approximately one-third black, one-third Hispanic, and one-third white. It has received strong support from city government, local foundations, and other philanthropic organizations. The media have often provided favorable support. The University of Wisconsin-Milwaukee (primarily, though not exclusively, through the authors of this book) has provided information through various research activities. With the support of diverse local actors, its primary tools have been two federal statutes (the Home Mortgage Disclosure Act or HMDA and the Community Reinvestment Act or CRA) enacted in response to a national community reinvestment movement. Collaboration, on several fronts, has contributed to concrete changes in the availability of credit in Milwaukee.

The Birth and Growth of the Fair Lending Coalition

Shortly after the *Atlanta Journal/Constitution* reported in 1989 (Dedman 1989) that blacks were rejected twice as often as whites in their mortgage loan applications, the Democratic mayor of Milwaukee and the Republican governor of Wisconsin assembled a Fair Lending Action Committee (FLAC) consisting of lenders, regulators, civil rights groups, researchers, and others (including the lead author of this book) to develop recommendations for closing Milwaukee's racial gap. After two years of discussion and a report proposing several procedural reforms, but little evidence of implementation of these reforms or changes in lending practices, frustration grew within Milwaukee's minority community. Two veteran community organizers (along with Squires) concluded that the missing link in Milwaukee's reinvestment effort was an independent organization that had the capacity to utilize the recently enacted federal legislation to "encourage" community reinvestment. Such an entity would complement voluntary initiatives that in fact would soon follow.

In 1991 representatives of several community groups in Milwaukee and the university drafted a proposal that would fund both the research and organizing capacity to permit ongoing, independent monitoring of lending activity and, where appropriate, the filing of challenges under the CRA. A local union provided the first small grant and a local nonprofit organization provided office space. The City of Milwaukee and the Milwaukee Foundation then provided funds to hire an executive director and carry out the essential research. Later that year the coalition was born.

Collaboration between the Fair Lending Coalition
and the University

The Fair Lending Coalition has pursued a fairly straightforward strategy. Each year university faculty and staff prepare a set of tables based on the most current HMDA reports. These tables provide, for each HMDA reporting institution, the number and dollar volume of mortgage loans (in absolute numbers and percentages of each institution's total lending), which went to economically distressed census tracts (the City's Target Area) and to racial and ethnic minorities throughout the area: Hispanics, American Indians, and Asians, as well as whites. Application rejection rates are also reported for each racial group by income level.

When lenders file applications with their regulatory agencies, a cursory review of their lending record is performed by coalition staff. Where an applicant reports lending activity substantially below industry-wide averages, additional information is sought. Comparisons with other institutions are utilized to minimize criticisms that low levels of lending to low-income areas or minority groups are accounted for simply by the association between these particular demographic characteristics and credit or financial related problems. Clearly, racial and economic lending disparities can be accounted for in part by economic considerations that safe and sound lending must take into consideration. But if other lending institutions are serving these communities, or at least are doing so more extensively than a given institution, it raises a question of whether or not the racial or income disparities of that institution pose problems that can be remedied. Since individual loan files are not available to the general public, unlawful discrimination is difficult to prove on the basis of HMDA data and other public sources of information. But to the extent that lending disparities are industry-wide phenomena, comparing an individual lender to an industry-wide average constitutes a conservative approach. That is, individual lenders are being compared on the basis of a standard that already reflects significant disparities if not unlawful discrimination. Where substantial differences are found between the record of a particular institution and the industry average, a visit is often made to the lender.

While visiting the institution information is taken from the CRA files, lenders are asked for copies of their underwriting guidelines (which they do not have to make public but they occasionally provide), locations of other branches are identified, recent CRA evaluations and responses to them by the lender are collected, and other

information is solicited. Lenders have generally been quite coopera-
tive in responding to these informational requests.

At this point coalition staff examine the quantitative and qualitative
evidence to decide if a challenge is warranted. The information is then
presented to the Board for a final decision. If the decision is to go
forward, coalition staff prepare the challenge, generally a five- to ten-
page statement identifying deficiencies in the institution's lending
record.

Five challenges have resulted in successful negotiation of eleven
reinvestment agreements. (Six lenders contacted the coalition and
voluntarily initiated discussions that resulted in signed agreements.)
Each has been a five-year program with commitments for new loans
totaling over $160 million in mortgage and small business loans. In
addition to the loan commitments, each agreement has specific provisions in which the lenders agreed to some or all of the following
actions: creation or expansion of basic or lifeline banking services for
low-income residents (e.g., free or low-cost checking accounts, cashing
government checks), implementation of an affirmative action program
to increase the number of minority employees, expansion of their
contracting for goods and services with minority-owned firms, and in
three cases lenders agreed to open a new branch in the central city.
Each of those branch offices is currently open for business.

While aggressive organizing and intensive research are two critical
elements to these reinvestment agreements, other actors are also essential. In addition to providing financial support, the mayor has openly
criticized local lenders for their failure to meet their responsibilities
under the law and has praised the work of the coalition. Good relationships have been developed with the local media which have provided substantial and positive coverage of coalition activities. And
volunteers who are drawn from all parts of the city have effectively
negotiated and monitored the agreements.

The impact of these organizing efforts can be illustrated by comparing the performance of those lenders who have entered into reinvestment agreements with other institutions. The increase in lending to
blacks, Hispanics and the Target Area on the part of the eleven financial
institutions that entered into lending agreements with the Fair Lending
Coalition equaled or exceeded the industry average. Between 1990 and
1997 lenders with CRA agreements increased the proportion of home
purchase loans to blacks by 1.9 percent which was also the industry
average. And loans to Hispanics increased 2.5 percent among lenders
with CRA agreements compared to no increase for all lenders. For the
Target Area comparable increases were 0.7 and 0.3 (see table 9.1).

Table 9.1 Home Purchase Loans by Lenders with CRA Agreements and with All Other Lenders, 1990 and 1997

	1990			1997			Change between 1990 and 1997		
	Percent Black	*Percent Hispanic*	*Percent Target Area*	*Percent Black*	*Percent Hispanic*	*Percent Target Area*	*Percent Black*	*Percent Hispanic*	*Percent Target Area*
Lenders with CRA Agreements	6.3	2.2	2.4	8.2	4.7	3.1	+ 1.9	+ 2.5	+ 0.7
All Lenders	5.5	1.9	2.9	7.4	2.9	3.2	+ 1.9	0.0	+ 0.3

SOURCE: 1990 and 1997 HMDA

A Win-Win Situation

Several individuals and groups, and indeed the city generally, have benefited from these activities. Local lenders have benefited from the additional business found in areas they previously had not adequately served. No doubt, their involvement with the coalition also aided them in the CRA examinations conducted by their respective regulatory agencies. The city of Milwaukee also gained from the additional branch banks and loan dollars that have been and will continue to be made available in economically distressed areas.

Obviously, these changes cannot be attributed solely to the coalition. During these years lenders launched a number of programs on their own and in collaboration with others to reach these markets. Lenders and several community organizations began mortgage counseling programs for first-time homebuyers. Much of this activity reflects the efforts of one particular coalition noted in previous chapters, New Opportunities for Homeownership in Milwaukee (NOHIM). And the Milwaukee efforts both reflect and reinforce a nationwide community reinvestment movement that has resulted in $1 trillion in new loan commitments in approximately 360 agreements across the nation since the CRA was enacted (Silver 1999).

Coalition and Collaboration: Keys to Success

If there is a single key to the achievements of the Fair Lending Coalition it is the collaborative nature of the operation. The credibility of the coalition begins with the broadly representative nature of its board and supporting volunteers. That credibility is enhanced by the research services of the university. Basically, the Fair Lending Coalition has the facts. The collaborative nature of the operation is also evident in the Coalition's external relations. City government, the local media, private foundations, and other institutions and individuals have played vital roles.

There is an interactive dimension to these internal and external characteristics. Outside groups support the coalition because of the representative nature of its board and the factual base of its operation. The coalition, in turn, is doing work that serves the interests of these other organizations and individuals.

The Fair Lending Coalition is a multilegged stool. Remove one of the legs and the entire structure becomes less stable. At the same time, each piece is strengthened by its association with the whole. Research, in the absence of effective organizing, would become little more than an academic exercise. And the organizing, without a strong research foundation, would be far less effective. Obviously, financial support from public and private sources facilitates the entire operation, which in turn makes at least a small contribution to the health and stability of the community in which all these actors live.

The Fair Lending Coalition has had an impact on community reinvestment efforts in Milwaukee. But it has been less aggressive at the end of the decade that it was during the mid 1990s. Structural changes that have occurred in the industry, and more dramatic changes that may soon occur in the way financial services are provided and regulated, pose serious challenges to the Community Reinvestment Act and community reinvestment activities generally, as will be discussed in the final chapter. Saul Alinsky once observed there are no permanent friends and no permanent enemies. Some lenders who previously fought reinvestment activities are now among the strongest supporters. However, with a change in administrations government agencies might not be as supportive. Foundation priorities shift. Newspaper editorial perspectives evolve. It appears that the success of reinvestment efforts in Milwaukee and other urban communities will continue to depend on aggressive organizing. Such organizing must encompass both challenges to the behavior of financial institutions and their regulatory agencies as well as effective partnerships with those same entities. Achieving and maintaining fair access to capital is unlikely to occur in any other way.

10

The Uncertain Future of Community Reinvestment

ESIDENTS OF MILWAUKEE'S LOW-INCOME communities account for approximately 12 percent of all households in the metropolitan area and in 1997 they received just over 4 percent of all mortgage loans and 2 percent of loan dollars. Blacks also account for close to 12 percent of all households and they received just over 7 percent of all loans and 3 percent of loan dollars. Hispanics account for almost 3 percent of households and they received just over 2 percent of all loans and 1 percent of all loan dollars. Each of these gaps has closed during the 1990s. But significant disparities persist.

Obviously, financial institutions are not solely responsible for these differences. Geographic variations in the quality of schools, discrimination in labor markets, unevenness in the quality of public services, other actors in the housing market, and many other factors contribute to variations in the credit-worthiness of mortgage loan applicants. At the same time, however, lenders do not always respond the same way to similarly situated borrowers from different communities. And the vagaries of public policy influence the responsiveness of financial institutions. Clearly the opportunity structure of urban communities for

171

financial services, and other goods and services, reflects cumulative causation (Galster 1998). But financial institutions are critical actors. Lenders, their regulatory agencies, community advocacy groups, and consumers all have roles to play in determining the extent to which community reinvestment proceeds in the future.

Barriers to Reinvestment

If there has been progress on the community reinvestment front in Milwaukee and around the nation, the proverbial dark clouds are on the horizon. The Community Reinvestment Act, which most observers agree has been critical to any success, is under constant attack. Legislation has routinely been introduced in Congress calling for a "safe harbor" (e.g., immunity from CRA challenges) for institutions with "Satisfactory" or better CRA ratings, which would include 98 percent of all lenders in 1998, up from 87 percent in 1987 (Woodstock Institute 1998). Small bank exemptions are also frequently proposed. Depending on the definition of a small business, such proposals could exclude up to 85 percent of all covered lenders (Bradford and Cincotta 1992: 267). Other proposals would permit comment on bank applications only at the time the CRA evaluation is conducted. Some have proposed that lenders be able to "self-certify" their compliance with the CRA. Elimination of the disparate impact standard of the Fair Housing Act has been offered (Silver 1999). While no serious public effort has yet been launched to eliminate CRA altogether, the direction of most proposals is evident; less is more. And with the bank modernization bill that did pass in 1999, some provisions of CRA have been rolled back.

Lenders, sometimes through their trade associations, have begun to organize in opposition to community reinvestment and fair lending initiatives. Following the Chevy Chase settlement, the Savings and Community Bankers of America—a trade association representing thrifts and banks—created a $100,000 war chest to fight at least some fair lending enforcement actions. These funds will be used to defend selected institutions and may also be used to support research, public relations campaigns, or a friend-of-the-court brief as part of an advocacy campaign (Meredith 1994). Edward L. Yingling, the chief lobbyist for the American Bankers Association, recently stated, "We've gone from a decade in which the consumer activists were really able to push their legislative agenda to a point where they not only can't push forward but we can begin pushing back" (Garsson and de Senerpont Domis 1994).

More recently the chairman of the Senate Banking Committee stated that under the CRA, "We have had rampant extortion, fraud, and kickbacks," claiming neighborhood groups use the law to shake down banks for loans (Dodge and Power 1998). The chairman, Republican Senator Phil Gramm of Texas likened CRA proponents to the Mafia and said the rules were "an evil like slavery in the pre-Civil War era" (Wayne 1998). Gramm has called for the Federal Reserve to conduct a study in which financial institutions could testify, in confidence, about the prevalence of such activities and he has considered holding hearings on proposed revisions of the law.

Finally, and for the first time since the CRA was enacted in 1977, Congress did enact legislation that rolled back its authority. Arguing that international competitiveness and maximum efficiency, ultimately for the benefit of consumers, require financial service providers to be able to offer banking, insurance, securities, and other services under one roof, financial service providers lobbied Congress for more than twenty years to repeal the Glass-Steagall Act and other post-Depression-era legislation that prohibited such integration. In 1999 Congress enacted and the president signed the Financial Services Modernization Act permitting banks, insurers, and securities firms to more freely enter each others' business. Such conglomeration had been proceeding piecemeal through various regulatory exemptions and loopholes under previous law. Now financial institutions will be able to more freely offer a range of services to their customers.

There are many potential dangers to this path. Opponents have expressed concern for the safety and soundness of at least some of the financial service companies that such legislation would permit. One basic fear is that subsidiaries of a holding company would engage in something other than "arms length" transactions when lending to, insuring, or otherwise financing another arm of that corporation, thus weakening the financial status of that subsidiary or even the entire holding company. Such "crony capitalism" or any number of other developments could lead to more institutions being viewed as "too big to fail" resulting in more taxpayers' subsidized bailouts similar to the estimated $180 billion bailout of savings and loans in the 1980s. A related consumer concern is that current prohibitions against "tying" where in order to obtain one financial service a customer would have to agree to purchase others from that company, would be weakened (Bush 1999).

A more direct CRA-related concern is the enhanced opportunity for such providers to shift assets out of institutions covered by the law into those entities (e.g., independent mortgage companies, insurers) not currently covered (Bush 1999; Taylor 1999a). In fact, institutions that traditionally provided for the vast majority of mortgage loans—savings and commercial banks which are covered by the CRA—now make less than half of such loans (Fiechter 1994: 7). One possible response would have been to establish CRA or CRA-like requirements for all providers of financial services, or at least to the lending activities of these firms, resulting in a level playing field that would not disadvantage the federally regulated depository institutions that are now the focus of the law. Instead, the law weakens the CRA requirements for those institutions to which it does apply.

Under the new law small banks, those with assets below $250 million, will be examined once every five years if they have an "Outstanding" rating and once every four years if they have a "Satisfactory" rating. Under previous rules they were examined every two years. A so-called "sunshine" provision requires lenders and community groups engaged in reinvestment agreements to file with the regulatory agency supervising the lender a report of the terms of their agreements and annual statements on how the funds are utilized. This will have a chilling effect on the desire of either community groups or lenders to form such partnerships in part because some lenders do not want their competitors to know all the details of their marketing plans (Taylor 1999b). The extent to which the CRA has been harmed by these changes can be debated. More significant than these particular changes, however, is the fact that, for the first time in more than twenty years of effort to do so, the CRA has been weakened, and no doubt Congress will consider further CRA "reforms" in the near future.

Another closely related threat to community reinvestment is the wave of consolidation and merger activity among financial institutions that preceded bank reform and no doubt will be encouraged by that legislation. The decline in the number of banks, mergers involving mortgage lenders and insurers, and the new legal environment that will encourage mergers previously prohibited by law, raise questions about commitments to community reinvestment.

The number of banks in the United States has declined from almost 20,000 in 1970 to 9,100 by the end of 1997. While some of this decline was due to bank failures, most of this decline is accounted for by mergers among healthy institutions (Bradford and Cincotta 1992: 261; Meyer 1998b). Milwaukee has not been immune from this trend. In 1997 the area's largest savings bank, First Financial, was taken over by the Green Bay-based Associated Bank Corporation (*Business Journal* 1998: 66). And in 1998 the largest bank holding company, Firstar

Corporation, announced that it would be taken over by the Cincinnati-based Star Banc Corporation (*Business Journal* 1998: 69).

The merger of Citicorp Bank and Travelers Insurance to form Citigroup, resulting in a $750 billion corporation engaged in banking, insurance, and securities, raised concerns to a new level both because of the scope of the entities involved and the diversity of financial services that will be offered under one roof. In fact, some claimed the merger was illegal under banking law at the time of the merger (Seiberg 1998).

Interestingly, many of the institutions currently engaged in mega-mergers have made unilateral CRA pledges for what appear to be substantial commitments. Citicorp and Travelers announced a $115 billion commitment to low-income and minority communities over the next ten years. Nationsbank and Bank America topped this when they announced a $350 billion commitment as part of their merger plans. But it is difficult to know what these large, national commitments actually mean. These announcements were made without any prior research and planning by, or discussions with neighborhood groups. Precisely what counts in these commitments and how these pledges relate to previous lending practices (that is, do they represent an increase in community reinvestment and, if so, how much) remain unclear. And mechanisms for monitoring and evaluation are unclear. For example, these commitments sometimes include credit card debt and loans to wealthy nonwhite households. Community groups in the local communities where these dollars may go would not necessarily view these commitments as responding to current needs (O'Brien 1998).

Milwaukee has experienced something like this in the recent past. In 1993 a coalition of inner-city churches (Milwaukee Innercity Congregations Allied for Hope—MICAH) and eight local lenders announced a $500 million, five-year loan commitment. But the requisite homework was not done. A closer inspection of the previous lending records of these institutions revealed that this "commitment" would actually amount to a lower level of lending than these institutions had provided in prior years (Norman 1993; Squires 1993). One lender conceded, "The dollars we pledged are the amounts we were asked to by MICAH. Maybe MICAH didn't seize the negotiating advantage they had. They could have squeezed more" (Norman 1993). Not surprisingly, over the next few years the lenders frequently and proudly announced that they were well ahead of meeting their MICAH goals.

The advent of electronic banking poses potential problems. Lenders are reducing their reliance on brick and mortar branch offices and tellers or real people at various levels to provide basic banking services.

Increasingly they utilize telephones, stored-value or "smart" cards, computers, and the internet to provide depository, bill paying, lending, and other services. More employers provide paychecks electronically and government agencies are increasingly distributing various benefits (e.g., grants, pensions, welfare payments) electronically as well. Low-income and minority households, which are less likely to be "wired," run even greater risks of being locked out of traditional banking services as this trend develops, as it no doubt will (Stegman 1999a).

Other problems, some longstanding and others relatively new, threaten community reinvestment initiatives. Racial steering and other discriminatory practices remain facts of life with black and Hispanic homeseekers encountering some form of unlawful discrimination in approximately half their encounters with real estate agents (Fix and Struyk 1992; Yinger 1999). Property insurance discrimination has been documented in cities across the nation with three of the nation's six largest insurance companies (Allstate, State Farm and Nationwide) settling fair housing complaints since 1995 following the pathbreaking settlement with American Family Mutual Insurance Company in Milwaukee that year (Squires 1997). Arbitrary and discriminatory appraisal practices persist undercutting property values in minority areas. In a project carried out by the Cleveland Federal Reserve Bank, one property in that city was valued at $36,000 by one appraiser and $83,500 by another (Pittinger 1996; Appraisal Process Task Group 1994). Each of these practices makes it more difficult for minorities and residents of low-income areas to build financial assets, qualify for mortgage loans, and become homeowners.

Predatory lending, another longstanding practice, has increasingly caught the attention of consumer organizations, fair housing advocates, and law enforcement agencies in recent years. "Reverse redlining" whereby lenders provide lower rates through one banking arm in white communities and higher rates through another subsidiary in nonwhite communities, points and other fees that far exceed the risk involved, negative or nonamortizing loans where borrowers end up owing more than the original loan amount, and many other practices have been documented that exploit minority and low-income markets, thus recreating the dual housing finance markets that prevailed twenty-five years ago (Peattie 1998; Saunders 1998; U.S. Department of the Treasury 2000). These practices are actually worse than the refusal to provide service. Families subject to these practices frequently find themselves in homes they cannot afford and ultimately lose their homes along with the life savings they have invested in them.

One indication of the increasing level of predatory lending is the growth in subprime lending. Subprime loans carry higher costs than conventional loans and are generally targeted at potential buyers with credit problems. No doubt to some extent such practices make credit available to borrowers who would not otherwise be able to borrow money. But the line between legitimate risk-based pricing and predatory lending is often crossed. In the Milwaukee metropolitan area subprime lenders doubled their share of the refinancing market in just one year; from 6.1 percent to 12.7 percent between 1996 and 1997. In low- and moderate-income areas their share grew from 13.6 percent to 25.2 percent. And among minority borrowers their share increased from 22.6 percent to 44.1 percent (Kamp 1999).

The advent of new technological tools has also generated controversy. Credit scoring and automated underwriting are increasingly used by mortgage lenders. With credit scoring lenders use credit reports to determine certain cut-off points to determine who is automatically eligible and who requires a second look. Automated underwriting involves the utilization of credit scores and other information about borrowers and the properties they want to purchase in the development of computer-generated models for assessing eligibility. Lenders maintain these practices allow them to process many more applications, and to do so in a more scientific, unbiased manner (Fannie Mae undated; Fair, Isaac and Company 1997). Others are not so sure. Concerns are raised regarding the inaccuracy of many credit reports. Since the factors that go into the models are generally confidential, it is not clear if each variable in fact reflects ability to repay or if nontraditional credit-related variables are excluded that would enhance the credit record of minorities. Even if no discrimination is intended, some models could have a disparate impact on minorities. And questions remain regarding what happens to those who have borderline scores (Fishbein 1996).

Barriers persist. Challenges remain. But they need not be prohibitive.

Fighting Back, Again

"Community organizing has been the driving force of the reinvestment movement from the beginning," according to two of the movement's pioneers, Calvin Bradford and Gale Cincotta (1992: 235). This remains true today. As they go on to observe, "At any given point, a legislator, an agency official, or some government agency can play an important part in an issue or policy; but over the long haul, community reinvestment remains a movement determined by people power" (Bradford and Cincotta 1992: 270). They quote one of their colleagues, Shel Trapp, who in his book *Blessed Be the Fighters* offered the following observation:

> "Confrontation was good for the '60s, but this is the . . . age of partnerships." That really sounds great, but the basis of partnership is equality and respect. My experience in the '60s, '70s, and '80s has been that while we are willing to form partnerships with anyone who is willing to come to the table and seriously discuss the issues, I have not seen too many of our opponents come to the table willingly. . . . Partnerships are great as long as there is mutual respect. Community organizations usually have to fight to get that respect. It reminds me of the story of the farmer who was asked why he hit his mule over the head with a two-by-four. His response was, "That is just to get his attention." In all the partnerships we formed, we first had to get the attention of our opponents. Translated, that means we've had to confront them. (Trapp 1986: 13–14)

No doubt, Shel Trapp would echo these sentiments for the new millennium.

An immediate focus of this struggle is the Community Reinvestment Act itself. This law was enacted as a result of community organizing, it has been neighborhood based activity that has fought off several efforts to dilute it, and no doubt such "people power" will be essential to preserve it. But community organizations, alone, are unlikely to preserve and build upon the fragile victories that have been won. They need partners.

In recent years local officials in Milwaukee and elsewhere have been critical to the success of grassroots organizations. The U.S. Department of Justice has negotiated vital settlements. Local and national media have kept these issues alive. Research by supportive academics has assisted many efforts, though as Shel Trapp noted, "Expecting research without organizing to accomplish something is like expecting a eunuch to become a father. It just doesn't work" (Trapp 1986: 14–15). The changing attitudes and behavior of some lenders have lent support. But it is depressingly clear that the struggle for community reinvestment is far from over.

The wide and persisting gaps in Milwaukee and elsewhere, despite the very real gains that have been achieved, are all too painful reminders of the work that remains. It is unlikely that we will return to the days of racially restrictive covenants and overt racial discrimination and redlining. But it cannot be assumed that the future will bring nothing but progress.

The value of such organizing efforts is reflected in a comparison of the performance of those lenders who have entered into reinvestment agreements with other institutions. As indicated in the first chapter, nationwide there is evidence that those who have negotiated CRA agreements with community groups are lending more to low-income and minority communities (Schwartz 1998). And the previous chapter demonstrated that the same pattern holds in Milwaukee. The eleven financial institutions that entered into lending agreements with the Fair Lending Coalition increased their lending to nonwhites and to the city's Target Area to a greater extent than the industry as a whole in the Milwaukee metropolitan area.

No outcome is preordained. What will happen in the future depends on decisions that real, live people make; decisions that will be the aftermath of continued, contentious political debate. Hopefully that debate will be informed by careful research documenting what is happening in the marketplace (with Shel Trapp's proviso securely in mind) and not just by the passive acceptance of policy statements and unilateral, unaccountable pledges.

Far more remains to be learned on a number of issues. In terms of the structure of the financial services industry it remains unclear how size of institutions, the trend towards consolidation and absentee ownership, the advent of electronic banking and the declining significance of brick-and-mortar branch offices, and relationships with community groups affect lending. The impact of each of these structural characteristics of lending institutions on the number and share of loans to low-income and minority markets needs to be more thoroughly examined. Chapter 7 found that institutions employing relatively more racial minorities were more likely to approve loan applications from minority borrowers. But it remains unclear if lenders with more branch offices in low-income communities do a better job of serving those communities. Do small lenders do better because of their intimate knowledge of their communities or do large lenders have more sophisticated underwriting, pricing, and marketing practices that enable them to better serve distressed areas? Similarly it remains unclear if multi-state institutions fare better or worse than institutions that are headquartered in and serve just one community. If lenders that have solid working relationships with community groups serve those areas better, the cause remains unclear. Is it the knowledge of the lending institutions that enable them to market their products better, the endorsement of a trusted local church which encourages residents to seek out those lenders, or some other set of dynamics that accounts for the performance?

New loan products are being introduced often requiring lower downpayments, mortgage insurance costs, and other fees. The impact on community reinvestment and the safety and soundness of the providers needs to be examined. Also, questions remain as to what extent, if any, unqualified buyers are encouraged to make a purchase they ultimately cannot afford, resulting in default and loss of their investment and substantial savings.

A key issue that has been virtually unexamined is the potential discriminatory impact from various pricing practices. As more lenders utilize risk-based pricing and create subprime products and institutions, will more people be able to obtain credit albeit at higher prices or will predatory lending grow resulting in some paying unfairly high interest rates, points, and related fees? Currently no cost data are available from HMDA. Consequently, cost data are available only from loan files which are available to regulators and litigants, but not the general public. If some measure of cost (e.g., interest rate, points) were added to HMDA, much more would be known about variations in this critical feature of loan products.

Lenders and regulators are developing new investigative tools and they need to be evaluated. Credit scoring, automated underwriting, and risk-based pricing may offer certain efficiencies, but possibly at the expense of fair lending. Far more remains to be learned about the impact of such technological developments.

Change may be the only constant in financial services. The better informed, the more effective these changes can be for all parties involved. The potential for win-win scenarios to play out in communities throughout the country exists. Hypersegregation and disinvestment serve the interests of a privileged few, and perhaps nobody in the long run. Balanced development across communities and equitable treatment of all residents is in virtually everyone's interest. Whether this vision will prevail remains to be determined.

Notes

Chapter 5

1. The methodology employed in this report is a slightly modified version of the methodology utilized by the National Community Reinvestment Coalition (1996) in its report *America's Worst Lenders*.

2. HMDA reports do not include loans made through the Wisconsin Housing and Economic Authority (WHEDA—a state affiliated organization that provides financial resources to stimulate and preserve affordable housing and small business lending) but which are effectively originated by conventional lenders. WHEDA mortgage loans accounted for 2.6 percent of all loans in the Milwaukee metropolitan area in 1996 (City of Milwaukee 1998: 5, 29-44; Federal Financial Institutions Examination Council 1996b). Although some lenders may have been ranked differently on some measures if WHEDA loans were included, the changes were likely small. For example, TCF Bank ranked first in the proportion of loans in the Target Area with or without the inclusion of WHEDA loans. Associated Bank ranked sixteenth or last with just 0.7 percent of its HMDA loans in the Target Area. Including WHEDA loans Associated ranked fifteenth with 1.3 percent of its loans in the Target Area compared to 1.1 percent for Norwest Bank.

3. In order to test the reliability of these variables or the extent to which each variable measures the same underlying phenomenon, the Chronbach's alpha statistic was calculated. When this statistic reaches a level of .70 or greater it is generally assumed that the variables on which the statistic was calculated are each multiple measures of the same phenomenon. In this case the alpha is .81, indicating that these rankings reflects multiple measures of community reinvestment activity.

Chapter 8

1. The *Business Week* cover story "Two Tier Marketing" described the emergence of a bifurcating system that is emerging across several industries

182 Notes

where "retailers are selling to 'two Americas' divided along economic lines" (Leonhardt 1997, 2). The story analyzed how the polarization of income in the 1990s has caused many retailers to develop a dual marketing strategy—one at the high end and one at the low end—and move away from a longstanding approach of appealing to one broad middle class of consumers.

2. Information on services offered, requirements to qualify for those services, charges and other fees, and hours of operation for banks and check-cashing outlets was obtained from telephone interviews with employees of each bank and personal visits to each check-cashing business during the fall of 1996.

Although some banks do offer virtually free checking accounts, they solicit information on customers' previous banking history. In those cases where there is a history of problems, such as the cashing of a series of checks where there are insufficient funds in the account to cover them, banks often submit those names to a nationwide service known as Check Systems. Similarly banks frequently consult Check Systems to verify whether or not a potential customer has been listed by another institution. While the guidelines among banks differ, once a person has been listed with Check Systems—for whatever reason—it is unlikely that such an individual would be able to obtain an account with any bank.

3. The formula used to determine the effective rate of interest is:

$$i = (1+r)^m - 1$$

where i = effective rate of interest
r = interest rate for a given period
m = number of pay periods
(Kellison 1970, 16)

(Since "i" is computed in decimal form multiplying by 100 will convert the number to a percentage.)

The large difference in the effective annual rate of interest in these examples is explained by the difference in both the interest rate for a given period, e.g., *20 percent* at one check cashing business and *1.5 percent* at a credit card company, and the frequency with which interest is paid, e.g., *bi-weekly* for the check cashing business and *monthly* for the credit card business. Compounding by 20 percent every two weeks will result in a far greater effective annual interest rate than compounding at 1.5 percent every month.

For example, if someone borrows $10 at 20 percent interest for two weeks, after the first two weeks the person owes the original $10 plus $2 in interest. If the new balance of $12 remains unpaid at the end of the next two-week period then 20 percent is added to the $12 making the new balance $14.40. By the end of only eight weeks the effective interest will have reached over 100 percent.

If, on the other hand, someone borrows $10 at 1.5 percent interest per month then after the first month the person owes the original $10 plus $.15 in interest. If the new balance of $10.15 is unpaid at the end of the following month and 1.5 percent is added then the new balance is $10.30. This makes the effective rate of interest after two months only 3 percent compared with over 100 percent when the rate is 20 percent every two weeks.

Bibliography

American Family Insurance Companies. Undated. "The People Plan," 1–4.

Anderson, Elijah. 1999. *Code of the Street: Decency, Violence, and the Moral Life of the Inner City.* New York: W. W. Norton.

Ando, Faith. 1988. "Capital Issues and Minority-Owned Business." *Review of Black Political Economy* 16 (4): 77–109.

Appraisal Process Task Group. 1994. Report of the Appraisal Process Task Group, a subcommittee of the Residential Housing and Mortgage Credit Project of the Federal Reserve Bank of Cleveland (June 1).

Bates, Timothy. 1989. "Small Business Viability in the Urban Ghetto." *Journal of Regional Science* 29 (4): 625–643.

———. 1997. "Unequal Access: Financial Institution Lending to Black- and White-Owned Small Business Start-ups." *Journal of Urban Affairs* 19 (4): 487–495.

Benston, George J. 1997. "Discrimination in Mortgage Lending: Why HMDA and CRA Should Be Repealed." *Journal of Retail Banking Services* XIX (3): 47–57.

Binder, John. 1992. "An Analysis of CE Check Cashing Rates and the Proposed Decrease in the Maximum Rate for Government Checks." (August 10). Cited in Erin Mullen, Malcolm Bush, and Samantha Weinstein (1997). "Currency Exchanges Add to Poverty Surcharge for Low-Income Residents." Chicago: Woodstock Institute.

Black, Harold, M. Cary Collins, and Ken Cyree. 1997. "Do Black Owned Banks Discriminate against Black Borrowers?" *Journal of Real Estate Finance and Economics* 11: 189–204.

Blanchflower, David G., Phillip B. Levine, and David J. Zimmerman. 1998. "Discrimination in the Small Business Credit Market." National Bureau of Economic Research Working Paper No. 6840.

Board of Governors of the Federal Reserve System. 1996. *82nd Annual Report 1995.* Washington, DC: Board of Governors of the Federal Reserve System.

Bostic, Raphael W. and Glenn B. Canner. 1998. "New Information on Lending to Small Businesses and Small Farms: The 1996 CRA Data." *Federal Reserve Bulletin* 84 (1): 1–21.

Bradbury, Katherine L., Karl E. Case, and Constance R. Dunham. 1989. "Geographic Patterns of Mortgage Lending in Boston, 1982–1987." *New England Economic Review* (Sept./Oct.): 3–30.

Bradford, Calvin. 1979. "Financing Home Ownership—The Federal Role in Neighborhood Decline." *Urban Affairs Quarterly* 14 (3): 313–335.

Bradford, Calvin and Gale Cincotta. 1992. "The Legacy, The Promise, and the Unfinished Agenda." In Gregory D. Squires, ed., *From Redlining to Reinvestment: Community Responses to Urban Disinvestment.* Philadelphia: Temple University Press.

Bush, Malcolm. 1999. "The Challenges to Community Reinvestment from Bank Modernization." Memo prepared for the Woodstock Institute (February 5).

Business Journal. 1998. *Book of Lists.* Milwaukee: *Business Journal.*

Calomiris, Charles W., Charles M. Kahn, and Stanley D. Longhofer. 1994. Housing Finance Intervention and Private Incentives: Helping Minorities and the Poor. *Journal of Money, Credit and Banking* 26 (August): 634–674.

Canner, Glenn B. and Dolores S. Smith. 1992. "Expanded HMDA Data on Residential Lending: One Year Later." *Federal Reserve Bulletin* (November): 801–824.

Caplovitz, David. 1963. *The Poor Pay More; Consumer Practices of Low-Income Families.* New York: Free Press.

Carr, James H. and Isaac F. Megbolugbe. 1993. "The Federal Reserve Bank of Boston Study on Mortgage Lending Revisited." Office of Housing Research, Federal National Mortgage Association.

Caskey, John P. 1994. *Fringe Banking: Check-Cashing Outlets, Pawnshops, and the Poor.* New York: Russell Sage Foundation.

———. 1997. *Lower-Income Americans, Higher-Cost Financial Services.* Madison, WI: Filene Research Institute Center for Credit Union Research.

Causey, James E. 1999. "Neighbors Cheer Legacy Bank's Arrival." *Milwaukee Journal Sentinel* (August 2).

Cavalluzzo, Ken S., Linda C. Cavalluzzo, and John D. Wolken. 1999. "Competition, Small Business Financing, and Discrimination: Evidence from a New Survey." Paper presented at conference on "Business Access to Capital and Credit." Federal Reserve System, Arlington, VA (March 8).

Census of Housing and Population. 1990. Summary Tape File 3 on CD ROM (Wisconsin) prepared by U.S. Bureau of the Census, Washington, DC 1992.

City of Milwaukee. 1996. *Annual Review of Lending Practices of Financial Institutions.* Milwaukee: Office of the Comptroller, City of Milwaukee.

———. 1998. "Annual Review of Lending Practices of Financial Institutions." Milwaukee: City Comptroller.

———. Undated. *Fair Housing Impediments Study.* Milwaukee: Community Development Block Grant Administration: 49.

Cloud, Cathy and George Galster. 1993. "What Do We Know about Racial Discrimination in Mortgage Markets?" *Review of Black Political Economy* 22 (1): 101–120.

Coleman, Jonathan. 1997. *Long Way to Go: Black and White in America.* New York: Atlantic Monthly Press.

Conta and Associates, Inc. 1990. "A Study to Identify Discriminatory Practices in the Milwaukee Construction Marketplace." Milwaukee: Conta and Associates, Inc.

Cooper, Geoff. 1991. "A Pit Bull for Milwaukee's Central City: Fair Lending Project Uses Attack-Dog Tactics to Change Lending Trends." *Business Journal* (September 23).

Coulton, Claudia J., Julian Chow, Edward C. Wang, and Marilyn Su. 1996. "Geographic Concentration of Affluence and Poverty in 100 Metropolitan Areas, 1990." *Urban Affairs Review* 32 (2): 186–216.

Cummings, Scott, ed. 1988. *Business Elites and Urban Development: Case Studies and Critical Perspectives.* Albany: State University of New York Press.

Darity Jr., William A. and Patrick L. Mason. 1998. "Evidence on Discrimination in Employment: Codes of Color, Codes of Gender." *Journal of Economic Perspectives* 12 (2): 63–90.

Dedman, Bill. 1998. "Racial Bias Seen in U.S. Housing Loan Program." *New York Times* (May 13).

———. 1989. "Blacks Turned Down for Home Loans from S & Ls Twice As Often As Whites." *Atlanta Journal-Constitution* (January 22).

Denton, Nancy A. 1999. "Half Empty or Half Full: Segregation and Segregated Neighborhoods Thirty Years after the Fair Housing Act." *Cityscape* 4 (3): 107–122.

Derus, Michele. 1997. "Central City Home Values Rebound." *Milwaukee Journal Sentinel* (February 10).

"Discrimination in the Housing and Mortgage Markets." 1992. Special issue of *Housing Policy Debate* 3 (2): i–745.

Dodge, Robert and Stephen Power. 1998. "Gramm Takes Shot at CRA—Kirk Fights Back." *Dallas Morning News* (November 5).

Elverman, Tim. 1998. Personal interview with Sally O'Connor (October 27).

Evanoff, Douglas D. and Lewis M. Segal. 1996. "CRA and Fair Lending Regulations: Resulting Trends in Mortgage Lending." *Economic Perspectives* (Federal Reserve Bank of Chicago) XX (6): 19–46.

Everett, David, John Gallagher, and Teresa Blossom. 1988. "The Race for Money," *Detroit Free Press* (July 24–27).

Fair, Isaac and Company. 1997. "Credit Bureau Scores in Mortgage Lending: Strategies for Improving Operations." San Rafael, CA: Fair, Isaac and Company.

Fair Lending Action Committee. 1989. "Equal Access to Mortgage Lending: The Milwaukee Plan." Report to Mayor John Norquist and Governor Tommy G. Thompson.

Fannie Mae. 1999. "Fannie Mae Offers New Options." Associated Press (January 15).

Fannie Mae. Undated. "What are Credit Scoring and Automated Underwriting?" Washington, DC: Fannie Mae.

Federal Financial Institutions Examination Council. 1996a. *A Guide to HMDA Reporting: Getting it Right!* Washington, DC: Federal Financial Institutions Examination Council.

———. 1996b. HMDA data supplied by Federal Financial Institutions Examination Council.

———. 1996c. "Community Reinvestment Act Interagency Questions and Answers Regarding Community Reinvestment." Richmond: Federal Reserve Bank of Richmond (October 21).

———. 1997. "Findings from Analysis of Nationwide Summary Statistics for 1996 Community Reinvestment Act Data Fact Sheet." Washington, DC: Federal Financial Institutions Examination Council (September 30).

Federal Register. 1997. "Notices." Vol. 62, No. 193 (October 6).

Federal Reserve Bank of Chicago. 1998. "CRA Small Business Lending Profile." Chicago: Federal Reserve Bank of Chicago.

———. 1999. "Beginning a Legacy in Milwaukee." *Profitwise* 9 (1): 10–12.

Federal Reserve Board (2000). "Survey of the Performance and Profitability of CRA-Related Lending," Washington, D.C.: Federal Reserve Board (July).

Fiechter, Jonathan L. 1994. Remarks by Jonathan L. Fiechter, Acting Director, Office of Thrift Supervision before the Michigan League of Savings Institutions (July 19).

Fishbein, Allen J. 1996. "Is Credit Scoring a Winner for Everyone?" Stone Soup (Spring): 14–15.

Fix, Michael and Raymond J. Struyk, eds. 1992. *Clear and Convincing Evidence: Measurement of Discrimination in America.* Washington, DC: Urban Institute Press.

Galster, George. 1991. *A Statistical Perspective on Illegal Discrimination in Lending.* Washington, DC: American Bankers Association.

———. 1998. *An Econometric Model of the Urban Opportunity Structure: Cumulative Causation among City Markets, Social Problems, and Underserved Areas.* Washington, DC: Fannie Mae Foundation.

Garsson, Robert M. and Olaf de Senerpont Domis. 1994. "GOP Win Looks Good for Banks." *American Banker* (November 10).

Glabere, Michael L. 1992. "Milwaukee: A Tale of Three Cities." In Gregory D. Squires, ed., *From Redlining to Reinvestment: Community Responses to Urban Disinvestment.* Philadelphia: Temple University Press.

Goering, John M., ed. 1986. *Housing Desegregation and Federal Policy.* Chapel Hill: University of North Carolina Press.

Governor's Committee on Minority Business. 1988. *The Wisconsin Challenge: A Report on Minority Business Development.* Madison: Governor's Committee on Minority Business.

Gramlich, Edward M. 1998. Remarks by Edward M. Gramlich at Widener University. Chester, Pennsylvania (November 6).

————. 1999. Remarks by Edward M. Gramlich at the Second Annual Robert J. Lampman Memorial Lecture. University of Wisconsin, Madison, Wisconsin (June 16).

Greene, Zina G. 1980. *Lender's Guide to Fair Mortgage Policies.* Washington, DC: Potomac Institute.

Greenspan, Alan. 1998. "Remarks by Chairman Alan Greenspan At a Community Forum on Community Reinvestment and Access to Credit: California's Challenge. Los Angeles, California" (January 12). http://www.bog.frb.fed.us/boarddocs/speeches/19980112.htm.

Gunther, Jeffrey. 1999. "Between a Rock and a Hard Place: The CRA-Safety and Soundness Pinch." *Economic & Financial Review* (Second Quarter).

Gunther, Jeffrey, Kelly Klemme, and Kenneth Robinson. 1999. "Redlining or Red Herring?" *Southwest Economy* 3 (May/June): 8–13.

Haggerty, Maryann. 1998. "Local Lenders Often Discriminate, Study Says." *Washington Post* (March 25).

Hamilton, Susan and Stephen J. H. Cogswell. 1997. Barriers to Home Purchase for African-Americans and Hispanics in Syracuse. *Cityscape* 3 (1): 91–130.

Harney, Kenneth R. 1994. "Lenders Bending Over Backward to Make It Easier to Buy a Home." *Washington Post* (October 1).

Harrison, Bennett and Barry Bluestone. 1988. *The Great U-Turn: Corporate Restructuring and the Polarizing of America.* New York: Basic Books.

Hellmer, Ray. 1996. Licensed Financial Examiner. Department of Financial Institutions, State of Wisconsin telephone interview (August 20).

Henningsen, Margaret. 1998. Personal interview with Sally O'Connor. (January 26).

Housing Policy Debates. 1992. Special issue on Discrimination in the Housing and Mortgage Markets. 3 (2): i–745.

Hoyt, Homer. 1933. *One Hundred Years of Land Values in Chicago.* Chicago: University of Chicago Press.

Hudson, Michael. 1996. *Merchants of Misery: How Corporate America Profits from Poverty.* Monroe, Maine: Common Courage Press.

Hunter, William C. and Mary Beth Walker. 1995. "The Cultural Affinity Hypothesis and Mortgage Lending Decisions." Working Paper Series, Federal Reserve Bank of Chicago (July).

————. 1996. The Cultural Affinity Hypothesis and Mortgage Lending Decisions. *Journal of Real Estate Finance and Economics* 13: 57–70.

Immergluck, Daniel and Marti Wiles. 1999. *Two Steps Back: The Dual Mortgage Market, Predatory Lending and the Undoing of Community Development.* Chicago: Woodstock Institute.

Immergluck, Dan. 1998. "Comment on 'New Information on Lending to Small Business and Small Farms: The 1996 CRA Data'." Chicago: Woodstock Institute (Feb. 12).

Immergluck, Dan and Erin Mullen. 1997. "New Small Business Data Show Loans Going to Higher-Income Neighborhoods in Chicago Area." Chicago: Woodstock Institute.

Jackson, Kenneth T. 1985. *Crabgrass Frontier: The Suburbanization of the United States.* New York: Oxford University Press.

Jargowsky, Paul A. 1996. *Poverty and Place: Ghettos, Barrios, and the American City.* New York: Russell Sage Foundation.

Joint Center for Housing Studies of Harvard University. 1998. *The State of the Nation's Housing.* Cambridge: Joint Center for Housing Studies of Harvard University.

Judd, Dennis R. 1984. *The Politics of American Cities*: Private Power and Public Policy. Boston: Little, Brown & Co.

Kamp, Marv. 1999. *Mortgaging the Future of our Low-Income Communities: An Analysis of Subprime Home Equity Lending in Wisconsin.* Monona, WI: Wisconsin Rural Development Center.

Keating, W. Dennis, Norman Krumholz, and Philip Star, eds. 1996. *Revitalizing Urban Neighborhoods.* Lawrence: University Press of Kansas.

Kellison, Stephen G. 1970. *The Theory of Interest.* Homewood, IL: Richard D. Irwin, Inc.

Kennickell, Arthur B. and Martha Starr-McClure. 1994. "Changes in Family Finances from 1989 to 1992: Evidence from the Survey of Consumer Finances." *Federal Reserve Bulletin* (October): 861–882.

Kim, Sunwoong and Gregory D. Squires. 1998. "The Color of Money and the People Who Lend It." *Journal of Housing Research* 9(2): 271–284.

Knight, Jerry. 1994. "Lenders Agree to Anti-Bias Pledge. *Washington Post* (September 13).

Lee, Bill Lann. 1999. "An Issue of Public Importance: The Justice Department's Enforcement of the Fair Housing Act." *Cityscape* 4 (3): 35–56.

Leonhardt, David. 1997. "Two Tier Marketing." *Business Week* (March 17): 82–90.

Levine, Marc V. 1994. *The Crisis of Low Wages in Milwaukee: Wage Polarization in the Metropolitan Labor Market, 1970–1990.* University of Wisconsin-Milwaukee, Center for Economic Development, Briefing Paper #3.

———. 1998. *The Economic State of Milwaukee: The City and the Region, 1998.* Milwaukee: Center for Economic Development, University of Wisconsin-Milwaukee.

Lief, Beth J. and Susan Goering. 1987. "The Implementation of the Federal Mandate for Fair Housing." In Gary A. Tobin, ed., *Divided Neighborhoods: Changing Patterns of Racial Segregation.* Newbury Park: Sage Publications.

Litan, Robert E., Nicholas P. Retsinas, Eric S. Belsky and Susan White Haag (2000). "The Community Reinvestment Act after Financial Modernization: A Baseline Report," Washington, D.C.: U.S. Dept. of the Treasury.

Longhofer, Stanley D. 1996. Cultural Affinity and Mortgage Discrimination. *Economic Review* 32 (3): 12–24.

Ludwig, Eugene A. 1996. Remarks by Eugene A. Ludwig, Comptroller of the Currency, before the Consumer Banking Association. Chicago (September 30).

Lunt, Penny. 1993. "Banks Make Check-Cashing Work." *ABA Banking Journal* (December): 51–52.

Madison, Alvin and Gregory D. Squires. 1996. "African Americans and Hispanics Robbed by Housing Industries." *Milwaukee Journal Sentinel* (April 19).

Marsico, Richard D. 1996. "The New Community Reinvestment Act Regulations: An Attempt to Implement Performance-Based Standards." Clearinghouse Review (March): 1021–1033.

Massey, Douglas S. and Nancy Denton. 1993. *American Apartheid: Segregation and the Making of the Underclass.* Cambridge, MA: Harvard University Press.

McKnight, John. 1993. *Mapping Community Capacity.* Evanston: Center for Urban Affairs and Policy Research, Northwestern University.

McNeely, R. L. and Melvin Kinlow. 1986. *Milwaukee Today: A Racial Gap Study.* Milwaukee: Milwaukee Urban League.

Meredith, Robyn. 1994. "Thrifts Set War Chest for Fight on Fair Lending." *American Banker* (October 18).

Meyer, Laurence H. 1997. The Role of Banks in Small Business. Remarks presented at Conference on Small Business Finance, Berkley Center for Entrepreneurial Studies and New York University Salomon Center, (May 23).

———. 1998a. Remarks by Laurence H. Meyer Before the 1998 Community Reinvestment Act Conference of the Consumer Bankers Association. Arlington, Virginia (May 12).

———. 1998b. Remarks by Laurence H. Meyer at the Bank Administration Institute, Finance and Accounting Management Conference. Washington, DC (June 9).

Mishel, Lawrence, Jared Bernstein and John Schmitt. 1997. *The State of Working America, 1996–97.* Armonk, NY: M. E. Sharpe.

Morics, W. Martin. 1996. "City of Milwaukee Annual Review of Lending Practices of Financial Institutions." Office of the Comptroller, City of Milwaukee.

———. 1998. "City of Milwaukee Annual Review of Lending Practices of Financial Institutions." Office of the Comptroller, City of Milwaukee.

Morrison, Joanne. 1999. "U.S. 1998 Homeownership Rate Hits Record 66.3 Percent." Reuters Limited (January 27).

Mortgage Bankers of America and U.S. Department of Housing and Urban Development. 1994. "Fair Lending—Best Practices Master Agreement." Unpublished document. Washington, DC: Mortgage Bankers of America and U.S. Department of Housing and Urban Development (September 14).

Moskowitz, Erik. 1995. "One-Stop Shops Offer Check Cashing and More." *Christian Science Monitor* (August 23): 9.

Mullen, Erin, Malcolm Bush, and Samantha Weinstein. 1997. "Currency Exchanges Add to Poverty Surcharge for Low-Income Residents." Chicago: Woodstock Institute.

Munnell, Alicia H., Lynn E. Brown, James McEneaney, and Geoffrey M.B. Tootell. 1992. "Mortgage Lending in Boston: Interpreting HMDA Data," Working Paper Series, Federal Reserve Board of Boston (Oct.).

Munnell, Alicia, Geoffrey M.B. Tootell, Lynn E. Browne, and James McEneaney. 1996. Mortgage Lending in Boston: Interpreting HMDA Data. *The American Economic Review* 86 (1): 25–53.

NAACP v. American Family Mutual Insurance Company. 1992. Statement taken from case files. Milwaukee, Wisconsin.

NAACP Insurance Settlement Class Committee. 1999. *Greenlining: A Progress Report Insuring Homes and Improving the Community.* Milwaukee: NAACP.

National Commission on Neighborhoods. 1979. *Building Neighborhoods: Final Report to the President and Congress of the United States.* Washington, DC: U.S. Government Printing Office.

National Community Reinvestment Coalition. 1994. *Catalogue and Directory of Community Reinvestment Agreements.* Washington, DC: National Community Reinvestment Coalition.

———. 1995. "CRA Dollar Commitments Since 1977." Washington, DC: National Community Reinvestment Coalition.

———. 1996. *America's Worst Lenders.* Washington, DC: National Community Reinvestment Coalition.

———. Undated. *CRA Commitments 1977–1998.* Washington, DC: National Community Reinvestment Coalition.

National Training and Information Center. 1991. *The Community Reinvestment (CRA) Handbook.* Chicago: National Training and Information Center.

New Opportunities for Homeownership in Milwaukee. 1998a. "Milwaukee and Freddie Mac Forge Multi-Million Dollar Alliance." Press release (October 8).

———. 1998b. "NOHIM 1997 Annual Report." Milwaukee: Community Development Block Grant Administration, City of Milwaukee.

Norman, Jack. 1989. "Congenial Milwaukee: A Segregated City," in Gregory D. Squires, (ed.) *Unequal Partnerships: The Political Economy of Urban Redevelopment in Postwar America.* New Brunswick: Rutgers University Press.

Norman, Jack. 1993. "Lending Pledges Are a Step Back, Group Says." *Milwaukee Journal* (August 17).

———. 1997. "Group Demands More Banking Services, Not Check-Cashing Center." *Milwaukee Journal-Sentinel* (April 23): B3.

———. 1998. "City Lowest in Loans to Firms in Poor Areas," *Milwaukee Journal Sentinel* (May 25).

Norquist, John O. 1998. *The Wealth of Cities: Revitalizing the Centers of American Life.* Reading, MA: Addison-Wesley.

O'Brien, Timothy L. 1998. "For Banks, a Big Nudge to Do More." *New York Times* (July 5).

Office of the Comptroller of the Currency. 1998. "OCC Economics Unit Will Focus on Fair Lending Exams." Press release (May 4).

Oliver, Melvin L. and Thomas M. Shapiro. 1995. *Black Wealth/White Wealth: A New Perspective on Racial Inequality.* New York: Routledge.

Orfield, Myron. 1997. *Metropolitics: A Regional Agenda for Community and Stability.* Washington, D.C. and Cambridge, Mass.: Brookings Institute Press and The Lincoln Institute of Land Policy.

Parry, Carol. 1997. Personal communication with Carol Parry, executive vice-president, Chase Manhattan Bank, at meeting of the Consumer Advisory Council of the Federal Reserve Board (April 16).

Peattie, Earl. 1998. Navigating the Subprime Mortgage. Washington, DC: Consumer Mortgage Education Consortium.

Pittenger, William L. 1996. "Managing the Appraisal Component of Fair Lending Compliance." *ABA Bank Compliance* (March/April): 11–15.

Pogge, Jean. 1992. "Reinvestment in Chicago Neighborhoods: A Twenty-Year Struggle." In Gregory D. Squires, ed. *From Redlining to Reinvestment: Community Responses to Urban Disinvestment.* Philadelphia: Temple University Press.

Policy Statement on Discrimination in Lending. 1994. *Federal Register* 59: 73 (18266–18274).

Porter, Michael E. 1995. The Competitive Advantage of the Inner City. *Harvard Business Review* May–June: 55–70.

Quinn, Lois M. 1997. *Employment and Training Needs of Central City Milwaukee Workers.* University of Wisconsin-Milwaukee, Employment and Training Institute (February).

Reno, Janet. 1998. Speech delivered before the Seventh Annual Conference of the National Community Reinvestment Coalition (March 20).

Ries, Leo. 1999. Personal interview with Sally O'Connor (January 26).

Ritter, Richard. 1995. "Redlining: The Justice Department Cases." *Mortgage Banking* (September): 17–25.

Rusk, David. 1999. *Inside Game Outside Game: Winning Strategies for Saving Urban America.* Washington, D.C.: Brookings Institution Press.

Saunders, Margot. 1998. Testimony before the Subcommittees on Housing and Community Opportunity and Financial Institutions and Consumer Credit, House Committee on Banking and Financial Services regarding the Rewrite of Truth in Lending Act and Real Estate Settlement Procedures Act. Washington, DC (September 16).

Schafer, Todd and Jeff Faux, eds. 1996. *Reclaiming Prosperity: A Blueprint for Progressive Economic Reform.* Armonk, NY: M. E. Sharpe.

Schultze, Steve. 1994. "Judge Orders George to Pay Delinquent Loan." *Milwaukee Journal-Sentinel* (June 29): 1b.

Schwartz, Alex. 1998. "Bank Lending to Minority and Low-Income Households and Neighborhoods: Do Community Reinvestment Agreements Make a Difference?" *Journal of Urban Affairs* 20 (3): 269–302.

Seiberg, Jaret. 1998. "City-Travelers Gets the Nod For Financial Powerhouse." *American Banker* (September 24).

Seward, Quinta. 1996. "CRC Under Cover." *Community Reinvestment News.* San Francisco: California Community Reinvestment Committee.

Sharma-Jensen, Geeta. 1998. "The Door Is Closing: Milwaukee-Area Home Prices Outpace Pay, Cutting Affordability, Worrying Observers," *Milwaukee Journal-Sentinel* (July 5): D1.

Shelly v. Kramer 334 U.S.1 (1948).

Shlay, Anne B. 1999. "Influencing the Agents of Urban Structure: Evaluating the Effects of Community Reinvestment Organizing on Bank Residential Lending Practices." *Urban Affairs Review.* 35 (2): 247–278.

Shlay, Anne B., Ira Goldstein, and David Bartelt. 1992. "Racial Barriers and Credit: Comment on Hula." *Urban Affairs Quarterly* 28 (1): 126–140.

Silver, Josh. 1999. E-mail message to membership of National Community Reinvestment Coalition (January 26).

Smith, Pam. 1998. Personal interview with Sally O'Connor. (November 30).

Squires, Gregory D. (ed). 1989. *Unequal Partnerships: The Political Economy of Urban Redevelopment in Postwar America.* New Brunswick: Rutgers University Press.

———, ed. 1992. *From Redlining to Reinvestment: Community Responses to Urban Disinvestment.* Philadelphia: Temple University Press.

———. 1993. "MICAH's Lending Agreements." Memorandum to the Fair Lending Coalition.

———. 1996. "Policies of Prejudice: Risky Encounters with the Property Insurance Business." *Challenge* (July/August): 45–50.

———, ed. 1997. *Insurance Redlining: Disinvestment, Reinvestment, and the Evolving Role of Financial Institutions.* Washington, DC: Urban Institute Press.

———. 1998. "Milwaukee, Wisconsin," in Neil Larry Shumsky (ed.) *Encyclopedia of Urban America: The Cities and Suburbs.* Santa Barbara: ABC-CLIO, Inc.

Stegman, Michael A. 1999a. *Savings for the Poor: The Hidden Benefits of Electronic Banking.* Washington, DC: Brookings Institution Press.

———. 1999b. *How Electronic Banking Can Help the Poor Build Wealth: Getting the Most Out of Electronic Benefits Transfer.* Washington, DC: Brookings Institution Press.

Streeter, William W. 1993. "Toward Bias-Free Banking." *ABA Banking Journal,* vol. LXXV (10: 19).

Taylor, John. 1999a. Testimony before the Committee on Banking of the U.S. House of Representatives. Washington, DC (February 11).

———. 1999b. Letter to William Jefferson Clinton (October 29).

Tisdale, William. 1989. "Divided City: Reversing the Trend." Masters Paper, Department of Urban Affairs, University of Wisconsin-Milwaukee.

Trapp, Shel. 1986. *Blessed Be the Fighters.* Chicago: National Training and Information Center.

Trotter, Joe William. 1985. *Black Milwaukee: The Making of an Industrial Proletariat, 1915–45.* Urbana: University of Illinois Press

Turner, Margery Austin, Raymond Y. Struyk, and John Yinger. 1991. *Housing Discrimination Study.* Washington, DC: Urban Institute.

U.S. Bureau of the Census. 1992. Census of Population and Housing, 1990. Summary Tape 3A.

U.S. Department of Housing and Urban Development. 1998. "Cuomo Announces Record $2.1 Billion Lending Discrimination Settlement and Commemorates Thirtieth Anniversary of Fair Housing Act," press release (April 3).

U.S. Department of Housing and Urban Development and Guaranty Bank. 1999. "Fair Lending Best Practices Agreement." Washington, DC and Milwaukee: U.S. Department of Housing and Urban Development and Guaranty Bank. (June 8).

U.S. Department of Justice. 1998. Lending discrimination cases, personal communication from Robert Berman to Gregory D. Squires. (April 1).

U.S. Department of the Treasury (2000). "Predatory Lending Report," Washington: D.C. U.S. Department of the Treasury (July).

U.S. Federal Housing Administration. 1938. *Underwriting Manual.* Washington, DC: U.S. Government Printing Office.

U.S. General Accounting Office. 1996. *Fair Lending: Federal Oversight and Enforcement Improved but Some Challenges Remain.* Washington, DC: United States General Accounting Office.

United States v. Blackpipe State Bank C.A., No. 93-5115 (D. S.D. 1994).

United States v. Chevy Chase Federal Savings Bank et al., C.A., No. 9-1-1824JG (D. D.C. 1994).

United States v. Decatur Federal Savings & Loan Association C. A., No. 1:92-CV-2198 (N.D. Ga. 1992).

United States v. First National Bank of Vicksburg C.A. No. 5:94 CV 6(B)(N)(W.D. Miss. 1994).

United States v. Northern Trust Company C.A., No. 95C3239 (E.D. Ill. 1995).

United States v. Shawmut Mortgage Company C.A., No. 3:93 CV 2453 (D. Conn. 1993).

Wayne, Leslie. 1998. "Panel Clears Overhaul Bill On Banking." *New York Times* (September 12).

White, Sammis, M. Marc Thomas, and Nicholas A. Thompson. 1995. "Changing Spatial Patterns of Employment Location: Milwaukee, Wisconsin 1979–1994." Urban Research Center, University of Wisconsin-Milwaukee.

Williams, Richard A. and Reynold F. Nesiba. 1997. "Racial, Economic, and Institutional Differences in Home Mortgage Loans: St. Joseph County, Indiana," *Journal of Urban Affairs* 19 (1): 73–103.

Wilson, William J. 1987. *The Truly Disadvantaged: The Inner City, the Underclass and Public Policy.* Chicago: University of Chicago Press.

Wilson, William J. 1996. *When Work Disappears: The Work of the New Urban Poor.* New York: Alfred A. Knopf.

Wisconsin Housing and Economic Development Authority. (1998). *1997 Annual Report.* Madison: Wisconsin Housing and Economic Development Authority.
———. 1999. Unpublished data.

Wise, Denise. 1998. Personal interview with Sally O'Connor (October 16).

Woodstock Institute. 1998. "Community Reinvestment in an Era of Megamergers and Financial Modernization." Presentation at the Nonprofit Center of Milwaukee (November 12).

Wyly, Elvin K., Norman Glickman, and Michael L. Lahr. 1998. "A Top 10 List of Things to Know About American Cities," *Cityscape* 3 (3): 7–32.

Yinger, John. 1995. *Closed Doors, Opportunities Lost: The Continuing Costs of Housing Discrimination.* New York: Russell Sage Foundation.

———. 1999. "Testing for Discrimination in Housing and Related Markets." In Michael Fix and Margery Austin Turner, eds., *A National Report Card on Discrimination in America: The Role of Testing*. Washington, DC: Urban Institute Press.

Zahn, Michael R. 1994. "George Owes $6,000 on Loan, Judge Declares." *Milwaukee Journal-Sentinel* (February 15): B1.

Index